# Practical Business Ethics for the Busy Manager

# Practical Business Ethics for the Busy Manager

M. Neil Browne
Andrea Giampetro-Meyer
Carrie Williamson

PEARSON
Prentice
Hall

Upper Saddle River, New Jersey 07458

Library of Congress Cataloging-in-Publication Data

Browne, M. Neil
    Practical business ethics for the busy manager / M. Neil Browne, Andrea
    Giampetro-Meyer, Carrie Williamson.--1st ed.
        p. cm.
    Includes index.
    ISBN 0-13-048109-2 (alk. paper)
        1. Business Ethics.    I. Giampetro-Meyer, Andrea. II. Carrie Williamson. III. Title.

    HF5387 2004
    174'.4—dc22

                                                                    2003063247


Editorial Director: Charlyce Jones Owen
Senior Acquisitions Editor: Ross Miller
Assistant Editor: Wendy Yurash
Director of Marketing: Beth Mejia
Senior Marketing Manager: Chris Ruel
Editorial Assistant: Carla Worner
Production Liaison: Louise Rothman
Manufacturing Buyer: Christina Helder
Cover Design: Bruce Kenselaar
Production Supervision and Composition: Preparé Inc.
Printer/Binder: Courier Companies, Inc.-Stoughton
Cover Printer: Phoenix Color Corp.


Credits and acknowledgments borrowed from other sources and reproduced in this textbook with
permission appear on appropriate page within text.

---

10 9 8 7 6 5 4 3 2 1

ISBN 0-13-048109-2

# Contents

## CHAPTER 4
## Classical Ethical Guidelines:
## Initial Steps Toward Good Work   *62*

## CHAPTER 5
## Moral Mentors in American Corporations
## and Organizations: The Models for Good Work   *79*

## *Part TWO: Application*

## CHAPTER 6
## Getting the Facts Necessary for Good Work   *100*

# CHAPTER 7
# Determining the Issue that Requires Good Work   *109*

# CHAPTER 8
# Locating the Relevant Law:
# The Framework for Doing Good Work   *118*

# CHAPTER 9
# Identifying the Alternative Options for Good Work   *136*

# CHAPTER 10
# Applying Personal Ethical Principles to Doing
# Good Work   *146*

# Preface

Many college students aspire to careers in business organizations. Professors who teach ethics classes assign reading material giving students some awareness that they are likely to struggle with dilemmas pitting their own values against the ethical norms of the organizations that employ them. For those of us who teach graduate students with careers already underway, we hear story after story confirming our perception of ordinary business life and our fears for our undergraduate students who do not appreciate the stress they may face beyond college.

The stress of everyday ethical dilemmas is overshadowed by news stories of serious corporate misconduct, scandal, and failure. Students are bombarded with depressing evidence of managerial amorality. As professors, we want to give students the tools they need to respond to the ethical dilemmas they will or currently face. Our primary objective in writing *Practical Business Ethics for the Busy Manager* is to present a practical, action-oriented approach to business ethics that will help prospective managers respond to business problems in a range of areas, including accounting, finance, marketing, and management.

As professors with a passion for lifelong learning, we appreciate many of the business ethics books that are currently available for use in higher education. Many excellent business ethics texts take an academic approach, explaining complex ethical theories to prospective managers. We find this academic approach meaningful to our own thinking. Unfortunately, though, we have discovered that this approach does not work for most of our students. At best, students play along with us when we use an academic approach, realizing that what they perceive to be overly complex, decontextualized reading is simply "stuff from school." They endure the lessons, pass the class, and move on to the next course.

At worst, a highly academic approach to business ethics pushes students down the road to cynicism. "Yeah, right. Let's imagine what Aristotle would say if he ran WorldCom." Sometimes, students rebel and refuse to play along with the complex reasoning academic business ethics books present. Instead, they trash all the material as remote, otherworldly, and useless. The worst students then resort to simplified, often relativistic, responses to ethical dilemmas. These responses show a very low regard for reason and lead to despair among faculty.

*Practical Business Ethics for the Busy Manager* is written in two parts. Part One includes five chapters laying the foundation for the practical, action-oriented approach to business ethics we present in Part Two. The book's first chapter introduces students to our general approach for considering ethical dilemmas. It emphasizes the need for individual business leaders to identify and develop their personal ethical perspective. This introductory chapter explores what it means to "do good work" from an ethical perspective. Chapter 2 aims to help students understand the context in which ethical dilemmas arise. It describes American business culture in an attempt to encourage students to see why they might be vulnerable to corporate cultures that are motivated by goals other than doing good work.

The book's third chapter introduces students to basic language units of ethics, including interests, roles, and values. Chapter 3 encourages students to identify their personal value priorities and consider how to act upon these priorities in daily business practice. Chapter 4 presents classical ethical guidelines that are initial steps toward good work. The final foundations chapter, chapter 5, presents material we believe is unique to our business ethics book. Chapter 5 encourages students to find, emulate, and become moral mentors—individuals who model "good work" and bring out the moral best in others.

Part Two of *Practical Business Ethics* gives explicit advice about what to do in the face of probable conflict within the business organization. Chapters 6 through 10 present the individual components of the FILOP process we outline (e.g., facts, issues, law, options, principles). The book's final chapter, chapter 11, shows students what the FILOP process looks like in action. FILOP directs prospective managers toward good work by asking them to develop an awareness of the facts of an ethical dilemma, an appreciation for the scope of the issue, and an understanding of the relevant law governing the issue, a consideration of the options available, and a selection of applicable ethical principles.

Throughout both Part One and Part Two of *Practical Business Ethics*, we are mindful of our intent to write a book that is readable, understandable, crisp, practical, and optimistic. Each chapter includes examples from a range of business disciplines. This book can be used across the business curriculum. Another motivating factor was our desire to write a book that any business professor can incorporate into the current course plan. We wanted to the book to be small, and largely self-teaching. We wanted the book to make a significant impact on students' business education, with minimal cost to the already overloaded professor. Finally, we wanted the book to be filled with current and classic examples from the business world to give the reader a sense that we are standing in the trenches with them as they face dilemmas.

Given our interest in making the book small, we selected features that would provide the most value-added material to the book. We designed features that would allow us to highlight key themes and emphasize the relevance of our approach to our students' working lives. *Practical Business Ethics* includes the following text boxes.

1. **Global.** As a business manager, prospective managers will communicate with businesspeople from various countries and cultures. Legal and social norms within these different cultures may influence their business interactions in ways they might not expect. Thus, we have included global boxes in each chapter to heighten students' awareness of the role of culture in ethical decision making. For example, chapter 5's Buddhism Global box demonstrates the role of religion in shaping beliefs about ethical work behavior. Other boxes explain Islam's prohibition of charging interest and the creation of relationship obligations in China.

2. **Values in Action.** Values, such as honesty, efficiency, fairness, security, and freedom, may conflict with regard to a particular business dilemma. To help students better identify the role of values in business decisions, chapters contain a "Values in Action" box that presents a business leader or company emphasizing the role of values. For example, chapter 3's Values in Action box explains how Dr. Jeffrey Wigand's key values of honesty, collective responsibility, and security led him to blow the whistle on the tobacco industry.

3. **Meet the Leader.** While we frequently hear examples of clearly wrongful ethical behavior, we do not so often hear about instances when successful businesspeople engage in ethical business behavior. One way prospective managers can learn to resolve ethical dilemmas is to mimic the ethical behavior of others. Thus, each chapter contains a "Meet the Leader" box that introduces the student to a successful businessperson who behaves ethically and articulates what it means to be a responsible, ethical employee. For example, chapter 2 presents Alfred P. Sloan, Jr., former head of General Motors, and his unique management style.

4. **Critical Thinking.** Ethical dilemmas frequently involve conflicting facts and interests. Consequently, students need to use reasoning skills to identify information in order to make an ethical decision. Therefore, each chapter contains critical thinking boxes to provide opportunities for students to develop these reasoning skills.

Who would find *Practical Business Ethics* especially beneficial? Our primary audience is the business professor with almost no ethics training, who wishes to supplement his or her marketing, management, accounting, or finance course with a readable book that addresses the problem of the distressing lack of concern about ethics among business majors. Similarly, a business school dean who wants to encourage conversations across a curriculum may suggest that faculty members assign the book in core business courses.

Business ethics professors who have grown weary of negative, anticapitalism books may see this book as a refreshing change. We believe that improving ethical decision making is a worthwhile goal. We do not see the point of telling students they are morally corrupt simply for working in business. We are counting on the excellent students we encounter on a daily basis to do and model good work in the business world. Finally, prospective managers and managers currently working in business may find this book useful, especially when someone is asking them to respond to an ethical dilemma *now*.

Several of our students have offered suggestions for how to improve the book, and we thank them. We are especially thankful for students in two classes who used the manuscript when it was in rough draft form—(1) students in Professor Nancy Kubasek's undergraduate Introduction to Business course at Bowling Green State University in Fall 2002, and (2) students in Professor Andrea Giampetro-Meyer's graduate ethics and social responsibility class at Loyola College in Maryland in Spring 2003. We also offer thanks to Nancy Kubasek, who provided helpful constructive feedback. We would like to acknowledge the assistance of the following Prentice Hall reviewers:

Paul L. Schumann, Minnesota State University, Mankato
Robin Radtke, University of Texas, San Antonio
Amy H. Moorman, Doane College
Richard Wilson, Towson University
Thomas D. Cavenagh, North Central College, Illinois.

Professor Moorman offered especially careful, insightful advice about how to improve the book. Finally, we would like to thank the students who offered especially thoughtful suggestions—Sarah Mercier and Steve Weigand.

M. Neil Browne
Andrea Giampetro-Meyer
Carrie Williamson

# Practical Business Ethics for the Busy Manager

# Part One • Foundation

## CHAPTER 1
# Doing Good Work

Ethics requires us to think about others. We already pay attention to our interests and desires; we need no training to do so. We are all very important to ourselves.

But doing good work, behaving each day as an ethical businessperson, seems to require training. Evolution has imprinted crude self-interest in our heads and hearts. To combat this natural tendency to look inward, parents, religious institutions, governmental leaders, and schools all try to focus our attention on the good and the right. They urge us to look outside ourselves before we act. They try to teach us that in looking outward, we improve our quality as individuals and contribute to creating a better community in the process.

In today's increasingly global business world, the outward view of ethics is both especially important and difficult to put into practice. The Global Boxes throughout this book highlight the necessity of thinking about the increasing complexity of conductiong business while looking outside ourselves. When we work and trade in many cultural settings, doing good work in a global economy requires us to familiarize ourselves with the interests of others that we are just starting to know.

The most basic ethical guidelines, such as the Golden Rule, which urges us to act toward other people the way we would hope others would act toward us, are framed in terms of human interactions. We are important, and so are other people. Now, how can we best live together? Answering that question is the subject matter of ethics.

## THE CONNECTION BETWEEN BUSINESS AND ETHICS

Business ethics refers to the "shoulds" that businesspeople will be guided by when they make commercial and financial decisions. But these "shoulds" are only occasionally clear. Studying the framework of doing good work provides guidance in those difficult managerial moments when we see strengths and weaknesses for each of the business options we are considering.

This lack of clarity about what businesspeople should be doing in their production, labor relations, and distribution policies; our living in a culture that often emphasizes moneymaking above all else; and the temptation to watch out for number one all raise doubts about the ethics of businesspeople. Some people have concerns about the extent to which ethics can flourish in an environment where "making the deal" is paramount. Will businesspeople intent on the bottom line have the time and inclination to wonder about the ethics of their decisions exchange? Does a market culture permit adequate consideration of honesty, justice, caring, and community? Can business maintain its traditional role of innovator, employer, and producer, while also focusing on the social significance of the means they use when fulfilling that role?

Many of us, for instance, simply accept the idea that there is one part of life where you can be ethical and then there is another part, a very different part called "business," where you do what you are told. This dichotomy can be carried to an extreme. For instance, when Enron's CFO, Andrew Fastow, played a major role in establishing Enron's offshore accounts, he harmed a large number of investors and employees who were depending on his decisions. Yet, people who knew Fastow away from work adamantly defended him as being a generous, caring, community-oriented person.[1] He helped to create a synagogue and was very active in various charities. One friend described how Fastow was the first person to offer help when a friend's son was diagnosed with a rare disease.

Although Fastow might have been an upstanding and compassionate citizen away from the office, he had a very different reputation among Enron employees. Employees described him as arrogant, volatile, aggressive, and vindictive. He had a reputation for being dangerously ambitious, as illustrated by his involvement in Enron's corporate misdeeds. Fastow has also been accused of using Enron's personnel review system to get back at people who disagreed with him.[2]

Although Fastow, like many businesspeople, might not have been particularly proud of the distinction between the ethical sphere and the business sphere, both he and others are adamant about the reality of the separate spheres.[3] This attitude suggests that business ethics is relevant only to classroom discussions or corporate responsibility seminars.

If for no other reason than the vast scope of business activities, stories of business misconduct, from embezzlement by a local citizen to falsification of records by top executives such as Fastow, are numerous and visible. Television, news magazines, and local newspapers have no short supply of lurid tales, documenting the venality of a chemical, meatpacking, or construction firm, which they do not hesitate to share with the public.

As a result, exposure to a seemingly large number of business wrongdoings makes us all wonder about the extent of business ethics. For example, Eric Schlosser's recent book details the brutal working conditions in many meat production companies.[4] Illustrations such as these are so powerful that their influence on people's conception of business far exceeds the statistical significance of the misdoings. In other words, stories of business crimes remain in the minds of the people as a description of daily business behavior, even though a close look at the frequency of such misconduct suggests they are the exception, and not the rule, as a description of typical managerial behavior.

Although none of us has any terrific evidence establishing how frequently businesspeople are or are not ethical, we DO believe that all of us share an interest in encouraging more thought and action in the area of business ethics. Ethical conduct by a businessperson is often good business, strengthens the community, and heightens our sense of self-worth. Hence, we all need to figure out a process whereby business conduct can become more ethical and then increase our understanding of how as an individual businessperson we can contribute to that process.

We begin to unify business and ethics by emphasizing the reality of business behavior in our particular historical era. All too frequently, business ethics is discussed in such an abstract form that it doesn't seem to have much to do with accounting, finance, marketing, and management problems. Business decisions are goal directed and action oriented. In contrast, much discussion of business ethics seems remote and foreign. We need a method that can be used on a daily basis, quickly and efficiently.

Even in the business world, ethical training may be considered only in the abstract. When a company provides ethics training for its management, the ethical guidelines presented for employees and executives may not be effectively enforced. In a survey of 100 corporate ethics officers, 54 percent believed that if Enron senior management had received ethical training, little to no difference would have been made to prevent that company's demise. Furthermore, 56 percent of these executives never survey employees about the effectiveness of their ethical guidelines, and 54 percent include no measurement for ethical compliance in their performance appraisals.[5]

Clearly, a better method is needed to develop a sense of ethics in the business world. We believe that such a method would take advantage of who businesspeople want to become. Specifically, our most fundamental premise is the belief that businesspeople at all levels possess an inclination to seek what is right and to do what is good. They are people first and businesspeople second.

In other words, when a person works for a business at any level, she or he does not thereby lose membership in other groups. Businesspeople have loyalties and duties to friends, family, and country. These obligations are always in the background of a business decision, pulling and pushing the businessperson into making choices that will affect others far beyond the financial and physical boundaries of the firm itself. As a result of this complicated interaction among social groups, businesspeople require a practical format for weighing these responsibilities.

## BUSINESSPEOPLE DO GOOD WORK

Yes, businesspeople can be ethical. Writing that sentence is awkward for us. But we feel a need to explain why we include such an observation. In speaking with publishers, students, and colleagues about our intentions for this book, we made it clear that we intended to include instances of businesspeople behaving ethically. Our logic quite simply is that a central way we all learn is by modeling or mimicking. Therefore, we wanted to include illustrations of businesspeople doing good work throughout this book. By showing that successful businesspeople behave in an ethical manner, these illustrations will provide you with the courage and imagery you will require when ethical dilemmas arise for you at work. The need for living models of good work is seen clearly in the South African experience described in the following global box.

When we told friends and colleagues about our plans for this book, we were taken aback by the common response to our intentions: Are there really businesspeople who behave ethically? Will you be able to actually find the ethical models you seek?

Prospective businesspeople need to know that the loud and certain answer to that question is "YES." In fact, one of our goals is to assure future businesspeople that one can be a successful businessperson *and* an ethical person at the same time. Consider Bill Ford, Jr., the Chairman of the Board for Ford Motor Company. In the redesign of the Rouge River complex in Dearborn, Michigan, Bill Ford led the company in creating an environmentally friendly manufacturing center that included, among other innovations, a "living roof," which is able to affect the local watershed by absorbing several inches of rainwater. Bill Ford's Rouge River complex is an excellent example of an ethical

**GLOBAL BOX**

## SOUTH AFRICA

For years, South Africa operated under a system of racial segregation, also known as apartheid. The global business community placed harsh sanctions on South Africa to express their disapproval for the apartheid system, which barred many businesses from entering the global market. Rather than accepting this fate, however, South African businesses began to look for ways around the sanctions. People in business seemed to admire and encourage shrewd colleagues who took advantage of loopholes in the sanctions. The practice of skirting the sanctions is alleged to have augmented the South African business community's tolerance for unethical behavior.

Though apartheid has ended, white-collar crime remains an epidemic problem for South Africa. Reported cases of fraud increased from 33,000 in 1986 to 55,300 in 1992. Researchers estimate that other white-collar crimes have increased by 50 percent over the same time period (De Beer, 1994).

The South African business community is caught in a vicious cycle where the standard for ethical behavior continues to fall, thereby making normally unethical practices appear acceptable. This complex situation is illustrated by a 1996 survey of marketing professionals. Although the professionals attest to the need for robust ethical norms, their responses to other questions indicate that their own standards for ethical conduct are quite low.

Within the last several years, scholars, government officials, and businesspeople have condemned corruption with the hope of breaking this cycle. Business ethics is now being taught in universities and discussed in public forums. Part of the discussion has considered the extent to which businesses have a responsibility to the community.

One area in which South African businesses have been asked to exercise social responsibility is the country's efforts to rectify racial inequality. Businesses are expected to take an active role in reducing inequalities and supporting government antidiscrimination programs. Although businesses have apparently been cooperative in this effort, the country is far from espousing itself as a trustworthy business center. Unfortunately, dramatic change will be difficult as long as South African businesses lack real-life models of ethical behavior.

*Sources:*

G. J. Rossouw, "Business Ethics in South Africa," *Journal of Business Ethics*, 16, no.14 (1997): 1539–1547.

Edden Van Zyl and Kobus Lazenby, "Ethical Behaviour in the South African Organizational Context: Essential and Workable," *Journal of Business Ethics;* 21, no.1 (1999): 15–22.

E. De Beer, "Stealing South Africa Blind: The Scourge of White Collar Crime," *Servanus;* 87, no.9 (1994): 44–45.

Michael H. Morris, et al., "Modeling Ethical Attitudes and Behaviors under Conditions of Environmental Turbulence: The Case of South Africa," *Journal of Business Ethics*, 15, no.10 (1996): 1119–1130.

business decision that included consideration of the local community and environment.[6]

To appreciate the link between successful business behavior and business ethics, we must be willing to acknowledge those situations in which businesspeople do behave in a manner that is much more than an act of narrow selfishness. Although we can certainly read negative motives into many neutral or positive actions, the inclination to do so makes less of us all. If we strain hard enough, it is possible to see any human action as egoistic and grasping. Imagine, for example, how easy it is to mock the kindness of a parent playing Santa Claus for her children. We could say, "Oh sure, she is just investing in the probability that her children will take care of her when she is old."

Because reading the incorrect motivation into a decision is an easy mistake to commit, good ethical decisions are difficult to distinguish from sly dealings for personal gain. As a result, ethical business decisions are often mislabeled. One such tricky example from the business world is Enron's strong support of the Kyoto treaty on global warming, which originally appeared to be praiseworthy environmental responsibility. Enron was also praised for being an active member of several environmental associations. However, Enron was the owner of Enron Wind Corp., one of the world's largest wind-power suppliers, and had large financial gains or losses at stake from the acceptance or rejection of the Kyoto standards.[7] With this information, we should wonder whether Enron's support was based on concern for profit before any real concern for the community.

Those skeptical of the ethics of businesspeople wonder, "Is it even possible to make human decisions apart from personal profit motivation?" Such a perspective suggests that caring, kindness, and compassion are to never be trusted at face value. We do not agree. Of course, those ideas can be abused, but they represent humans at their highest level of achievement from our perspective. As human motivations, they are just as real as any set of more self-serving objectives.

We are not urging naivete. We are all too aware that when an oil company announces that it is tearing down all its billboards in the Rocky Mountains because "we too want to enjoy the beauty of our national heritage," that actual reason may be that the billboards were not an effective marketing strategy. Rather than silently changing strategy, the firm may be seizing advantage from the situation by posing as a lover of natural beauty. However, it is also possible that the billboards were cost effective, but management wished to take a stand on behalf of the opportunity for later generations to see relatively unspoiled scenic vistas.

All we are maintaining is that, first and foremost, businesspeople are members of a much larger community than just the business world. Although the business world moves them in particular directions, several other powerful aspects of their humanity serve as competing motivations for business decisions. Consequently, business decisions reflect a weighing and sorting among all the various motivational influences that together lead to the potential for good work.

## DISCOVERING GOOD WORK BY CONVERSATION

This weighing and sorting occurs best through conversation. Listening and evaluating what others see as good work provides access to multiple perspectives, you will have the optimal building blocks for becoming an ethical businessperson. There is no set of ethical rules that are so clearly correct and reliable that all we need do is discover and apply them. Instead, when conversing about ethical dilemmas, we are forced to clarify, explore, argue, and rethink our position.

As Deborah Stone points out in *Political Reason and Policy Paradox*, announcing our loyalty to such virtues as freedom or justice is just the beginning of ethical analysis. Instead, a declaration of our core values is nothing more than an invitation to a moral conversation, either within our own minds and consciences or with others affected by or interested in the prospective decision.

The outcome of a moral conversation among people is a better decision to the extent that we have clarified certain things during the discussion.

- Clarity of purpose—We need to know what kind of life we want to live.
- Honesty from all participants—We need to be open about our concerns.
- Reasons for the decision—We need a thoughtful basis for our choices.
- Consistency of the decision with ethical guidelines—We need to align ourselves with traditional pathways to finding good work.
- Initial respect for all views in an ethical conversation—We need to listen first and then react.
- Attention to the weaknesses of our own positions—We need to think critically about our preferred business decisions.

Omit any of these prerequisites from a conversation about business ethics, and little is left besides noise.

To meet the preceding prerequisites, conversation about good work requires a common language. Imagine trying to provide an accounting analysis for a firm, but having almost no knowledge of accounting, its concepts, or its issues. The resulting panic and subsequent resistance to doing the accounting analysis is entirely understandable. The analogy to conversation about business ethics is direct. To engage in an ethical conversation, we need a basic vocabulary, a format for using the vocabulary, and a lot of practice.

The basic language units of ethical discussion are *values*, the name we give to the positive abstractions that capture our sense of what is good or desirable. Ethical discussion would be empty without some conception of where we are headed. It is just inconceivable that we could think carefully about business ethics unless we had first considered the importance of such values as honesty, efficiency, fairness, security, and freedom when choosing among alternative business decisions. Our priorities with respect to these and other values are our goal. They propel us in the direction of particular kinds of good work.

To guide these discussions about value priorities and consequent business decisions, we will present alternative formulations of values that businesspeople and various cultural groups have suggested as optimal value priorities. For example, the Romans' preeminent values were piety, devotion to family, and loyalty to the state. Every such list carries with it the implicit question: Are these value priorities ones that you should make your own?

Our purpose here is to demonstrate that thoughtful people disagree about value priorities, as their varying visions of a better world predict they would. But the desirable response is not to just throw up our hands and say, "Well, then, I guess I can have any value priorities I want." Instead, we want to improve ethical conversation by encouraging both the recognition that there is more than one set of reasonable ethical positions and that an ethical businessperson is always looking for a better one from among those alternatives.

## THE NEED FOR PRACTICAL BUSINESS ETHICS

Suggestions for better ethical conversation are just one way that we want to emphasize the creation of a practical approach for *better* business ethics. There is no way we can promise and deliver a technique for businesspeople to be master ethicists. As we will explain later, that activity is a full-time occupation unto itself. We want to distinguish the approach in this book from those intricate theoretical procedures that hold out a standard of reflection and analysis that is not achievable in a business setting.

Multiple constraints prevent the businessperson from making altogether terrific ethical decisions. When businesspeople make decisions, they are not in some classroom where they have large amounts of time to discover optimal ethical moves. On the contrary, time pressures are of the essence. A colleague or supervisor is looking you in the face, asking you to do something NOW. Although you might be able to buy some thinking time before you act, decisions must be made quickly. Therefore, you will need some kind of fundamental and simple ethical process that you can actually use at work. Providing that practical format is our objective. It will not be perfect, but we believe that attempts to achieve perfect ethical decisions should be left to professional thinkers.

### The Role of a Personal Ethical Perspective

To begin the process of developing a practical ethical system, we want to emphasize the need for individual business leaders to identify and develop their personal ethical perspective. This step is crucial preparation for those instances when personal beliefs about what is ethical clash with the organization's inclinations, as given voice by someone who is their boss. Without previous use of an effective ethical format to understand personal standards, it is too easy to just obey whenever the organization shouts, "Make your numbers." By obeying such mandates, businesspeople will be internalizing the ethical habits of their firm reflexively. As a result, the individual moral self loses identity.

To resist this somber outcome, our text will suggest approaches to greater self-understanding. After all, each of us brings a personal perspective to work each day; we may just need a reminder and a process to activate it. Business ethics will be guided in major part by how successfully we can apply a personal ethical stance in our business decisions.

### The Interrelated Role of Business Culture

It is important to understand not only your personal ethical standards but also those of your employer. A business organization has an ethical history and an ethical vision. Both these factors create a climate in which business decisions will be made. The interaction between personal ethics and the ethical environment encouraged by the business organization are the crucible in which business ethics will be determined. That interaction is a partnership; the individual business leader cannot entirely create an ethical climate. Similarly, the organization, regardless of its degree of hierarchy, cannot entirely reconstruct the ethical views brought to the business by its individual members.

We want to make certain to emphasize the personal economic reality of being tied to a particular business organization as employee, customer, or investor. Although in an extreme case a person may want to sever relationships with a business because the ethical gap between personal and organizational ethics is too great to tolerate, that action will almost always be a final resort. Hence, a practical business ethics must include capabilities for changing and adapting to the business organization with which you have an ethical partnership.

## An Ethical Partnership between Self and Organization

To apply the concepts of the right and the good agreed upon by the employer-employee partnership, we as moral agents must somehow decide which of several potential ethical perspectives to use in a specific business context. Then we must decide how to put the chosen perspective into operation. No ethical theory provides a simple single ethical answer to a business problem. Thus, naming a preferred ethical perspective would be only a first ethical step for reflective businesspeople. They would still need much guidance concerning the making of an ethical business decision.

This book attempts to provide that guidance. The first half (chapters 1 to 5) provides background information that puts ethical decision making into an appropriate context. The second half guides the reader through an actual decision-making process. It provides an ethical format that integrates several practical activities that, when used together, promote better business ethics. Specifically, it recognizes that a practical business ethics requires the following.

1. Awareness of the **F**acts of the ethical dilemma
2. Appreciation for the scope of the **I**ssue
3. Understanding of the relevant **L**aw governing the issue
4. Consideration of the **O**ptions available
5. Selection of applicable ethical **P**rinciples

We call our approach FILOP to acknowledge both the importance of each element and the integrated manner in which they work together to create a practical strategy. As any set of steps, they are stronger when used together. Readers who are facing an ethics "emergency" at this moment may want to skip to Part 2 of the book and save Part 1 for a time when they can read, study, and reflect.

## THE PROFIT MOTIVE AND ETHICS

What is the profit motive, and how does this concept fit into a practical strategy for business ethics? The profit motive is just that. It is a single possible stimulus for operating a business. Many who look at business from outside assume that firms always maximize profit. However, that assumption is far too simple to capture the reasons why businesspeople behave in particular ways.

Management texts give the profit motive its proper due, placing it in the midst of a long list of business objectives, including ethical goals. In addition, management texts clearly explain that the necessity to make a profit is quite distinct from the effort to maximize profit. Of course, firms wish to make a profit, but a host of competing objectives limit the desire to *maximize* those profits.

Indeed, profit maximization is most socially desirable *only when markets resemble mom-and-pop grocery stores*. In that form of market, what economists call pure competition, profit maximization compels businesspeople to provide high-quality products at the lowest possible prices in the amounts desired by consumers. In purely competitive markets, should a business fail to be responsive to consumer inclinations, it would not survive. In such an ideal setting, profit maximization forces the businessperson to serve the desires of consumers.

However, in other forms of markets, firms that attempt to maximize profits would be able to use stronger means than their mom-and-pop predecessors to manage or control the marketplace for the benefit of those directly involved with the firm. In other words, as soon as businesses become powerful by departing from purely competitive markets, their profit maximization activities run the risk of doing social harm. Therefore, the importance of making ethical decisions for businesspeople is increased significantly.

Bayer, a chemical manufacturer, is one example of a powerful company that might have benefited from more consideration of ethical decision making. This company caused serious harm when it marketed a highly lethal pesticide to illiterate Peruvian agricultural communities. Bayer's packaging of the white-powder chemical gave little or no warning of its toxicity to their target market, small farmers in the Andean Mountains who could not read the Spanish labeling. Although Bayer increased profits by this marketing decision, 24 children died after accidentally ingesting the pesticide, which resembled powdered milk.[8]

However, not all profit-enhancing decisions have such high levels of disregard for public safety and well-being. Many businesspeople appreciate the complexity of profit maximization and are careful to spell out the multiple objectives that guide their decisions.

Businesses that ignore the complex nature of profit maximization and instead portray themselves as one-dimensional profit machines will face a steep uphill climb if they expect the rest of us to believe that they will be honest or dependable. Yet, we should not underestimate the power of the profit maximization language in serving as a justification for business decisions. So as frequently as is appropriate, we will stop in this book to highlight the tension that often exists between profit maximization and particular ethical perspectives.

One thing we want to avoid in these discussions of profit maximization is any implication that profit is unethical or that profit maximization never has an ethical justification. Thus, to place those "profit moments" in proper perspective, we should all remind ourselves about the potential social advantages of profits in general and profit maximization in particular. *Under the right circumstances*, profits can stimulate socially desirable innovation, efficiency, and consumer sovereignty.

## LAW AS AN ETHICAL GUIDE

The idea that business can use the law as an ethical guide, much like the idea that businesses can be both ethical and profit maximizing, is often viewed with skepticism or disdain. Law provides a very important ethical guideline, not something to be sneered at as if it is ethics light. Law is one potent public voice about what particular communities see as good and right.

Because the law represents important social norms, expectations, and rules of the game, it provides a reading of what behavior should be discouraged and which is to be encouraged. The creation of legal sanctions and the rejection of proposed legislation, courtroom decisions, and damage awards spell out the boundaries of what businesses are permitted to do. Consequently, we will urge you to consider law as a significant contributor to ethical guidelines.

In no manner are we suggesting that laws are always ethical, nor are we claiming that law and ethics are the same thing. Law evolves; that evolution is one important element to consider when ethical business-people act. Legislatures and courts are continually revising the law because they recognize that law is always a work in progress.

However, as a guideline for what is good and right, businesspeople can start by identifying the relevant law. At a minimum, a businessperson can fairly say: "I have paid attention to ethics to some extent, for I have obeyed the law."

For example, Party City, a store in Maryland, has large bins of latex balloons for sale.[9] Although balloons are a recognized choking hazard for young children, they are also essential as party supply items. How should the manager decide the best policy for selling balloons? In this case, the Child Safety Protection Act of 1994 requires that all balloons be sold with a particular warning label: Choking hazard, inappropriate for children under eight. Whatever decision the manager reaches about selling balloons at Party City, posting safety labels that comply with the law is a good place to start.

## BUSINESS AND TRUST

In the late summer of 2002, national polls reported high degrees of public mistrust of upper management in major American corporations. Fully 75 percent of respondents claimed that corporate executives would be willing to say anything that would make their conduct appear innocent. So what?

Business has an important role to play in any organized society. It functions in three important domains. The first two are standard functions in the market exchange process:

1. As prospective *producers*, they must interact with potential investors, existing owners, suppliers, and employees.

2. Once a good or service is produced, businesses must successfully negotiate with consumers a price and quality of output that will permit businesses to be *sellers*.

In anticipation of a point we will make throughout this book, you should notice that these two functions alone highlight the variety of people affected by any business decision.

But a third business function is at least as important as the first two because of its symbolic effect on our national reputation, our future as an economic pacesetter, and the general ethical climate in our neighborhoods. This symbolic effect is expressive; it serves as a signal to others, telling them who we are and what we care about.

3. The prominence of business as an institution in our culture results in its inescapable role as an *educator*. Businesspeople are leaders in what we might think of as social reproduction, the passing of understandings and expectations from generation to generation. They are major voices in training young people to appreciate which aspirations are acceptable and which go beyond what respectable people in our situation do.

The wave of recent corporate scandals illustrate how corporate misdeeds can send compelling signals about the norms and priorities of American business. For many people, the scandals indicated that corporate executives cannot be trusted because they care only about their short-term financial gains, regardless of the long-term impact. This message has powerful implications on global, national, and personal levels.

Consider the story of Ameet Shah.[10] Three years ago he graduated from Duke University and landed a job at J. P. Morgan Chase in New York City. He took home a big paycheck and was able to work on prominent business deals. Nonetheless, the corporate scandals made Ameet question his whole purpose for being in corporate America. As he explains, "I saw people who put 15 years of service into the company get laid off in a day because of the irresponsible behavior of corporate executives. I started thinking that I didn't want to be associated with that." In fact, Ameet was so turned off by the behavior of prominent members of corporate America that he quit his job and joined Teach for America. He is now teaching in the South Bronx. Ameet's departure from corporate America illustrates the potential impact of business's symbolic effect.

The social roles of producer, seller, and educator performed by businesspeople are dependent on high degrees of trust. If those with whom businesspeople interact cannot depend on the claims businesses make, then resources are unnecessarily wasted. For example, the time that could have been spent arriving at an agreement is spent strategically estimating the level of self-dealing and dishonesty present in the behavior of the businesspeople with whom we are trying to work.

Consider how focused on the actual terms of the trade you can be when you are buying a car from a friend. The trust you have in your friend is a lubricant for the exchange; trust creates efficiency on the road to "yes." But the situation would be very different if you were buying the same car from a businessperson whom you expected to attempt to extract more money from you than the car would be worth in a competitive market (where all relevant information about the vehicle is available for everyone thinking about purchasing the car). In this situation, you do not trust the businessperson. Therefore, you must spend large amounts of time and energy attempting to protect yourself from the financial exploitation that you believe the businessperson has in mind for you. None of us likes the feeling that others are out to use us in this fashion. Instead, when we are able to trust one another, we maintain confidence in the results of business dealings.

The importance of trust is not limited to the business roles as producer and seller. It is also a necessity for businesspeople to be effective educators. When businesspeople are at their best, they model the values of diligence, responsibility, creativity, and efficiency. Although the worth of those values for our community does not require that we trust businesspeople, the positive effect businesspeople can have as illustrations of these values is very much affected by whether we trust those same businesspeople.

One positive example of a company that creates public trust is Fannie Mae, a financial corporation that aims to further low-income and minority home ownership through its $2 trillion program, the American Dream Commitment. Over 51 percent of Fannie Mae's financing in 2001 went to low- and moderate-income households as part of the corporation's goals to provide financing to borrowers who would otherwise be hindered from borrowing or subject to predatory loan rates.[11] Fannie Mae's financial success highlights the positive role that a business can have in furthering community trust.

Values are not just abstractions; they usually come to our attention through some human model—a person whom we trust and admire. When citizens, customers, employees, and students see businesspeople as working only for their personal interests, the educational potential of business is tarnished. Few people will want to mimic the values and patterns of those they have learned to distrust. When businesspeople treat others as objects or instruments for their own needs, they become the villainous characters that Hollywood so often portrays when businesspeople are represented in films.

## A SAMPLE BUSINESS ETHICS DILEMMA

This first chapter concludes with a sample business dilemma. Notice its complexity. No easy answers come to mind. However, highlighting our theme, businesspeople do not have the option of punting or running for cover when such dilemmas arise. Businesspeople need to act. Hence, they need a practical approach they can use to do good work.

## THE H. B. FULLER CASE[1]

Forty million children live in the streets of Central America. These children, orphans and runaways, survive by finding small jobs, begging, stealing, and prostituting their bodies for food. In an economy with rampant unemployment, and with few government or charity programs to help them, their lives are constantly threatened with cold, hunger, and fear. Vulnerable to attacks from both nature and other human beings, these children must sleep in doorways, abandoned buildings, and sewer pipes and are often physically and sexually abused, even by the police.

Around 70 percent of these Central American street children have found escape from the pain of these conditions by addiction to glue. The children buy solvent-based contact cement intended for shoe making and repairs, which is packaged by retailers in small plastic bags and baby food jars. When the children inhale the fumes of this glue, they experience relief from incessant hunger and are consoled in their loneliness.

However, this euphoria comes at a high cost. The fumes also destroy their lungs, livers, and brains. The chemicals in the glue, especially toluene, one of the solvent bases used in manufacturing the glue, are highly toxic. Not only does their use as narcotic agents burn the skin, nose, throat, and eyes, but also, once inhaled, the fumes go quickly through the bloodstream to the brain. Side effects include memory loss, hearing loss, brain damage, and, sometimes, sudden death. Addicts frequently lose physical coordination and suffer muscle weakness and permanent nerve damage. The chemicals also interfere with blood cell production, inducing a life-threatening form of anemia. Death can result because inhaling the glue sometimes leads to sudden liver failure or cardiac arrest.

The physical harm of these chemicals is not even necessarily the most serious hazard to those who sniff the glue. Children intoxicated by these narcotics are also much more vulnerable to death from sources other than just the toxic fumes. For example, children high on glue are more likely to drown in drainage ditches and sewers or be killed in traffic or by violence.

In the early 1980s, newspapers in Honduras began to run stories about child addicts. These newspapers referred to the children as "los resistoleros"—after Resistol, a line of glues manufactured by H. B. Fuller S.A., a subsidiary of Kativo Chemical Industries, S. A. Kativo is one of Central America's 500 largest corporations and is wholly owned by H. B. Fuller Company of St. Paul, Minnesota.

While Resistol glues may be a popular choice of addicts, they are by no means the only products so abused—addicts in Honduras and other Central American countries also abuse glues, paint thinners, and other chemical products made by other companies.

However, despite Kativo's protest of the label, the name Resistoleros stuck. The strong marketing position of H. B. Fuller's products turned into a marketing nightmare as child addiction became synonymous with the

Resistol glue products. Child advocacy groups, most noticeably Covenant House (or Casa Alienza in Spanish-speaking countries), began to organize protest against H. B. Fuller and other companies who were marketing the solvent-based glues destroying the street children of Central America.

Despite H. B. Fuller's reputation in the United States as a corporation devoted to ethical integrity and concern for the wider community, the company's response to the public outcry in Latin America was less than satisfactory. While the company did stop using toluene, the highly toxic solvent, in some of the adhesives, the substitute for toluene, cyclohexane, is only slightly less poisonous when inhaled, causing many of the same irreversible damages to the health of the street children.

H. B. Fuller looked even worse when its chief competitor, another multinational corporation, stopped selling solvent-based glues in Central America, offering instead a water-based adhesive. Henkel Corporation is based in Dusseldorf, Germany. When its company image came under increasing fire from both the Central American and German press, Henkel decided to switch to non-solvent-based products, first in Central America, then globally.

In 1992, H. B. Fuller's board of directors announced that the glue would be discontinued "wherever these products are known to be abused as inhalants." This statement was initially welcomed by the press, but ended up hurting H. B. Fuller's case further, as availability of the Resistol glues in Central America continued almost unhindered. H. B. Fuller stopped retail sales only in Honduras and Guatemala—the two countries in which Casa Alienza is active. Production and marketing continued in four other Central American countries, and in Honduras and Guatemala, street children could buy the glue from retailers who purchased the glue in large drums and repackaged it.

Efforts were also made to have H. B. Fuller add an irritant to the toxic glues that would make them too obnoxious to inhale. Airplane glue manufacturers in the 1960s added oil of mustard to their glue to avoid abuse of the glue as a narcotic. H. B. Fuller refused to reformulate its glues with this oil. In March 1989, the Honduran Congress even passed a law requiring oil of mustard to be included in all solvent-based glues made or imported for sale in the country. However, H. B. Fuller protested changing its formula, and the law was not enforced.

H. B. Fuller's mission statement declares, "The H. B. Fuller Company is committed to its responsibilities, in order of priority, to its customers, employees, and shareholders. H. B. Fuller will conduct business legally and ethically, support the activities of its employees in their communities, and be a responsible corporate citizen." It is possible that this statement is no more than corporate wallpaper covering crass profit seeking; the company's history in other areas seems to indicate otherwise. H. B. Fuller's consistent policies as an employer and community benefactor have earned it 13th place in Business Ethics magazines "100 Best Corporate Citizens" for 2002. This knowledge raises an important ethical question: How closely linked are H. B. Fuller's decisions about glue in Central America to this corporate responsibility? To better answer this question, we must first examine several reasons for H. B. Fuller's continued sale of a solvent-based glue.

One of H. B. Fuller's protests is that the legitimate users of Resistol in Central America will be harmed if the product is discontinued. Solvent-based contact cements provide rapid set, strong adhesion, and water resistance—characteristics H. B. Fuller has tried without success to match with a water-based glue. If the glue is not available for legitimate public and industrial use, economic growth in Central America might be hindered.

At the same time that solvent-based adhesives are vital to some Central American businesses, drug addiction is so prevalent among street children that they will turn to any available narcotic substance. If shoe glue were not available, H. B. Fuller argues, street children would get high on the paint thinners and other solvents used even now as alternative narcotic substances.

Furthermore, in 1994, when Fuller substituted cyclohexane for toluene in its glues, the price of the glue also increased by 30 percent. In addition to the increase in price, cyclohexane also lacks the sweet smell of toluene. While Casa Alianza is right to point out that cyclohexane is still highly toxic, H. B. Fuller argues that this change in formula has made the glue less attractive to children than the other manufacturer's glues available on the streets.

In the 1980s, when the effort was made to persuade Fuller to add allyl isothiocyanate (oil of mustard) to its glues, Fuller presented evidence that the additive was significantly hazardous to the health of employees and consumers. Oil of mustard was found to be carcinogenic in studies run with rats. Furthermore, a toxicology report offered evidence that the chemical was extremely destructive to the tissue of the upper mucous membranes and the upper respiratory tract, eyes, and skin; caused burns, nausea, dizziness, and headache; and could be fatal if swallowed or inhaled. Finally, adding allyl isothiocyanate would shorten the shelf life of the glues to a maximum of six months.

In further attempts to demonstrate their concern for the problem of glue addiction, H. B Fuller executives have met with both government leaders and antidrug advocates in Central America. In 1987, the company started community affairs committees with Kativo employees in Central America, stating, "We want to be a company with recognized values, demonstrating involvement, and commitment to the betterment of the communities we are a part of." As part of their involvement, the company has made public statements and helped draft legislation in favor of increased education for street children about drug abuse. H. B. Fuller also makes regular contributions to homeless shelters for street children in Central America.

A thorough examination of this dilemma will show that drug addiction of Central American children is part of the larger problem of poverty, neglect, and abuse found in these countries. But how do H. B. Fuller's decisions either relieve or exacerbate the problem? Is the supposed concern for "community" shown by Fuller and its subsidiaries genuine? Or is the company taking advantage of current conditions in Central America to further its own profits?

*Sources:*
[1] Marjorie Kelly, "Though H. B. Fuller May Wish It, Resistol Issue Won't Go Away," *Minneapolis Star Tribune*, December 4, 1995; *Casa Alianza*, http://www.casa-alianza.org/EN/index-en.shtml.

## CRITICAL THINKING QUESTIONS

A case like H. B. Fuller presents a lot to think about. Even after we ask key ethical questions about the effects of the firm's behavior on the many constituencies the firm has, we still must wade through a weighting of the often-conflicting interests of those affected parties. No rule book is available to give us unambiguous rules to follow in making these assessments of what is the good thing to do for the community.

But our best hope for more ethical business decisions is the use of our listening and reasoning skills to arrive at judgments consistent with our best efforts to be curious, open, and reflective. To assist you in this endeavor, we will end most chapter with *critical thinking quesitons*. These questions move us toward an evaluation of the alternatives we are considering. They require us to compare evidence and reasons in pursuit of improved business ethics.

## ENDNOTES

[1] Wendy Zellner, et al., "The Man Behind the Deal Machine," *Business Week*, Feb. 4, 2002, 40–41.

[2] John A. Byrne, "Corporate Culture: Enron & Beyond," *Business Week*, Feb. 25, 2002, 118.

[3] Wendy Zellner, et al., "The Man Behind the Deal Machine," *Business Week*, Feb. 4, 2002, 40–41.

[4] Eric Schlosser, *Fast Food Nation: The Dark Side of the All-American Meal* (Boston: Houghton Mifflin, 2001).

[5] "Top Corporate Ethics Officers Tell Conference Board That More **Business Ethics** Scandals are Ahead," *LEXIS Financial News* (June 17, 2002): http://web.lexis-nexis.com/universe/document?_m=52e748bdf2eb03a8c330d45b96f747c2&_docnum=16&wchp=dGLbVlb-lSlzV&_md5=6664cfacdb950bad255505f7917150c5 (accessed September 24, 2002).

[6] R. J. King, "Huge Project Revitalizes River Rouge," *Detroit News*, July 9, 2000.

[7] John Berlau, "Is Big Business Ethically Bankrupt?" *LexisNexis* (March 18, 2002): http://web.lexis-nexis.com/universe/document?_m=be57b235c6101c20e7fc1f7a5e33b2b0&_docnum=1&wchp=dGLbVlb-lSlzV&_md5=652d634b81fa7ab73487e7ea108a1032.

[8] Kara Sissell, "Product Liability," *Chemical Week*, 163, no. 41 (Nov. 7, 2001): 17.

[9] "Trouble in Toyland: The 2001 PIRG Survey of Potential Toy Hazards Found in Stores," http://www.toysafety.net/ (accessed September 2, 2002).

[10] Rachel Lehmann-Haupt and Warren St. John, "Corporate Bad Guys Make Many Seek the Road Less Traveled," *New York Times*, July 21, 2002, 9–1.

[11] "In Brief: Fannie Surpasses Minority Targets," *American Banker*, 167, no. 17 (January 25, 2002): 11.

# CHAPTER 2

# American Corporate and Organizational Culture: The Employment Context

**THE FOCUS:**
Why might good people do bad things when they become employees in corporations and organizations?

When you go to work, you intend to provide services in return for compensation and a sense of satisfaction that you have made a contribution to a human enterprise. You know very well that your behavior will be organized and judged by the organization for which you work. But to what extent will you be asked to make decisions that are inconsistent with your personal sense of ethics? How will you respond? As you begin this chapter, think about these questions in terms of the following scenario.

You have landed the job of your dreams. Upon graduation from medical school, you will work as a researcher for one of the nation's top medial research centers. Under the direction of a nationally known star in the area of cancer research, you will help create new strategies for curing the disease. You have long maintained, "My lifelong ambition is to advance science." This goal is especially important to you because a number of your relatives have died of cancer, and you are honoring their memories by contributing to advances in cancer research.

As you think about your role in the quest to advance science, you wish you had a mentor who could help you sort out some of your concerns about the challenges you may face as you start your career. In particular, you have some concerns about the increasing links between business and medical research.

Your new employer, Dr. Valerie Mill[1] of the University Research Center, is the kind of medical researcher whose work attracts the interest of venture capitalists. These venture capitalists want to invest in tomorrow's possible medical breakthroughs.[2] In your interview for the research position, Dr. Mill explained her belief in enlightened self-interest. Dr. Mill likes to say, "There is nothing wrong with advancing science and generating wealth at the same time. It's a win-win for doctors and patients."

You are not so sure about the claim that enlightened self-interest is likely to yield a win-win. There's one particular case from a medical ethics class you took a few years back that haunts you. It is the case of Dr. Hugh Davis, the physician at Johns Hopkins University who played a primary role in inventing the Dalkon Shield, a contraceptive device.

Dr. Davis invented the Dalkon Shield in the late 1960s with the best of intentions—he wanted to advance women's health and family planning.[3] Unfortunately, Davis created a defective design for his invention, and as a consequence of his work, thousands of women suffered. The device's multifilament string, which was supposed to keep it in place and make removal possible, resulted in infections that caused some women to become sterile, others to miscarry, and some to die. Eventually, the injured women sought damages from A. H. Robins, the company that bought the Dalkon Shield from Davis and his collaborators. The company eventually went bankrupt, and Dr. Davis's career was ruined.[4]

You remember the case well because, like most ethics disasters, it was complicated and left you feeling confused and uncertain. For example, you remember that government regulators had failed to monitor Dr. Davis and other inventors. Also, A. H. Robins had failed to ensure it was offering a safe product to the public.

You also recall that Dr. Davis was a complicated person for you to judge. On the one hand, he seemed like you—an inventor with a passion for medical advancement. Although he enjoyed financial benefits from his invention, he was not a bottom-line, money-oriented man. The case was never a simple "ethics versus greed" dilemma. On the other hand, writers who have described Dr. Davis have pointed out that he was arrogant,[5] lied when it suited his interests,[6] became paranoid,[7] and demonstrated a general lack of empathy for those injured by the defective device he created.[8]

One key fact that troubled you was that Dr. Davis relied on his reputation as an expert scientist to tout the superior qualities of the Dalkon Shield, all the while failing to disclose his financial interest in the product. Both as a scientist and businessman, his acts eventually became a lose-lose-lose, with losses for women, A. H. Robins, and Dr. Davis.

As you consider the "enlightened self-interest" views of Dr. Mill and your concerns about the new job, you try to assure yourself that you could never be like Dr. Davis. Of could you? You think, "Am I deceiving myself? Is it possible I could become just like Dr. Davis?"

First, you realize that you are an American, joining an organization steeped in American traditions, both good and bad. You pride yourself on being a "rugged individualist," prepared to rise and fall according to your own talent, hard work, and decision-making skills. You also admit that, in spite of your rugged individualism, there have been times when you have conformed to the culture around you. Despite your desire for independence, you know you need to "play the game" to succeed in any profession.

Second, you realize that, like Dr. Davis, you are going to work for an American business. Your idealism and desire to become a force for positive change might get reshaped as you work for an organization that places a high priority on bottom-line results. You know that even not-for-profit organizations with noble visions care very much about generating revenues and minimizing costs.

Then you think about the individual within the organization. You wonder how good people end up engaging in bad acts. It is not as if a small band of evil men and women enters the business world, wreaking havoc until they crash and burn. What complicated process yields ethics disasters? Are individuals to blame? Are organizations and corporations to blame? Do certain situations that arise in the ordinary course of business lend themselves to ethics disasters?

To help you answer some of your concerns about business ethics, you want to get a sense of yourself compared to others who work in corporations and organizations. What are the typical smaller, daily dilemmas you are likely to face in your new job? You also wonder how other employees resolve the dilemmas they face in their working lives.

In the preceding role-playing situation, an awareness of the context for business ethics would help you answer many of your questions. The primary goal of this chapter is to explore this background information necessary for making good ethical decisions. It is important to note that the context in our example is an American one. In particular, it is an American *business* context. Most ethical dilemmas you will experience will occur within that particular context. Hence, understanding what the American business culture tends to expect from you is an important and helpful first step in developing a practical ethical system. You may also feel a sense of comfort, knowing the kinds of dilemmas you face are typical. In other words, you are not alone. Additionally, awareness of an American employment context can help you develop a moral partnership with your employer.

You may be especially interested in thinking about the individual within an organization. You are concerned about both large ethics disasters and the kinds of ethical dilemmas American workers face on a daily basis. Before we get to a list of those dilemmas, we must make clear what ideas make America unique, and how these ideals shape the good and bad traditions we see in corporations and organizations.

## KEY ELEMENTS OF AMERICAN CULTURE

*The idea of individualism is central to the American experience.*[9] **Individualism** is "a view of the individual person which gives unprecedented weight to his or her choices, interests, and claims."[10] In other words, what the individual wants is of utmost importance. It is not uncommon for Americans to say, "I'll do what I want," then, in response, other people will say, "And so you should!" Americans demonstrate a strong interest in **individual responsibility,** which is the idea that each person should control his or her own actions and be accountable for the consequences of those actions.[11]

In contrast, **collectivism** gives primary weight to the needs and objectives of certain societal groups, such as governments and churches. **Collective or community responsibility** is the idea that informal (e.g., clubs) or formal groups (e.g., churches, government agencies) should solve problems through means that show mutual trust and commonality of interests and priorities.[12] Individuals, from this framework, are strongly influenced by factors beyond their personal control.

For our purposes, a distinction between individualism and collectivism is important because citizens from different countries may frame and suggest different responses to ethical dilemmas. In the individualistic context of the United States, we tend to point fingers at individuals when something goes wrong (e.g., "How could Kenneth Lay have been ignorant of what was going on at Enron?").

By contrast, German citizens (see Global Box) are likely to focus on institutions when assigning blame. In Germany, a person considering the Enron collapse might ask, "What is it about American capitalism that yielded this kind of widespread wrongdoing?"

Individualism has powerful implications for American culture:[13]

1. There is a strong belief in systems that **protect private property.**[14] An individual who owns something deserves to do what he/she wants with it, as long as he/she acquired it fairly.[15]
2. We believe in **freedom,** which means we generally want our government[16] (and others) to "leave us alone."[17] Sometimes, however, we want the government to intervene when significant market failures occur. For instance, in 2002, in the face of visible corporate wrongdoing, there was bipartisan support for legislation asking for increased transparency and accountability in corporations. The freedom we tend to support most aggressively is a freedom *from*. This approach to liberty is always watchful that some group might prevent individual decisions.
3. We believe individuals should **advance based on their merits.**[18] Mobility (movement up and down the income scale) should be based on an individual's own talent and effort.

**GLOBAL BOX**

### GERMANY

Comparative studies in business ethics often look at differences in ethical rules across countries or business etiquette. Another revealing way to approach comparative studies is to consider how countries frame ethical problems. For example, when a business is accused of acting unethically, Americans tend to see the individual people involved as the source of the problem. Our legal system focuses on implicating individuals for their specific wrongdoings.

The American tendency to frame ethical problems as stemming from individual behavior differs from how Germans tend to frame ethical issues. When attention is brought to the unethical practices of a German business, the focus is on the norms, values, and policies of the entire business system. The administrative system in which the business operates is generally seen as the source of the problem. Germans are concerned with how institutional norms permit unethical behavior. German appeals for reform reflect the focus on institutional problems. Rather than rallying for the prosecution of individual wrongdoers, Germans tend to call on the government for legal and regulatory solutions to unethical practices.

The call for more effective regulation goes out to companies as well. Many German companies have responded by implementing official policies aimed at preventing unethical behavior. These policies include complete bans on accepting gifts valued at more than fifty marks and not permitting personal addresses to appear on business cards. These regulations reflect Germans' assumption that institutions are at the root of ethical business problems.

*Source:*
Fred Seidel, "Business Ethics in Three European Countries: A Comparative Approach," in *Working Across Cultures: Ethical Perspectives for Intercultural Management,* ed. Heiko Lange, et al., pp. 235–261 (Dordrecht, Netherlands: Kluwer Academic, 1998).

4. Our culture views individuals as equal in the sense that there is an **absence of rank**[19] (e.g., we do not have a caste system). Individuals can move from one social class to another.

In addition to these key individualistic descriptors, Americans are generally positive, in search of happy endings.

What are the sources of central cultural ideas? Curiosity about *where* we get our fundamental ideas provides us with insight into the extent to which we want to continue to be guided by these early influences or move onto a better source for our ethical vision.

In every culture important institutions, including business, religion, education, and the family, interact to teach us what is acceptable ethically in our particular setting. For example, in some cultures, business and religion are intertwined; in Middle Eastern/Islamic cultures religion plays a major role in guiding business decisions. In contrast, in America, although individual business leaders might vocally announce links between their religious views and the way they operate their business,[20] most business dealings are **secular or nonreligious.**

Business and education do interact extensively in American culture. In an increasing number of instances, corporations are purchasing access to today's students, who will become tomorrow's consumers. Schools that prefer not to influence their students' spending habits are in a difficult position because these schools will not be able to benefit from the financial assistance that corporate support brings.

Here is one example of just such an intersection between business and education. A computer company may desire to donate computers to a school, hoping to show students how much they might prefer a particular brand of computer down the road. *Microsoft* founder Bill Gates, for example, donated one billion dollars to 12,500 public schools throughout the country for the purchase of computers.[21] Not only does Mr. Gates's action invest in the future success of the company by familiarizing students with *Microsoft's* computers, it also benefits the school by providing a much-needed resource.

American firms are increasingly forming influential partnerships with families as cultural leaders. For instance, some businesses are responding to employees' expressed interest in balancing their work and family responsibilities. Some employers are providing on-site day care as an employee benefit. However, other businesses are more individualistic, expressing the belief that people who choose to have families should work out their own plan to balance work and family responsibilities. Few Americans would be shocked by individualism-based policies such as this one. However, as we mentioned previously, citizens of other countries have very different expectations regarding the good and right roles of social institutions.

The travelers' surprise at the generosity and compassion of the townspeople in the box foreshadows a dark side of the dominant American ideal of individualism.[22] The focus on the self championed by individualism creates some negative implications associated with American culture.

1. In spite of their rugged individualism, Americans tend to be **conformists.** Writers have described Americans as "intensely conformist,"[23] often demonstrating a "lack of independence of thought."[24]
2. Self-interest sometimes becomes **selfishness.** Writers have noted that "individualism carries with it a tendency to emphasize excessively the rights of the self against all comers ..."[25] and sometimes manifests itself in a "failure to recognize others' needs."[26]
3. The focus on the self can lead to **erosion of societal institutions.** Writers have suggested that "individualism has come to emphasize far too much of the gratification of the self over the needs of various important social institutions including, above all, the family."[27]

## VALUES IN ACTION

### Gander after 9/11—Americans are surprised and thankful after Canadians befriend strangers

Americans tend to focus so much on self-interest that we are often surprised when citizens of other countries look beyond self-interest and emphasize collectivism instead.

A good example of collective responsibility occurred the week of September 11, 2001, when citizens of Gander, Newfoundland, with a population of 10,300, welcomed 6,500 unexpected visitors from around the world.[1]

After the terrorist attacks in the United States, the American government prohibited pilots heading to the United States from landing in America. Soon after, pilots landed 200 planes in Canada, and 38 of those landed in Gander.

In the following four days, Gander residents opened their own homes to stranded travelers, mostly Americans. The town felt a sense of collective responsibility for the travelers. Residents served their surprise guests home cooked meals and offered comfort and friendship. Other groups also helped. For instance, local doctors and pharmacies refused payment when guests needed care and medicine. Also, bus drivers who had been on strike came off picket lines and offered their services. One bus driver said, "In times like this, that's what the Newfies believe in—helping people."[2]

One American remarked, "[Residents of Gander] literally stopped their lives to take care of us. ... I've never in my life met people so generous and giving."

This story shows that residents of Gander believe in **collective responsibility**—the town viewed itself as one unit, working together to help the travelers. It also shows that the residents of Gander value both **generosity** and **compassion.**

Sources:
[1] This text box is based on information from Marcella Bombardieri, "Unexpected Welcome—Canadians Befriend September 11 Guests," *Boston Globe*, December 23, 2001.
[2] Ibid.

4. Many Americans are more likely to celebrate **narcissists** than people who place a high priority on looking out for others. Narcissists are individuals who demonstrate an excessive amount of self-love and are often "vain, grasping, manipulative characters who have an inflated perception of themselves and little regard for others."[28] One writer points out that "[narcissists] are everywhere"[29] in our contemporary culture, and "have received a widespread stamp of approval ...."[30] In fact, "Narcissism ... is glorified."[31]

5. Americans sometimes demonstrate **denial** about barriers to equal opportunity. Many white citizens ignore racial discrimination and the extent that it serves as a barrier for equal opportunity for African Americans.[32] Also, many upper-class Americans refuse to acknowledge how inequality in public education compromises the ability of lower-class Americans to compete on a level playing field.[33]

6. **Americans tend to think very highly of themselves.** In fact, it would not be surprising to hear Americans argue against the five preceding points, suggesting that individualism does not really have a dark side.

Finally, it is important to note the overwhelming influence of profits in American culture. Financial success seems to matter to all organizations. As one writer points out, "Everything now has a 'bottom line,' even schools and voluntary organizations."[34] This ever-present goal of making a profit, which is common to American business, is not always such a high priority for businesses based in other countries. In Islamic countries, making a profit is not as important as following religious rules regarding business practice.

## AMERICAN BUSINESS CULTURE

### The Bureaucratic Ethic

American business culture benefits from the positive traits associated with individualism. For example, it embraces the values of freedom and individual responsibility. Many American workers enjoy the opportunities American business provides for upward mobility. Most Americans believe it is really true that anyone, no matter their background, has a chance to "make it" by working in business. This section focuses on problems with American business culture—the problems that lead to the ethical dilemmas that can undermine the positive aspects of business culture.

Sociologist Robert Jackall did the most important work on the topic of ethics in bureaucratic organizations in the late 1980s.[35] Jackall went into a number of organizations to study the ways though which organizational bureaucracies shaped managers' moral consciousness. He concluded that the days of the Protestant ethic, where workers viewed their jobs as sacred callings, are long gone. Instead, most large organizations operate under a bureaucratic ethic. In essence, this ethic means that "[w]hat is right in the corporation is what the guy above you wants from you."[36]

Jackall learned that in this kind of culture, it is important for managers who want to climb the hierarchy to devote a significant amount of time and energy to shaping other people's perceptions of them. In other words, how you present yourself is often more important than your natural talent and work ethic.

Although image is an important part of American business culture, Jackall found that the belief that managers must be team players is even more prevalent. Good corporate managers identify the goals of their

## GLOBAL BOX

### MIDDLE EAST/ISLAM

The formal study of business ethics has yet to take hold in the Middle East. Neither Arabic nor Hebrew has a term for business ethics. Middle Eastern universities do not offer courses in the subject. Few businesses have formal codes of ethical conduct. The lack of formal study does not mean that Middle Eastern businesses are bereft of ethics, though. Scores of businesspersons use their religion, mainly Islam, as their moral compass in business dealings.

Many Muslims see God, the universe, and the people of the universe as interrelated. The belief in interdependence is illustrated by the use of the phrase, "insha' Allah." Muslims often use this phrase, rather than giving a firm answer or when making a promise to do something in the future. The phrase's commonly accepted meaning is, "if Allah wills it." Its use implies that there are no guarantees on what is to come because Allah has ultimate control over the course of events—even business events.

Although Islam considers business a socially useful endeavor, the religion does demand that one adhere to the tenants of Islam while conducting business affairs. Islamic law addresses issues of taxation, fair trading, consumption, and production, among others. The production of goods and services is expected to comply with the following conditions. First, the use of the good or service must be lawful within Islam. Muslims, for instance, cannot produce wine because Islamic law forbids its consumption. Second, Islamic law dictates that if a resource can be productive, then it cannot be left unused in the name of private ownership. Thus, if a person owns fertile land, then he must make use of that land. The entire community would be deprived of the land's benefits if it sat unused. Third, it is impermissible to sell something that is currently unavailable or whose delivery is questionable. This rule seeks to protect buyers from overconfident sellers. Finally, Islamic principles dictate that a product or service sold by a Muslim cannot cause harm to others. Muslims struggle to reconcile these tenants with modern business norms.

*Sources:*
Gillian Rice, "Islamic Ethics and the Implications for Business," *Journal of Business Ethics* 18(4) (1999): 345–58.
Dove Izraeli, "Business Ethics in the Middle East" in *Perspectives in Business Ethics* (2nd ed.), ed. Laura P. Hartman, 752–756 (Boston: McGraw-Hill, 2002).
Jamal A. Badawi, "Islamic Business Ethics" in *Spiritual Goods: Faith Traditions and the Practice of Business*, ed. Stewart W. Herman, 295–323 (Bowling Green, OH: Philosophy Documentation Center, 2001).

supervisors and do whatever is necessary to meet them. Personal decisions become team decisions, which often means individual managers do not feel personally responsible for their decisions. Managers or teams of managers often undertake actions individuals may consider wrong or immoral outside the firm. However, these actions are acceptable and even laudable within the firm because what is moral is what the boss desires.

Jackall discovered that in most bureaucratic organizations, the level of conformity is high. Employees in the corporate world are often reluctant to speak up when they observe or participate in troubling behavior. Many people are unwilling to bring bad news to the powerful people in the organization because most large organizations do not reward dissent.

Even boards of directors are subject to these silencing pressures; they simply do not want to rock the boat. Consider the recent WorldCom scandal. In 2002, this company, one of the nation's largest telecommunication's companies, admitted to lying about its profits. In particular, WorldCom exaggerated its cash flow by almost $4 billion.[37] The case is one of the largest incidents of accounting fraud in American business history. Investigators discovered that WorldCom's board of directors was put on notice about understated costs, hidden debts, and backdated contracts over a year before the company's demise. A shareholders' lawsuit revealed these corrupt practices and was supported by the testimony of dozens of employees. Nonetheless, the board of directors did not want to ask the tough questions. They, too, conformed to the pressure and chose to simply enjoy the success of the company without questioning its practices.[38]

## Obedience to Authority: Why Do People Conform?

In 1960, Stanley Milgram conducted the most well-known experiments that tested individuals' willingness to obey authority figures. Study participants (subjects) were told to give painful and apparently fatal shocks of electrical current to other participants (experimental subjects), who were answering quiz questions incorrectly. The subjects gave the shocks, even though they could hear the experimental subjects screaming in pain. The subjects continued to give shocks because scientists in white coats (authority figures) told them they had to, or the experiment would be ruined. The experimental subjects were actually actors.

The Milgram experiments attempted "to see how far a person [would] proceed in a concrete and measurable situation in which he is ordered to inflict increasing pain on a protesting victim."[39] Milgram found that "ordinary people, simply doing their jobs, and without any particular hostility on their part, can become agents in a terrible destructive process."[40] Milgram found that in some situations, people's moral concerns shift from the question, "Is this right?" to "Am I living up to the expectations of the authority figure?"[41]

Milgram offered several explanations for why people conform. The most important explanation is that hierarchies within organizations help individuals survive. He wrote that "organized social life provides survival benefits to the individuals who are part of it...."[42] Thus, people often conform to the will of authority figures because they want to reduce friction and increase their chances of survival.[43] This rationale helps us reconcile the ideas of individualism and conformity. At first glance, the rugged individualist believes she would not conform to an authority figure because she "is her own person," yet she needs to conform to ensure her individual survival.

More recently, management scholars Joseph L. Badaracco, Jr., and Allen P. Webb surveyed managers who work "in the trenches"—young managers who work below the middle-manager level.[44] Badaracco and Webb's research confirmed many of Jackall's observations about the bureaucratic ethic in organizations.

Young managers from a wide range of industries indicated that (1) middle managers often exerted pressure on young managers to engage in behavior the young managers believed was sleazy, unethical and/or illegal; (2) corporate codes of conduct offer little in the way of help; (3) young managers described top executives as out of touch with regard to ethical issues; and (4) young managers relied on a simple sleep test to resolve the ethical dilemmas they face at work. They asked, "If I do this, can I sleep at night?"[45]

The managers Badaracco and Webb interviewed also made clear that the organizations they worked for placed primary importance on the young managers' ability to perform well ("making your numbers") and engage in team play. Few young managers felt their organizations would reward them for engaging in ethical behavior; they were not convinced that "ethics pays."[46]

It is possible the corporation or organization that employs you does not operate under a bureaucratic ethic. If your corporation or organization is different, one possible explanation is that it is less bureaucratic than the ones Jackall, Badaracco, and Webb studied. You may work for a smaller firm or a large company with few managerial layers. Or perhaps your organization has taken steps to safeguard against some of the harsh consequences of the bureaucratic ethic. For example, your company may reward individual managers who speak up when they see wrongdoing. Finally, it is possible your company keeps its eye on its long-term commercial viability. Included in every decision is the necessity to look beyond what will be best for the company in the short run. The long-run interests of a variety of constituencies are the ultimate responsibility for the ethical firm.

### Corporate Ethics Codes

In the context of a bureaucratic ethic, it is not surprising that corporate codes of ethics provide little help to a young or midlevel manager struggling to demonstrate good behavior. Whereas this book defines **ethics**

## MEET THE LEADER: ALFRED P. SLOAN, JR.

Although this chapter highlights some of the harsh consequences of a bureaucratic organizational structure, there was a time in American history when this organizational structure changed America for the better.

In the book *Leading Minds: An Anatomy of Leadership*,[1] cognitive psychologist Howard Gardner gives Alfred P. Sloan, Jr., credit for serving as a key founder of the corporate form we know today. As head of General Motors (GM) from 1923–1946, Sloan created an organizational structure that helped make the company the largest and richest corporation in the world.[2] This structure is one we take for granted today—it includes separate autonomous divisions, along with a large general office we now know as a corporate headquarters. This structure weaves features of both decentralization and centralization[3] to help the company prosper.

As the leader of GM, Sloan became a spokesman for American business and encouraged the American public to see the corporation as an important societal institution, one as important as the church and military. Sloan wanted Americans to know that business could be a force for good. He served as one of the first models of what we refer to today as stakeholder theory (e.g., that companies should look out for the interests of a wide range of constituencies, including consumers). Sloan also presented the idea that GM's prosperity was good for the country as a whole.[4] Gardner wrote that Sloan believed that "[a]t times of prosperity, all could seem to benefit from a rising tide...."[5]

As a leader, Sloan was known for his interpersonal style. He lived what he preached about the ideal corporate form. He listened to others. He used his power carefully. Gardner quotes Sloan, "I got better results by selling my ideas than by telling people what to do."[6] Sloan also gave back to the community by engaging in philanthropy. Sloan's relationship with GM dealers was so strong that when Sloan retired, they honored him by making a contribution to cancer research that was valued at over $1.5 million.[7]

*Sources:*

[1] Howard Gardner, *Leading Minds: An Anatomy of Leaderhip* (in collaboration with Emma Laskin) (New York: Basic Books, 1995).

[2] Ibid., 133.

[3] Ibid., 147.

[4] Ibid., 142.

[5] Ibid., 143.

[6] Ibid., 139.

[7] Ibid., 140.

as *what we owe one another in a world in which we are socially and globally interdependent as workers, businesspeople, and consumers*, most organizations and corporations have a much narrower definition of ethics.

To most corporations, *ethics consists of the rules an organization expects its employees to follow*. Lawyers hired to protect the firm often create and enforce ethics codes. However, these ethics codes may be

**CRITICAL THINKING BOX**
Often, authors do not have the space to make the lists they present complete. The list is missing information. Can you add to the list of reasons why a particular corporation or organization might not have a bureaucratic ethic?

difficult for young managers to apply in real-life situations. In addition, these managers are hard-pressed to find thoughtful counsel within the corporation because corporate ethics offices do not usually employ psychologists, philosophers, theologians, or experts in any field with expertise that would provide assistance to individual managers struggling with an ethical dilemma.

Most managers know corporate codes of conduct exist more as a part of the company's defense strategy than as a practical guide. If an individual manager violates the code, the company is "covered," in the sense that managers had been told not to violate a law or rule. In fact, many employees sign a form pledging that they know the organizational ethical rules. When a problem occurs, the company responds by firing the individual employee who violated a rule, often without looking at broader cultural issues that set the stage for the employee to violate the rule.

It is not too surprising to recognize that corporate ethics codes often assume that most unethical business conduct arises from the behavior of lower-level managers, not top-level executives. The "hypothetical" ethical dilemmas most companies create tend to show lower-level workers considering unethical behavior. Ethics codes and training programs are more likely to highlight the possibility that midlevel managers are taking company pencils home than that high-level executives are manipulating accounting practices to make sure they get their annual bonuses.

Even when corporate codes of ethics consider the behavior of high-level executives, these codes are often ineffective in terms of whether they prevent unscrupulous behavior. For instance, Enron Corporation's code of ethics prohibited certain conflicts of interest for high-level executives. However, on two occasions, the board of directors waived the company's code of ethics, allowing one of the company's top financial officers, Andrew Fastow, to also be president of one of the partnership companies. Clearly, this business arrangement is an example of a conflict of interest. Even codes of ethics that apply to high-level executives are sometimes intentionally suspended.

Another problematic assumption of corporate codes of conduct is that they are usually "good times ethics" programs.[47] These codes of conduct are useful, as long as the ethical dilemma is so superficial that a company would be delighted to have outsiders watch the "struggle"

between right and wrong that the company faces. In most ethics training programs, the morally correct response to the hypothetical dilemma the company poses is easy to identify and relatively painless for the
company to pursue. In essence, the programs are often public relations
tools, allowing outsiders to get a glimpse of the company at its moral
best. However, when the company faces a real moral crisis, the corporate code and its ancillary training and committees are not always
helpful.

As a consequence of the bureaucratic ethic, the nature of ethics
codes and programs, and the willful blindness that some high-level managers demonstrate, it is not surprising that many young and midlevel
managers are cynical about their work. Americans, who are usually optimistic and hopeful, work in the business world and often become cynical managers. This cynicism works like acid, making many workplaces
intolerable. Over the course of time, some managers start to view their
work as senseless.[48] Many ask, "What am I doing here?"

Unfortunately, managers with the strongest moral inclinations are
often the managers with the strongest desire to quit, whereas those with
the most questionable individual moral codes keep climbing. At the end
of his book, Jackall describes the most promotable managers as those
who (1) see opportunities in others' misfortunes, (2) have the nerve to
pretend nothing is wrong even when the world is crumbling, (3) are
willing to do virtually anything their organization demands, no matter
how morally questionable, and (4) live a life in which nothing is more
important than one's own survival and advantage.[49]

## THE INDIVIDUAL WITHIN THE ORGANIZATION

### Ethics Disasters

When the world watches as an ethics disaster unfolds, it is not long before people in and outside the business world ask, "How could this have
happened?" Recently, we asked that question with regard to Enron,
Arthur Andersen, WorldCom, Tyco, Global Crossings, HealthSouth, and
many others.

Usually, we offer explanations that fall under three general categories. We say (1) there's something wrong with the **people** who made
questionable decisions, (2) there's something wrong with the
**organization** that engaged in wrongdoing, and/or (3) there's something
wrong that is unique about the **situation** that made the disaster un-
fold. This third category includes *structural* issues (e.g., matters larger
than people and organizations).

Using the information we've learned about American business culture, let's go back to Hugh Davis and the Dalkon Shield and explore
possible explanations for that particular disaster.

*How might people be flawed?* We all enter the workplace with our unique personalities and carry with us the lessons we have learned over the course of our lives. Sometimes, who we are gets us into ethical dilemmas. It is possible that individuals are flawed in multiple ways.

1. Individuals may **lack moral awareness.** Some people have no idea they are even facing an ethical dilemma. This is especially likely when there is a proximity problem[50]—when a person is so far removed from the people they may be hurting that they do not realize that they are hurting real people.
2. Individuals may **lack moral maturity.** Individuals go through stages of moral maturity. They start at a young age "doing the right thing" because they fear punishment or want to maximize their self-interest.[51] If the person matures, they engage in morally good behavior because they want people to think highly of them and/or they want to avoid breaking rules. The most morally mature individuals "do the right thing" because of higher concerns, such as their moral duties to others. Some people get stuck in the moral development process and never get beyond the most basic, self-interested rationales for behavior.
3. In rare cases, individuals may suffer from **personality disorders** that lead them to make poor decisions. One personality problem occurs when the positive traits of narcissism (e.g., that it drives people to do things) is not counterbalanced with other traits, such as empathy. Sometimes, excessive narcissism (see box) leads to poor decision making.

With regard to Dr. Hugh Davis, we could ask, "What was wrong with him?" Did he lack awareness of what his invention was doing to flesh-and-blood women? Did he suffer from stunted moral development? Did he suffer from a personality disorder?

---

### NARCISSISM: AN INTRODUCTION

In chapter 5, we will consider extreme narcissism—the rare situation in which narcissism becomes a personality disorder. For now, let's take an initial look at narcissism.

Healthy narcissism refers to "the investments of energy in one's genuine self."[52] Mature individuals demonstrate healthy narcissism when they balance self-love with an appropriate sense of self-worth. They have a realistic sense of themselves, both achievements and weaknesses. They can laugh at themselves. They can also make unique, positive contributions to the world.[53]

When we call someone a "narcissist," we are referring to unhealthy narcissism. Unhealthy narcissism exists because some people have not yet fully developed emotionally or morally, even though they are adults in terms of their age.[54]

Sandy Hotchkiss, LCSW, has written about unhealthy narcissism. She describes the characteristics of a powerful narcissist in the work environment.[55] The narcissistic boss: (1) has poor interpersonal boundaries;[56] (2) maintains his/her feelings of superiority by dumping personal shame onto employees or coworkers;[57] (3) announces a grand, perfectionist vision then gets workers to work frantically, often at great personal cost;[58] (4) turns unremarkable employees into "golden" workers who get more than their fair share of rewards, primarily because they "make the boss look or feel more pumped up";[59] (5) exploits others, often using them mercilessly;[60] (6) screams, plays mind games, and creates manic excitement;[61] (7) demonstrates envy and engages in destructive behavior, like gossiping;[62] and (8) constantly seeks admiration.[63]

Of course, it would be unfair for us to pass judgment on someone without a huge amount of information. We do know that those who knew Dr. Davis offered multiple descriptions of him. A colleague stated that he had a strong ego, that "[h]e was convinced that everything he did was right."[64] As the lawsuits piled up,[65] Davis became paranoid. He was filled with rage and blamed greedy plaintiffs' lawyers for his problems.[66]

We also know that Davis never said he was sorry for his role in causing women's harm, and he never apologized for misleading others about his financial interest in the Dalkon Shield.[67] His son described him as "a person who [did] not care about how others feel."[68] It is possible that Dr. Davis lacked moral awareness and/or maturity. It is also possible that a narcissistic personality made him blind to others' pain.

*How might organizations be flawed?* When thinking about an ethics disaster, consider the following possibilities.

1. The organization as a whole **lacks moral awareness.** Sometimes, organizational dynamics make it difficult for individual actors to see potential problems. Sometimes, teams rally around a bad plan, assuring each other they are doing a great job when in fact they are heading for disaster. The more the company invests in a bad plan, the harder it is to admit a mistake and start fixing it.

2. The organization has created a culture in which **a bureaucratic ethic thrives.** When a bureaucratic ethic thrives, you can count on the fact that individuals will not feel personally responsible for decisions. Or they may make decisions that suffer from an overreliance on data (e.g., cost-benefit analysis). Also, the individuals may see their decisions as gamelike.[69]

3. The company has **failed to implement safeguards** to counter the harsh consequences of the bureaucratic ethic. In spite of their flaws, safeguards such as legalistic corporate codes do supply a moral

minimum—a floor below which corporate behavior cannot go.[70] Also, companies can establish hotlines that allow employees to voice dissent anonymously.

With regard to Dr. Davis, the relevant organization was A. H. Robins, the company that bought the rights to produce the product. We may want to learn more about the extent to which A. H. Robins was morally aware. We might also understand the Dalkon Shield disaster better if we knew the strengths and weaknesses of the company's culture.

*How might some situations lend themselves to ethical disasters?* We must look for structural problems that are larger than both individuals and organizations. Consider these situational factors/structural issues.

1. Powerful Americans tend to make **positive assumptions about privileged people.** Consider, for instance, our reluctance to send white-collar criminals to jail. Sometimes, businessmen and women who engage in morally flawed behavior are admired rather than ridiculed.
2. **Individualistic Americans want the government to "stay out of it,"** even though the law could harness the good in corporations and organizations. Often, people who work in business portray law as a nuisance, rather than a helping hand. Additionally, we often tend to ignore the ways in which financial contributions to political campaigns corrupt our democratic process. The laws regulators are supposed to enforce are often drafted with the interests of corporations in mind. Sometimes, it seems that companies are enacting their own limits, and these limits often fail to look out for a range of stakeholders.
3. **Markets often reward short-term profits,** rather than responsible, sustainable commercial success. As one writer points out, financial markets often reward companies that "abandon accountability to all stakeholders but one: the global financial market."[71] He writes that CEOs are "hell-bent on maximizing short-run financial returns to shareholders."[72] In this environment, high-level executives are more interested in outrunning rather than preventing big mistakes.

With regard to Dr. Davis and the Dalkon Shield disaster, we need to look at societal trends. At the time the disaster unfolded, it was unlikely that society was ready to hold doctors responsible for gross negligence. They were simply too powerful and admired. Also, at the time, the government regulated drugs, but not devices. Sometimes, we wonder too late what government regulators may or may not have been doing to protect consumers.

Finally, we need to look at the extent to which our market system operates the way it is supposed to—whether we can really vote with our dollars and put companies like A. H. Robins out of business. Unfortunately, it took years for many women to obtain the information they needed to know what was causing their medical problems.

With regard to today's environment and the hypothetical dilemma at the beginning of the chapter, we need to ask some important questions, including: Why are hospitals seeking revenue from business? What role are regulators playing in looking out for patients as hospitals become more entrepreneurial? What are the risks inherent in new relationships between business and medical researchers? What is the best way to advance science?[73]

### Everyday Ethical Dilemmas

Most managers do not face the kind of life-and-death dilemmas the Dalkon Shield case presents. Instead, managers generally face what we call "everyday dilemmas." Although these dilemmas have less-severe consequences, they still possess the power to erode an individual manager's sense of optimism and hopefulness about the American business culture.

Stop for a moment and think about a time when you discovered that the word *ethics* had something to do with your daily working life. Think through that moment: Where are you? What is happening? Who is with you? How do you feel at this moment?

Now, take a look at Table 2.1. We have reviewed a range of sources to generate a list of the kinds of daily ethical dilemmas managers say they face at work. Is the moment that you thought of similar to any of the dilemmas we present? Our point in asking you to engage in this exercise is to show you that you are not alone. Because most organizations discourage individual managers from discussing the everyday ethical dilemmas they face, managers may not realize that what they experience is typical.

That many individual managers experience daily ethical dilemmas is significant for a variety of reasons. For our purposes, we will focus on how managers feel about these moments.

Often, managers feel stress, anger, and anxiety about the daily ethical dilemmas they face. These negative feelings affect a company's productivity and an individual manager's sense of worth and have the potential to affect other stakeholders who might suffer if a manager's performance slips. How individual managers respond to daily ethical dilemmas can affect customers, other employees, and investors. Consequently, it is important for managers to establish a moral partnership with their firms. This partnership should harness the best in corporate and organizational behavior and make it easy for individual managers to do good work.

**TABLE 2.1** Everyday Ethical Dilemmas

| | |
|---|---|
| *Job security and/or employee discipline* | Should I lie or deceive employees who work for me about whether they will be laid off next month? |
| | Should I obey my employer and fire an employee when I believe this action is discriminatory? |
| | Should I speak out if I believe my employer is treating one of my colleagues unfairly by engaging in a sexual harassment investigation that is poorly designed and implemented? |
| *Issues that challenge a person's honesty and/or sense of discretion* | Should I misstate numbers in a report to make my department look as if it is accomplishing its goals? |
| | Should I look the other way if I see my boss accept gifts when my organization has a policy that forbids accepting gifts? |
| | Should I file government reports with incorrect information to help move my organization forward on an important project? |
| | Should I share privileged or private information with an outsider to enhance my own career or status? |
| *Product quality, health, and safety* | Should I ship products I know will not meet my customer's expectations and/or are defective? |
| | Should I overlook my company's infraction of environmental laws? |
| | Should I generate marketing materials that fail to let consumers know the risks of a product? |
| *Inappropriate use of company resources* | Should I take company property (e.g., computer software) home and make it my own? |
| | Should I follow the crowd and adopt a flexible approach to how to use my company expense account? |

## AMERICAN BUSINESS CONTEXT WRAP-UP

In this chapter, we have asked you to consider some unique traits of American business culture, especially the idea of individualism and its positive and negative influences on the business world. We have also asked you to see the complexity of ethics disasters. Often, those who are disgusted with business scandals want to point the finger at just one cause, when in reality both people and organizations may be flawed. Additionally, some situations lend themselves to ethics disasters. Finally, we wanted you to get a sense of "everyday" ethical dilemmas—the kinds of dilemmas managers face regularly.

In the opening of chapter 2, we asked you to think about links between business and medical research. Our hypothetical situation raised questions about relationships between medical researchers and venture capitalists. We encouraged you to think through an ethics disaster from the past (the Dalkon Shield disaster) and see its complexity— that people, organizational factors, and situational factors all played a role in the disaster. Our goal in asking you to think about these factors was to encourage you to see that good people often do bad things when they become employees in corporations and organizations. All managers, even busy ones, need to take the time to understand practical business ethics.

## CRITICAL THINKING QUESTIONS

1. What are the special strengths of an individualistic culture? At this stage of your life, you probably have a rough idea of the kind of business activity in which you hope to engage. If you are able to have the managerial role you are currently considering, can you foresee any particular ethical dilemmas that will require you to restrict the extent of your individualism?

2. The concept of "the team" as an organizational metaphor for business behavior is commonplace in texts and management seminars as well. To what extent is the bureaucratic ethic just another name for teamwork?

3. What does it matter if unethical business behavior is caused by a lack of moral awareness, a failing of the business organization, or a cultural habit that encourages such behavior? If you were to identify a primary cause for a misdeed, such as accounting fraud, how would that knowledge be helpful in building a more ethical firm?

## ENDNOTES

[1] This name is fictitious.

[2] Douglas M. Birch and Gary Cohn, "Of Patients and Profits: The Changing Creed of Hopkins Science. What was Once Heresy Is Now the Mission: A Partnership with Business to Advance Research," *Balitmore Sun*, June 25, 2001[hereinafter *Patients and Profits*].

[3] The facts in this introduction are from Michael Ollove, "Destroyed By His Own Invention," *Baltimore Sun*, October 25, 1998, 10G.

[4] Ibid. A. H. Robins ended up paying more than $3 billion to settle nearly 200,000 lawsuits filed by women or their families.

[5] Ibid.

[6] Ibid. Davis testified in favor of the Dalkon Shield and its effectiveness without indicating that he was a 35% owner in the Dalkon Corporation.

[7] Ibid.

[8] Ibid.

[9] Everett Carll Ladd, *The American Ideology: An Exploration of the Origins, Meaning, and Role of American Political Ideas* (1994)[hereinafter Ladd]. This monograph was produced by The Roper Center for Public Opinion Research in Storrs, CT.

[10] Ibid.

[11] Herbert J. Gans, *Middle American Individualism* (New York: Free Press, 1988).

[12] Ibid.

[13] This list summarizes some of Ladd's key findings. See Ladd, *supra* note 9.

[14] Ibid., 2.

[15] Ibid., 9.

[16] Ibid.

[17] Ibid., 7.

[18] Ibid., 11.

[19] Ibid.

[20] See, e.g., the influence of Jewish faith on how Aaron Feurstein runs Malden Mills. Chapter 5 highlights Feurstein and his philosophy of business.

[21] Charles Haddad, "Don't Let Microsoft Claim the Classroom," *Business Week Online*, Dec. 4, 2001.

[22] Ladd, *supra* note 9, 20.

[23] Ibid., 5.

[24] Ibid., 19.

[25] Ibid., 21.

[26] Ibid., 22.

[27] Ibid., citing Robert Bellah.

[28] Sandy Hotchkiss, *Why Is It Always About You? Saving Yourself from the Narcissists in your Life* (New York: Free Press, 2002), at xv [hereinafter *Why Is It Always About You?*].

[29] Ibid.

[30] Ibid.

[31] Ibid.

[32] Ladd, *supra* note 9, at 17–18.

[33] Jonathan Kozol, *Savage Inequalities: Children In America's Schools* (New York: Harper Perennial, 1992).

[34] Charles Handy, "A Better Capitalism," *Across the Board*, a publication of the Conference Board, April 1998, at 16, 17.

[35] Robert Jackall, *Moral Mazes: The World of Corporate Managers* (New York: Oxford University Press,1988) [hereinafter *Moral Mazes*].

[36] Ibid., 6.

[37] http://www.abc.net.au/pm/s591888.htm

[38] Neil Weinberg, "Asleep at the Switch," *Forbes*, July 22 2002, 38.

[39] Stanley Milgram, *Obedience to Authority* (New York: Harper & Row, 1974), 3–4.

[40] Ibid., 6.

[41] Ibid.

[42] Ibid., 131.

[43] Ibid., 124.

[44] Joseph L. Badaracco, Jr., and Allen P. Webb, "Business Ethics: A View from the Trenches," *California Management Review* 37 (1995): 9.

[45] Ibid., 18.

[46] Ibid., 12.

[47] This label came from John Swanson, former ethics officer at Dow Corning. He recounts his story in John A. Byrne, *Informed Consent: A Story of Personal Tragedy and Corporate Betrayal* (New York: McGraw-Hill, 1996). He uses the phrase "good times ethics" on p. 212–13.

[48] *Moral Mazes*, 201.

[49] Paraphrased from Jackall's last chapter, on p. 204.

[50] Art Wolfe, "The Corporate Apology," *Business Horizons* (March-April): 1990, 10.

[51] For a complete explanation of Lawrence Kohlberg's cognitive approach to moral development, see Howard T. Prince II, "Moral Development in Individuals," in, *The Leader's Companion: Insights on Leadership Through the Ages* ed. J. Thomas Wren, 484, 486–88 (New York: Free Press, 1995).

[52] *Why Is It Always About You? supra* note 30, xvii.

[53] Ibid.

[54] Ibid.

[55] See generally Ibid., at chapter 16: Narcissists at Work: The Abuse of Power.

[56] Ibid., 128–29. This person ignores the fact that you are a separate person, and often uses you.

[57] Ibid., 130–31.

[58] Ibid., 131–32.

[59] Ibid., 132.

[60] Ibid.

[61] Ibid.

[62] Ibid., 134–35.

[63] Ibid., 135–36.

[64] Ollove, *supra* note 3.

[65] Ibid., Ollove indicates that Davis was named as a codefendant "hundreds, if not thousands, of times."

[66] Ibid.

[67] Ibid.

[68] Ibid.

[69] See Wolfe, *supra* note 57.

[70] See Robert G. Kennedy, "Virtue and Corporate Culture: The Ethical Formation of Baby Wolverines," *St. John's Review of Business* 17 (1996): 10–15.

[71] David Korten, *When Corporations Rule the World* (San Francisco: Berrett-Koehler, 1995).

[72] Ibid.

[73] Birch and Cohn raise these questions in "Of Patients and Profits," *supra* note 2.

# CHAPTER 3

# Identifying Personal Values: The Individual Context

**THE FOCUS:** What are your personal value priorities? How can you use those value priorities in your daily life?

The decisions you make at work are inescapably *your* decisions. No matter how we might like to blame others for them if they are later exposed as ethically deficient, we must bear some responsibility for having said "yes," when a "no" was possible. Correspondingly, when you make an ethical decision at work, you deserve some of the credit, for you could have easily taken a less-ethical course of action.

Knowing more about yourself and understanding the reasons why you have chosen to be the kind of person you are goes a long way toward pushing you in an ethical direction. You can say to yourself: A person with values like mine would act this way and not that way. Values serve as guides toward correct behavior at work. Becoming more familiar with your own is the goal of the following story.

The chairperson of an Institutional Review Committee (IRC) at Indiana University-Purdue University Indianapolis (IUPUI) has asked you to serve as a community representative on the committee.[1] You are an administrator for a private educational service in Indianapolis and have been asked to offer the committee a layperson's perspective on some issues the committee faces with regard to drug studies. Before you tell the committee "yes," you want to review your knowledge of the committee's work and its relationship to Eli Lilly & Co.

The IRC came about largely in response to an article the *Wall Street Journal* published in 1996.[2] This article exposed Eli Lilly and Co.'s practice of using homeless men to participate in Phase One drug tests. The

Food and Drug Administration (FDA) requires U.S. pharmaceutical companies to engage in three phases of drug testing. In Phase I, companies test drugs on healthy volunteers to see whether they can safely test them on patients in Phase II. In Phase II, companies test the drugs on normal and sick patients to determine possible side effects of the drugs. In Phase III, pharmaceutical companies give drugs to sick patient to try to determine appropriate dosages. Today, Eli Lilly has a drug clinic at IUPUI, and the IRC reviews Eli Lilly's policies.

According to the 1996 *Wall Street Journal* article, by the mid-1990s, Eli Lilly's Laboratory for Clinical Research had become a refuge[3] for homeless alcoholic men. Many of the men became regular "volunteers" and willingly subjected themselves to testing to earn $85 per day, which at the time was the lowest per diem in the business.[4] The article told several stories of men who participated in the testing to earn a few thousand dollars of "easy money." They then left the testing clinic that had housed them for weeks, rented cheap motel rooms, and blew the money on alcohol and prostitutes.[5]

At the time, the company denied the allegations, asserting that 94 percent of its test subjects provided residential addresses.[6] However, Dr. W. Leigh Thompson, the company's retired chief scientific officer, responded differently.[7] He had expressed concerns that the company might be exploiting the homeless. He said that Eli Lilly's board, which oversaw the company clinic, as well as the company's top executives believed that using homeless men in drug testing was a philanthropic act. Dr. Thompson stated that he, too, took this position. He said, "Providing [homeless men] with a nice warm bed and good medical care and sending them out drug- and alcohol-free was a positive thing to do."[8]

After the *Wall Street Journal* published the article, a flurry of angry responses from different sectors of the American public inspired the company to create two panels of outside experts to advise them about whether to stop using homeless volunteers.[9] The IRC, which you have been asked to join, is one of those two committees.

You know the IRC has already engaged in important work. For instance, the IRC has already sought scientific advice about whether alcoholism could affect drug-testing results.[10] Additionally, the committee has consulted medical ethics experts to advise them on whether the company should pay the homeless to serve as test subjects.[11] Today, Eli Lilly's drug testing center, the Lilly Clinic, is no longer a mecca for homeless men. The company has changed its procedures for qualifying volunteers.[12]

In particular, the company now focuses on signing up female volunteers so they can test drugs geared toward women, such as drugs that respond to breast cancer and osteoporosis.[13] Also, the company has moved some of its early drug testing to clinics in Singapore and Europe.[14]

You do not know what the IRC's focus will be in the three-year term they have asked you to serve.[15] You have already decided to say yes, but now you know you must prepare to provide the kind of outside oversight the committee says it needs. You have never been the kind of person to rubber-stamp decisions, and you are not about to start to do that now. All the newspaper articles you are reading about corporate corruption are making you see the importance of acquiring and applying ethical knowledge to business decisions. You will need to take your new volunteer job seriously, including learning some practical ways to apply ethical concepts to business.

Business ethics focuses on a *process* for improved business conduct. We began this process by learning about American business culture as the context for our ethical dilemmas. Now chapter 3 continues this process by introducing you to some basic language units of ethics: interests, rules, and values. Additionally, the chapter asks you to work with these language units to see how they might function in real decision-making processes. To illustrate what this knowledge will do for you, we will consider a possible issue that our hypothetical IRC member will face. Then, in the dialogue box at the end of the chapter, we will use chapter concepts to respond to the hypothetical situation.

Suppose you decide to ask questions about why Eli Lilly has started engaging in early drug testing abroad.[16] You are truly an outsider, which means you have no idea why a pharmaceutical company would want to move drug testing to locations in Singapore and Europe. You wonder whether:

- Regulations in other parts of the world are more lenient with regard to drug testing.[17]
- It is cheaper to engage in drug testing abroad.
- The company shows more or less compassion to test subjects who are not American.
- Your past volunteer work with vulnerable populations will affect your work with the IRC.
- The company has clarified its value priorities.
- You can articulate your own value priorities.
- You will be able to contribute to the committee and remain true to your beliefs.

Now, let's learn some important concepts so you can think through this hypothetical situation.

## YOUR PERSONAL VALUE PRIORITIES

### Interests and Roles

Learning the language of ethics is the first step in the process of applying ethical concepts to business life. Two basic language units of ethics discussion are **interests** and **roles. Interests** refer to the involvement of all relevant parties in a decision. Ordinarily, we can expect any business decision to affect individuals and groups in diverse ways. Decisions typically help some people more than others and harm yet others. Identifying and weighing these interests are primary components of practical ethics. Many of you will encounter situations in which you have to weigh your personal interests against the interests of an entire business entity. CEOs who have large personal stakes in their corporations constantly struggle with these competing interests. A recent article entitled "The Good CEO" highlighted executives who are more interested in advancing their company's interests than their personal interests.[18] These executives help to remind us that interests are pertinent because we have an obligation consider and respect others' needs.

How do these interests arise? The many **roles** we play yield different interests. For example, every businessperson is both an employee of the business and much more. He or she is also a neighbor, a citizen, a customer, and perhaps a hiker, property owner, and mentor as well. Each of these roles has interests attached to it, interests that are often in conflict, even within the same individual. As a neighbor, I may not want you to buy that ugly brown fence you plan to place between our houses, but as the manager of the lumber yard from which you will buy the fence, I hope you buy our entire inventory of brown fence.

As actors in the business world make decisions, they should think about the different options in the context of roles and interests. Especially at early stages of decision making, actors have the power to think through which interests the potential decision advances and which are hurt. When David Simon's Brooklyn Carpet Exchange experienced lower profits after the September 11th attacks, he had to make financial decisions that would undoubtedly affect a variety of people. Taking his employees' interest into consideration, he decided against layoffs and instead cut employee salaries, including the salaries of top management.[19]

Listing the interests is a helpful first step in ethical conversation. Next, we must decide how to weigh those interests in conformity with our aspirations for our community and ourselves. To better define the aspirations we possess, we require the assistance of values, another basic unit of ethical discussion.

## Values

Ethical talk and thought is constructed from building blocks, and none is more crucial than **values.** Values are positive abstractions that capture our sense of what is good or desirable. They are *ideas* that underlie conversations about business ethics. Values such as honesty, efficiency, fairness, security, and freedom play key roles in shaping business decision making.

Just to make certain that you are comfortable with the idea of values, take this opportunity to jot down a few more values that might affect financial and trade decisions. If you need some help, just think about what positive abstractions you intend to emphasize to your children. If that vision is not helpful, imagine what you would want your friends to say about you, were they asked to speak about your special qualities as a person. What positive abstractions would be responsible for those qualities? We already mentioned a few additional examples in chapters 1 and 2. Can you remember them?

Conversations about controversial business ethics issues require you to choose among alternative options. Talk about our values would be simple if we could just make a list and say, "Well, there they are." But such a list is pretty meaningless because the concepts on our list are, by definition, values that everyone else has as well.

What makes organizations and individuals unique is the **priority** we attach to particular values. Every business has honesty as one of its values, but we know from rough experience that for some businesses this value is far down on the list of values that will guide their actual behavior. In addition, when people say, "I value honesty," they may not all be defining honesty in the same way. Therefore, before we focus on value priorities, we need to think through some basic definitions of important values.

In the area of business ethics, certain values play a particularly large role in reasoning. We have listed some key values following and have offered some preliminary definitions. You should view this list as a starting point. Feel free to add values and definitions to the list. We have also taken some of the everyday ethical dilemmas from chapter 2 and used them as examples of questions that highlight certain values. A few everyday dilemmas have been added, when necessary, to illustrate a particular value.

Also, note that our *American* business culture shapes the list of key values we present in this chapter. As you read the Global Box that describes business ethics in Russia, ask yourself which of the values in Exhibit 3-1 might not appear on a list of key values in Russia.

**EXHIBIT 3-1**   Alternative Forms of Key Values that Shape Business Decision Making[1]

| *Value* | *Alternative Meanings* |
| --- | --- |
| **Honesty** | To refuse to lie, steal, or deceive in any way |
| | To adhere to the facts |
| | To answer accurately any question directed to me |
| | *Example: Should I lie or deceive employees who work for me about whether the company plans to lay them off next month?* |
| **Freedom** | To act without restriction from rules imposed by others |
| | To possess the capacity or resources to act |
| | *Example: Should I follow the crowd and adopt a flexible approach to how to use my company expense account?* |
| **Security** | To be safe from those willing to interfere with your property rights |
| | To achieve the psychological condition of self-confidence such that you welcome risks |
| | *Example: Should I speak out if I believe my employer is treating one of my colleagues unfairly by engaging in a sexual harassment investigation that is poorly designed and implemented? Has my company assured me that it welcomes dissent?* |
| **Justice** | To receive the product of your labor |
| | To treat all human beings identically, regardless of class, race, gender, or age |
| | *Example: Does my employer have a separate and lower pay scale for workers of a particular race?* |
| **Efficiency** | To get the most from a particular input |
| | To minimize costs |
| | *Example: Should I ship products I know will not meet my customer's expectations and/or are defective, when fixing the problem will be costly?* |

Source:
[1] This exhibit comes from Nancy Kubasek, Bartley Brennan, and M. Neil Browne, *The Legal Environment of Business: A Critical Thinking Approach*, 3rd ed. Upper Saddle River, NJ: Prentice Hall, 2003.

In the next section, we encourage you to make sense of relationships between individual and organizational values. But first, here is a glimpse of values in the Russian context.

## RUSSIA

The notion of business ethics can be perplexing to the average Russian. Many Russians believe that a market economy is inherently corrupt and that adherence to ethics while doing business is nearly impossible. This perplexity stems, in part, from a lack of experience in a functioning market economy. Russians also lack visible models of businesses that do act ethically while performing successfully. Yet, there is a pressing need to inform Russians about the potential to reconcile business in a market economy with ethical behavior.

Many Western businesspersons express concern about unethical business practices in Russia. Their concerns are often a source of tension with Russians because the latter do not consider their behavior unscrupulous. For example, Russian business continues to rely on the exchange of favors between businesspersons, a practice known as *blat*, to accomplish business objectives. The informal system works when one person or institution pays another person or institution in exchange for some type of favor, such as waived interest fees or a high rating on a government inspection. The blat system developed under communism because it was difficult to get things done quickly in the centrally controlled government. The end of communism however, did not bring the end of this practice.

For American businesspersons, the common practice of paying for favors creates an ethical quandary. Although the practices may not be ethically sound by American standards, a person seeking access to Russian business may feel compelled to engage in these behaviors. Other ethically questionable practices, such as fraud, misappropriation of funds, and exploitation of company resources, raise questions about the benefits of doing business in Russia. In 1997, America Online (AOL) closed its Russian operations because of bank fraud and uncontrollable credit card number theft.

American businesses, like AOL, are quick to shake their fingers at Russians for unethical behavior, but Russians have their own qualms with American business practices. For instance, some Russians still question whether it is ethical for a business to make a profit. Under communism, profit was seen as a catalyst for selfish behaviors and, thus, in conflict with the interests of the state. Some Russians also find the high disparity in salaries that characterizes Western businesses unethical. For an executive to make a significant amount more than the employees suggests to Russians that the employees are being exploited for the executive's benefit. The idea of firing and laying off employees is also ethically questionable in Russia. A worker rarely lost his or her job under communism. Those who were fired had usually committed an egregious act. The shame associated with losing one's job persists in Russia, even though layoffs are frequent occurrences in a market economy. These differing standards, which arise from different value priorities, illustrate the complications that arise when doing business across cultures.

*Sources:*
Drew Wilson and Lloyd Donaldson, *Russian Etiquette and Ethics in Business* (Chicago: NTC Business Books, 1996) pp. 79–80, 138
Elia V. Chepaitis, "Ethics across Information Cultures" in *International Business Ethics: Challenges and Approaches*, ed. Georges Enderle, (Notre Dame, IN: University of Notre Dame Press, 1999) 42–50.
Shelia M. Puffer and Daniel J. McCarthy, "Finding the Common Ground in Russian and American Business Ethics," *California Management Review*, 37, no. 2 (1995): 29–46.

---

### A SPECIAL SET OF VALUES: THE CARDINAL VIRTUES

The appendix in chapter 4 introduces you to the major ethical theories, including virtue ethics, which focuses on how to become the kind of person who can do the right thing.[1] People who care about developing virtue in themselves and others often focus on a particular set of values, known as the cardinal virtues.

Dr. Robert Kennedy, a business ethics professor at the University of St. Thomas, explains that the traditional names of the cardinal virtues are fortitude, temperance, prudence, and justice, but that he presents them as courage, discipline, wisdom, and fairness. We present Kennedy's definitions following because we believe they might assist you as you think through your own value priorities.[2] When you learn more about virtue theory, you will understand why Kennedy uses the word *habit* in each definition.

**Courage:** The habit of moderating the emotions of fear or boldness to achieve a rational goal.

**Discipline:** The habit of moderating the emotions of enjoyment and denial to achieve a well-ordered personal or professional life.

**Wisdom:** The habit of recognizing good ends and choosing effective and efficient means of achieving them. Kennedy explains that the opposite is false wisdom or shrewdness, which is when a person is skilled at choosing efficient and effective means, but is confused or indifferent about the goodness of the goals.

**Fairness:** The habit of giving to others what they are due.

*Sources:*
[1] Robert G. Kennedy, "Virtue Theory and Corporate Culture: The Ethical Formation of Baby Wolverines," *St. John's Review of Business* (Winter 1995/1996): 12.
[2] All definitions come verbatim from Kennedy, Ibid., 13–14.

---

## INDIVIDUAL VALUES; ORGANIZATIONAL VALUES

When we go to work for a particular organization, we do not enter the workplace as a blank slate, waiting for the organization to tell us what we believe and how we should behave. Rather, we bring a lifetime of experiences with us. As a result, we enter the workplace with strong ideas about what is good and right. We developed these strong ideas with the help of schoolteachers, parents, friends, and/or religious counselors.

Consequently, people who work in businesses usually have a strong sense of self. We often hear people say, "I know who I am." In fact, many people define their self-worth and importance using terms that are values. For example, most of us would be proud to know that others see us as a person who acts on the values of honesty, dependability, and compassion. These are also the values we most want to see observed by our children and neighbors. We might also be proud to announce to our peers our commitment to a particular value, such as equality or efficiency.

Values do not guide only individuals; businesses also possess their own set of values and value priorities. Businesses have an ethical history and an ethical vision. In some organizations, company leaders announce a vision that shows respect for a particular set of values. The Pillsbury Company demonstrated their values when the company donated over 140,000 pounds of food to the charity *America's Second Harvest*, which feeds people throughout the United States.[20] Other organizations have mission statements or codes of ethics that show a preference for certain values. Less frequently, upper-level executives ask managers in the middle or lower ranks of a hierarchy to develop a set of value priorities so that eventually, when these managers work their way up the hierarchy, their value priorities become those of the entire organization.

These days, it is common for people in business to walk around with a list of their employer's guiding values in their wallet on a laminated card. Some businesses post their preferred values on the organization's walls. The idea of posting values comes from a variety of sources. One such source is businesses that have been on the cutting edge in the field of ethics. Levi Strauss & Co. is a good example of these pioneering businesses.

The following example from Levi Strauss shows a particular set of business values, as announced by company leader Robert D. Haas. Read about Robert D. Haas. As you read, think about these questions: What values does Robert D. Hass list for Levi Strauss? What challenges does the company face by pursuing a values-based approach to engaging in business? If you agree with his idea of responsible commercial success, which values are you likely to prefer?

Robert D. Haas did not come up with value priorities for Levi Strauss all by himself. One of his strengths is that he realized the importance of creating a moral partnership between the company he leads and the employees who follow him. Haas realized that business decision making requires an ongoing exchange of ethical talk between individuals and organizations. For this conversation to take place, individuals and organizations need to come to the discussion with an open mind and the desire to use reason in forming their decisions. Remember that a moral partnership requires enough collaboration that employees should see a fit between their personal values and the organization's values. Employees should not be one person at home and a completely different person at work.

To move toward a moral partnership, employers and employees will need to discuss a range of issues related to values. A good place to start a moral partnership is practice in recognizing value conflicts. This practice will lead to improved decision making.

## MEET THE LEADER: ROBERT D. HAAS

A *Business Week* article written in the mid-1990s describes Robert D. Haas, Chairman of the Board and now former Chief Executive Officer of Levi Strauss & Co., as a tall, gangly, cerebral man with a mild manner, who "doesn't fill up the room with his charisma." Yet, you should imagine Robert D. Haas as a strong leader. He is a man with definite views about how corporations should behave. His beliefs have changed Levi Strauss & Co. Haas believes in what he calls "sustained responsible commercial success." He believes that each person who works in business wants her legacy to be that she helped a company act responsibly and in an "ethical way that serves [the] enterprise's long-term interests."

Haas believes that responsibility includes a commitment to maintaining high ethical standards. To achieve such high ethical standards, Haas abandons the traditional ethics program, which focuses on compliance with a set of rules. Instead, he advocates a values-oriented program. Rather than setting up ethics rules that employees must follow, Haas believes companies should cultivate and support a culture that embraces high ethical standards. He says, "High ethical standards can be maintained only if they are modeled by management and woven into the fabric of the company." Levi Strauss & Co. bases their approach to ethics on the company's six ethical principles, which are honesty, promise-keeping, fairness, respect for others, compassion, and integrity.

To reach a decision about a particular dilemma, the company first identifies which of the six ethical principles applies to a particular business decision. Then, the company determines which internal and external stakeholders' ethical concerns should influence the business decision. Finally, the company balances the ethical concerns of stakeholders with the company's key values. People in the field of business ethics recognize Haas for his approach to ethical decision making, "managing by values."

How does managing by values make Levi Strauss different from other companies? In keeping with the six core values, the company developed "aggressive diversity initiatives, which ensure that talent [will] not be impeded by race, ethnicity, or gender." Under the direction of Haas, the company has taken steps that have earned Haas the title "mild-mannered maverick." For instance, the company was a pioneer in the 1980s in developing an AIDS education program for employees, was later one of the first corporations to extend medical benefits to unmarried partners of employees, and was one of the first corporations to establish clear guidelines for the conduct of overseas contractors regarding the use of child labor.

Haas says that in business, "[e]thics must trump all other considerations. Ultimately, there are important commercial benefits to be gained from managing your business in a responsible and ethical way that best serves your enterprise's long-term interests. The opposite seems equally clear: the dangers of not doing so are profound."

Today, many businesspersons and writers still praise Levi Strauss for its great values. Unfortunately, however, the company enjoys less praise with regard to its financial performance. The company's sales have dropped significantly in recent years. However, as the company turned 150 years old in 2003, their continued existence shows that the company has held its own in the cutthroat fashion world.

*(continues on the next page)*

*(continued)*

Additionally, Robert D. Haas can be proud of the legacy he has helped create—that of a company with clear value priorities that it lives, in good times and in bad.

*References:*
"Ethics—A Global Challenge: Character & Courage," *60 Vital Speeches of the Day* (June, 1994) 506–509.
Russell Mitchell and Michael Oneal, "Managing by Values: Is Levi Strauss' Approach Visionary—or Flaky?" *Business Week*, August 1, 1994, 46–52.
Charles Stein, "Creating Real Value," *Boston Globe*, October 1, 2002, D.1.
Associated Press Newswires, "Famous Maker of 501s Turns 150," May 1, 2003.

## CRITICAL THINKING BOX

**If you read in the newspaper today that the Levi Strauss company laid off 1,000 workers and is considering closing one of its plants, would that be enough to take them off your personal list of "companies to admire"? Why or why not? How perfect must companies be for them to be admirable? To what extent do personal value priorities affect which companies we admire?**

## Value Conflicts

So, what have we established so far? We now know that

1. Values are the **basic language** we use to discuss business ethics.
2. Values are most illuminating when we think about them in terms of the **person's or organization's value priorities.**
3. Values are not self-explanatory; they have **multiple meanings** that require clarification.
4. Ethical business decisions are the **product of cooperation** between the values of business leaders and employees.

Most thoughtful individuals pledge allegiance to all the values we have considered so far—honesty, freedom, security, justice, and efficiency. But when faced with an ethical dilemma, these values often conflict. When you read about the value priorities of Levi Strauss and Robert D. Haas, it is not surprising that some would not want to be a Levi Strauss employee. For instance, if efficiency is your highest value priority, you might be troubled that Levi Strauss spent money on an AIDS education program. You might also be concerned that if the company cares too much about the way workers in developing countries are treated, it might lose the competitive edge that comes from hiring cheaper labor overseas.

People who work in business experience daily dilemmas that pit one value against another. In this situation, we would say that someone is experiencing a **value conflict.** For example, should a manager who discovers inappropriate handling of medical waste in the department she supervises bring the issue to the attention of managers even higher up in the organization?

On the one hand, the manager wants to make sure the problem is remedied. She values **security,** defined as "to achieve the psychological condition of self-confidence." Security comes about when we can trust business organizations to look out for community safety. In New York, for example, more than 60 restaurants donate a portion of their profits to the Restaurants Against Hunger Campaign.[21] These restaurants demonstrate their concern for the community and the safety of those in the community who lack enough food.

On the other hand, the manager supervising medical waste handling also values **efficiency.** She takes steps to make sure similar problems will not occur in the future. She then wonders whether it is worth the money to solve past problems that may or may not cause harm to others. After all, as a manager, she is responsible for minimizing costs.

Another example of a value conflict is the issue of whether a manager should tell a subordinate that his peers do not appreciate his contributions to the team. On the one hand, the manager wants to be **honest** to the subordinate. Letting the employee know the truth will help him develop professionally. On the other hand, the manager is concerned about **justice.** He wonders whether the team is treating people identically, regardless of their class, race, gender, and age.

In this situation, suppose the employee whose contributions are not valued by peers is fifteen years older than the average team member. The manager wonders whether peers are undervaluing the work of an older worker. He considers whether educating the team about their possible bias against the older worker might be a better course of action than having an honest discussion with the undervalued employee.

Consider also the example of an employee who knows one of her coworkers is falsifying expense reports and seeking reimbursement for expenses unrelated the business. On the one hand, the employee values **freedom.** She believes that each employee should be free to act without restrictions imposed on him or her by others. The employee wonders whether it is any of her business where a coworker decides to draw the line regarding reimbursement for business expenses. On the other hand, the employee values **efficiency.** She realizes that when some employees are in effect stealing company assets, other stakeholders are hurt in the long run. Minimizing costs related to unfair employee behavior ensures that the organization will be around in the long run to serve community needs.

One final example relates to affirmative action. Supporters of affirmative action want employers to treat people equally, regardless of their race or gender. Unfortunately, some employers consider factors like race and gender, and consequently overlook qualified women and nonwhites for jobs and promotions. Affirmative action, defined as a policy that requires employers to treat all employees equally and refrain from overlooking applicants based on their race or gender, shows a commitment to **justice.** Employers often want **freedom** more than justice. They want to be able to act without rules imposed by others. Employers may want to make decisions using time-honored traditions such as word-of-mouth referrals or a preference for candidates who make them feel at ease. Unfortunately, this tradition often means less-qualified candidates get the job or promotion. As the following Global Box shows, conversation about the value conflicts surrounding affirmative action is relevant in many countries around the world.

## GLOBAL BOX

### EUROPEAN UNION

The issue of affirmative action is a controversial one in the European Union (EU), just as in the United States. In 1997, the EU codified its antidiscrimination policy in the Amsterdam Treaty. The treaty included a clause outlawing discrimination based on sex (among other characteristics) in employment. The Amsterdam Treaty also amended the EU's mission statement to include the achievement of "equality between men and women" as an EU goal. The treaty allows for "positive action" to be taken to ensure equal employment and pay. This allowance has raised a contested question: Within what boundaries can this positive action occur? European Court of Justice (ECJ) has offered some clarifications to this question in two of its decisions.

In 1995, the ECJ heard the case of *Eckhard Kalanke v. Freie Hansestadt Bremen*, which involved an affirmative action program in the German state of Bremen. The program gave women unconditional favorable treatment in public sector employment. The ECJ invalidated the program when it ruled that unconditional preferential treatment violated the EU's codified commitment to equal treatment. Europeans were acutely critical of the decision.

Two years later, the ECJ had the opportunity to reevaluate its ruling when it heard a case involving a law in the German state of North-Rhine Westphalia that gave women preferential treatment in public sector jobs. The ECJ upheld this law. In its reasoning, the court pointed to the law's flexible quotas as justification for its legality. The ECJ cautioned that affirmative action laws and programs should still be considered on a case-by-case basis.

Supporters of affirmative action for European women were relieved by the ECJ's 1997 decision. They point out that business in Europe is still dominated by males. Across the EU, women hold less than 2 percent of senior management positions and less than 1 percent of board seats. The 1997 law approved by the ECJ is limited to the public sector, though, and did not have direct implications for private European companies.

*Source:*
Edmund L. Andrews, "European Court Backs Hiring Women to Correct Past Discrimination," *New York Times*, November 12, 1997.

Now, it is time for you to practice identifying conflicts. This section presents a few of the everyday ethical dilemmas from chapter 2, then asks you to identify and explain a major value conflict that underlies the dilemma. We will answer the first question to show you what we mean. Note that you are allowed to add values and definitions.

1. *Should I file government reports with incorrect information to help move my organization forward on an important project?*

   **One conflict:** honesty versus financial security

   **Explain:** On the one hand, you value honesty, which means to adhere to the facts. On the other hand, you also value financial security. Of course, some firms may require honesty for advancement. But if your firm focuses on short-run profit figures, it will probably reward you if you obey a supervisor who asks you to submit a report that misleads and thereby saves the firm some money, at least for now.

   **Now, you try.**

2. *Should I obey my employer and fire an employee when I believe this action is discriminatory?*

   **One conflict:**

   **Explain:**

3. *Should I share privileged or private information with an outsider to enhance my own career or status?*

   **One conflict:**

   **Explain:**

4. *Should I overlook my company's infraction of environmental laws?*

   **One conflict:**

   **Explain:**

5. *Should I take company property (e.g., computer software) home and make it my own?*

   **One conflict:**

   **Explain:**

## Value Priorities

The recognition of underlying value conflicts in dilemmas like the preceding examples is only the beginning of business ethics. You must next decide which value priorities *you* prefer. When we read a list like the one in Exhibit 3-1, we recognize that the list carries with it an implicit question: How should I prioritize these values? As you were reading the list, you probably found yourself weighing which alternative forms of these values you prefer and apply in your business life.

Remember that values are the basic unit of ethical talk, and the **weight** attached to the particular value varies with the business problem and the business organizations themselves. Honesty and security might be uppermost in the mind of a family owned firm, but only minimally valued by large, publicly held companies or companies in highly competitive markets.

For example, the Enron Corporation executives probably valued financial security over honesty. The company's top executives overstated earnings on Enron's financial statements to maintain higher stock prices, thereby illustrating that the executives placed more weight on efficiency than they placed on disseminating honest information.

Ethical talk can become confusing because the person sitting next to you will probably choose different priorities and different definitions of key values. Thoughtful people disagree about value priorities. However, they do not give up on conversation because they believe that their ethical views can still be improved. Toward this end, the next section provides a few reminders for thinking and talking about value priorities in daily life.

## VALUE PRIORITIES IN DAILY LIFE: WORDS OF CAUTION AS YOU MOVE FORWARD

### Practice Listening to Others with an Open Mind

Once you start talking about interests, roles, and values, it will become clear that, from moral philosophers to an intelligent coworker, even the most thoughtful people disagree about value priorities. However, the desirable response is not to just throw up our hands and say, "Well, then, I guess I can have any value priorities I want." Once you see that ethics requires you to notice that there is more than one set of reasonable ethical positions, you must remember to respect reason and other people. Respect should shape and mandate your personal, flexible commitment to a particular set of value priorities. In other words, try not to stick stubbornly to opinions you carried into the conversation. A quest for moral maturity requires you to ask yourself, "How might I be wrong?"

### Offer Definitions of Values and Ask Others to Do the Same

Many values are ambiguous. In Exhibit 3-1, we modeled for you the importance of providing definitions for values. So, when you are engaged in conversation, definitions will add clarity to your argument.

Try this format: "I believe in freedom, which I define as the ability to act without restrictions imposed by others. Given my view of freedom, I will now express my view on the issue you raise . . . ." Then, in response, another person might say, "Okay, I understand your position, and I believe in freedom too. However, in this situation, I value equality more. By equality, I mean that individuals should be treated equally, regardless of traits over which they have no control, such as gender and race. Now, let me clarify my position, given my value priority . . . ."

### Refrain from Congratulating Yourself for Merely Announcing Particular Value Priorities

Saying you believe in particular values is not enough. You must **do your best to act on your values.** Some corporate leaders are especially good at announcing their and their company's value priorities, but mediocre at acting on those values. For example, many companies were quick to point out their commitment to transparency and oversight in financial reporting after their fellow companies fell into disrepair. However, some companies' actions do not reflect this alleged commitment.

For example, Anita Roddick, founder of the cosmetic franchise The Body Shop, expresses enthusiasm for improving the world with regard to human rights, environmental concerns, and the rights of indigenous people.[22] Journalist Jon Entine, who has followed Roddick's work for years, argues that Roddick's "do-right rhetoric"[23] is more marketing spin than reality. Over the years, he has gathered solid evidence in support of his conclusion. For example, he has gathered information to point out the questionable quality of The Body Shop's products. Entine also cited an EPA lawyer who said that the company's claims regarding to environmental protection are "window dressing"[24] and outlined a gap between the company's statements about human rights and their real reputation with Third World producers.[25]

In fairness to The Body Shop, there is no denying that it is difficult for companies in competitive industries to live a social vision, and we do not want to require unattainable perfection. On the other hand, we should not applaud businesses for simply saying they care about a variety of stakeholders and values. Similarly, you, as an individual, should make sure your expressions of value priorities are genuine. To the extent possible, you should act on the value priorities you express, rather than using them to create a false persona.

Now, that you have been introduced to values and practiced using this important unit of ethics, it is time for you to consider the chapter as a whole: interests, roles, and values. As you read about Dr. Jeffrey Wigand in the Values in Action box, think through your answers to these questions: What interests did Dr. Wigand have in promoting safer cigarettes and prohibiting the use of particular additives in tobacco products? What roles yielded these different interests? What roles did he play, in addition to his role as a businessman? Can you add to the list of values we suggest guided Dr. Wigand as he decided what steps to take in response to his concerns about the practices of Brown & Williamson and the tobacco industry? How do you define the values you added? What primary value did Brown & Williamson probably hope Wigand preferred? In other words, what value might have encouraged him to keep quiet? Finally, we have provided some information in Exhibit 3-2 that indicates that simply reacting to situation by telling all, an action known as whistle-blowing, is seldom a simple and effective response to ethical dilemmas.

You now know that interests, roles, and values are the basic language unit in conversations about business ethics. You also know why conversations about values are both important and difficult. You know some complexities of values (e g , that their definitions are often ambiguous). You also now know that, in the field of ethics, answers are seldom easy. You are starting on the right track if, when faced with an ethical dilemma, you are confused and uncertain.

In the next chapter, we will give you some additional tools to help you work through your bewilderment. Be prepared, though. If we do our job well, you will remain confused and uncertain. Yet this disorientation will not leave you paralyzed, unable to respond reasonably to an ethical dilemma. The next chapter will teach you some classical ethical guidelines, which are likely to come in handy in your daily working lives.

## Values, Interests, and Roles Wrap-up

In this chapter, we have introduced you to the concepts of interests, roles, and values. These three concepts are basic language units of language. We have also encouraged you to work with these language units, to think about value priorities and conflicts. Finally, we have encouraged you to think about the cooperative relationship between employers and employees, which allows them to articulate an organization's value priorities.

In the opening of chapter 3, we asked you to think about how you would behave if a company like Eli Lilly asked you to play a role in reviewing its decisions. After reading this chapter, you are starting to learn material that will prepare you to provide the kind of oversight companies really need. At a minimum, companies need outsiders who understand the concepts of interests, roles, and values. This understanding helps you when you are working in an oversight capacity, as our opening scenario describes. It also helps you in many other situations,

## VALUES IN ACTION
### Dr. Jeffrey Wigand Blows the Whistle on Big Tobacco

Dr. Jeffrey Wigand became a nationally known figure in the mid-1990s after he blew the whistle on tobacco executives and the tobacco industry for lying to the public about the extent to which they have known about the specific health dangers of cigarettes. He blew the whistle after his employer, Brown & Williamson, fired him in 1993 for disputing his employer's use of a tobacco additive, Coumarin, in pipe tobacco. By blowing the whistle on both his former employer and the tobacco industry, he acted on his value priorities. Three of Wigand's key values are **honesty, collective responsibility, and security.**

We define honesty as "to refuse to lie, steal, or deceive in any way."[1] Dr. Wigand refused to lie about the health hazards of cigarettes. In addition, he exposed lies by tobacco industry executives. Wigand was in a unique position to know the truth. His advanced degree in medicine and biological sciences put him in a position to understand complex scientific issues related to the health and safety of cigarettes. Additionally, he was the highest-ranking former tobacco executive willing to speak truthfully about the health and safety of cigarettes.

We define the second key value, collective responsibility, as "the idea that informal or formal groups should solve problems through means that show mutual trust and commonality of interests and priorities."[2] Wigand showed his belief that the government should solve certain social problems by deciding to help the Food and Drug Administration (FDA) understand complex documents related to health hazards of smoking. Wigand's decision made it possible for the FDA to establish jurisdiction over tobacco, which is now considered a drug. Government regulation of the tobacco industry promises to prevent future harm to consumers.

Finally, we define security as "achieving the psychological condition of self-confidence such as you welcome risks."[3] Wigand wants consumers to enjoy self-confidence when they make decisions about which products to purchase. In the past, many Americans continued to smoke, in part because they did not believe tobacco products are addictive. Wigand's willingness to speak out helped make clear the true dangers of nicotine, additives, and smoking. Consumers can purchase products with confidence only when they know the true risks of products. Wigand hopes that once consumers realize the dangers of smoking, they will stop buying tobacco products. He currently strives to educate the public about the risks of smoking by working through the nonprofit organization he formed, Smoke-Free Kids, Inc.

You may know of Dr. Wigand because Disney presented his story in the 1999 movie *The Insider.*

Sources:
[1] See Exhibit 3-1.
[2] This is the definition from chapter 2, American Corporate and Organizational Culture.
[3] See Exhibit 3-1.

including when you are working as a manager within an organization. As you practice using the language of ethics, you will be better able to state clearly your personal value priorities and use them in your daily life.

**EXHIBIT 3-2**   Why Whistle-Blowing is Seldom an Easy Answer to Complex Ethical Dilemmas

**Whistle-blowing** is "the reporting by an organizational member of illegal, immoral or illegitimate activity to parties who can take action."[1] Potential **whistle-blowers** are individuals who are thinking about blowing the whistle to an outsider. When a person blows the whistle, he or she has usually exhausted all possible avenues for resolving problems within the organization.

Management professors Greenberger, Miceli, and Cohen have conducted some of the most important research on whistle-blowing. Their work considers how the attitudes and behaviors of a person's coworkers affect the attitudes and behaviors of potential whistle-blowers.

**Generally, what makes a person speak up within an organization when he/she discovers a problem?** Greenberger, Miceli, and Cohen found out that three factors are important: the work group's characteristics, the potential whistle-blower's characteristics and relationship with the group, and the situation's characteristics.

A potential whistle-blower is *more likely* to speak up within an organization and point out problems when that person works in a group that is weak, lacks cohesion, and does not offer rewards the potential whistle-blower values. The crucial point here is that people are more likely to speak up when they do not fear negative consequences. For instance, the likelihood that someone will speak up goes down if that person is in a work group with the power to make decisions that affect coworkers' performance evaluations.

A potential whistle-blower is *more likely* to speak up within the organization and point out problems when that person perceives she is competent, independent, and distinct/separate from others. She may also be more likely to speak up if she has already established herself as a team player. In this situation, the group is less likely to reject her concerns.

A potential whistle-blower is *more likely* to point out problems when she engages in work that does not require mutual assistance from a work group. Also, a person is more likely to speak up when the wrongdoing is unambiguous (e.g., when it is difficult to argue about the facts). Finally, the chances that someone will speak up internally go up when outsiders are not threatening the group. For instance, if a group of angry consumers is threatening from the outside, insiders might band together more tightly, thus making it more difficult for a potential whistle-blower to speak up within the organization.

**If a person threatens to blow the whistle, in what circumstances is she likely to promote change?** It is important to note that potential whistle-blowers do not all experience the same consequences. A person who points out wrongdoing can sometimes get the group's support, and then change can occur within the organization. That means whistle-blowing (telling an outsider) would not be necessary for change to occur.

Generally, a person who points out a major problem is more likely to get group support for change the more he or she is like the other people

*(continues on the next page)*

(continued)

in the group. The potential whistle-blower is more likely to get the group's support if she is credible, confident, competent, and objective. She is also likely to get support when the situation is not ambiguous. The potential whistle-blower is also more likely to get group support the more she presents views with a flexible rather than rigid style of argumentation. Additionally, potential whistle-blowers do better when they get social support from others before announcing the problem. Overall culture matters too. The potential whistle-blower enjoys more support in a culture that welcomes dissent.

Organizations are often better off when they solve problems within the organization. That means they should want potential whistle-blowers to speak up within the organization, not to outsiders. Still, however, many organizations do not make it clear that the organization will reward employees who point out problems internally. Consequently, some employees feel they have no choice but to blow the whistle to someone outside the organization, such as a reporter or regulatory agency.

Of course, organizations are best off when they minimize wrongdoing, which reduces that possibility that an individual will feel the need to deviate from group norms.

Finally, even if whistle-blowing or attempted whistle-blowing does not promote change, it is still good for a person who values **integrity.** We will explore the definition of integrity fully in chapter 5. For now, we will define it as acting on your sense of right and wrong, no matter what the personal consequences and no matter whether the problem a person points out gets solved.

*Source:*
[1]David B. Greenberger, Marcia P. Miceli, and Debra J. Cohen, "Oppositionists and Group Norms: The Reciprocal Influence of Whistle-blowers and Co-Workers," *The Journal of Business Ethics* 527 (1987): 527.

## CRITICAL THINKING QUESTIONS

1. What additional information would you like to have before deciding whether Anita Roddick has value priorities similar to yours? Why is the information in this chapter insufficient for you to make a fair judgment in this regard?

2. When we attempt to discover our own value priorities as a prelude to making more informed ethical decisions at work, we are making some assumptions that may or may not be true. Try to identify some of these unstated foundational beliefs that would need to be true in order for us to follow the advice of this chapter. Hint: Is it possible that our personal ethical guidelines are not identifiable by ourselves?

3. What important lesson about the application of value priorities is contained in the brief legal history of affirmative action cases in the European Union Global Box? Hint: Why do the courts not apply one simple rule to all affirmative action disputes?

## ENDNOTES

[1] Facts for this scenario come from "Stuck for Money," *supra* note 2, and Jeff Swiatek, "Homeless Cut Down Participation in Indianapolis Firm's Drug Tests," Knight-Ridder Tribune Business News: *Indianapolis Star* and *News-Indiana*, September 5, 1999, available at 1999 WL 22013147 [hereinafter Eli Lilly Update]. The information about IUPUI and the review committee comes from Eli Lilly Update. This article refers to an administrator for a private educational service who really was asked to serve on a review committee.

[2] Laurie P. Cohen, "Stuck for Money: To Screen New Drugs for Safety, Lilly Pays Homeless Alcoholics," *Wall Street Journal*, November 14, 1996, at A1 [hereinafter "Stuck for Money"].

[3] Eli Lilly Update, *supra* note 1.

[4] Ibid.

[5] Ibid.

[6] Ibid. Men often gave addresses of homeless shelters or relatives.

[7] Ibid.

[8] Ibid.

[9] Eli Lilly Update, *supra* note 1.

[10] Ibid.

[11] Ibid.

[12] Ibid.

[13] Ibid.

[14] Ibid.

[15] This part of the scenario is fictitious.

[16] This question is purely hypothetical. We have seen no evidence that stakeholders are questioning Eli Lilly on this matter.

[17] You do know that federal policy does not prohibit the use of homeless populations in drug testing.

[18] Nanette Byrne, "The Good CEO," *Business Week*, Sept. 23, 2002, 80.

[19] "There Are Still Ways to Circumvent Layoffs," *USA Today*, Nov. 15, 2001.

[20] *See* Anonymous, "Pillsbury to Feed Children, Donate to Second Harvest," *Nation's Restaurant News* 52 (2001).

[21] *See* Anonymous, "N.Y. Restaurants Donate to Hunger-Relief Program," *Nation's Restaurant News* 19 (2001).

[22] Jon Entine, "Body Flop," *R.O.B. Report on Business Magazine*, at www.robmagazine.com/june02/story-cover_june02.html

[23] Ibid.

[24] Ibid.

[25] Ibid.

# CHAPTER 4

# Classical Ethical Guidelines: Initial Steps Toward Good Work

**THE FOCUS:**
When in a hurry, what can I do when faced with an ethical dilemma?

When you face an ethical problem at work, there is no need to feel alone. Thoughtful people have been struggling with such dilemmas since the first person considered optional courses of action. The appendix to this chapter presents a few of the major ethical theories that have emerged from the historical effort to create a better community. In addition, the chapter focuses on three classical ethical guidelines that are especially useful when you are in a hurry and cannot spare the time to reflect about the applicability of those ethical theories to your immediate situation. How would you decide the better course of action in the following narrative?

Your company has been busily working on plans for national production of a new product—a car that needs only one gallon of gas to travel 300 miles. Your role on the project is to use your skills as an engineer to test the new technology behind the environmental features of the car.

The results from initial testing excited you about the car's potential. You discovered that air pollution will decrease by 70 percent with use of the new car. Unfortunately, further testing raised serious concerns. After putting the components that are supposed to make the car an environmental success through rigorous testing, you are fairly certain that the car is not going to function the way the lead development crew expects.

In particular, your tests to date show that the car will function well and efficiently for approximately four years, but after that it is likely that the environmentally friendly components will fail. Moreover, the car will experience weakness that will cost individual car owners thousands of dollars in repairs. In essence, the car uses very little gas, but the design of the car cannot withstand normal wear.

You have discussed your preliminary findings with your boss and asked for more time to test the car. You believe you need another eight to ten months to complete testing and work with other engineers to come up with suggestions for change. Your boss has made it clear that you will not get the time. He wants to give the production plant the go-ahead on the car within the month.

Your boss has pressures of his own. He tells you that *Newsweek* has been calling him for weeks, begging for the first look at the car. The EPA has hinted that it will strongly support the sale of the car. You and your boss both wince when you consider the astronomical projected income from the car sales.

Your boss has an idea. He wants you to rerun the tests and "coax" the components through the testing procedures. He points out that by the time the car's problems surface, the company will have promoted him. He also says that you are old enough that you will surely be retired. Your boss is certain that, one way or another, you can both outrun this situation.

You are enough of an old-timer that the scenario your boss has outlined is eerily familiar. You remember a case that occurred in the late 1960s in which a B. F. Goodrich engineer coaxed aircraft brakes through testing procedures so the company could move forward and produce an A7D aircraft for the Air Force.[1] Initially, the engineer cooperated with company directives to falsify data. You recall that the engineer, Kermit Vandivier, complied because he was afraid he would get fired and thus be unable to support his family. Ultimately, Vandivier blew the whistle on the company and reported the falsified data to the FBI.

Remembering that case is making you feel anxious. You'd like to share the facts of that case with your boss, but you suspect he already has difficulty respecting you because of your age. He was in elementary school when Vandivier blew the whistle on B. F. Goodrich. He will view the facts as ancient history, rather than an important story that could guide you both now.

As you trudge back to your office, you think about how you have devoted much of your life's energy working for this company. You have given your work your all, often at the expense of your family. Now you feel too tired to put energy into a battle about testing of this car. However, you can't imagine your final few years at the company hoping that you are successful in outrunning this potentially huge mistake. In these years, you are likely to suffer from worrying about what might happen when the public learns the truth about the car.

In the meantime, your boss keeps reminding you that your company will lose a lot of money if production doesn't begin within the next month. The plants are ready to begin production, the media is buzzing, and you could play a major role in making the company's plans become reality. All you have to do is rework the data and rewrite the report.

You think, "Do I have any options? What if I 'coax' the components through the testing, as my boss suggests? What if the company begins production now and just ignores the problems the car will encounter in four years?" Unlike the Vandivier/B. F. Goodrich case, this problem is not life threatening. You've certainly seen worse problems in your time, such as the exploding Ford Pinto and cigarettes. Plus, the benefits of the new car might outweigh the limited life span. Because the new car uses much less gas than the typical car, consumers are likely to save money overall—even after expensive repairs are taken into consideration! Furthermore, sales of the car will make a huge dent in the air pollution problem. Four years can be a long time; perhaps within that time you can help the company figure out how to fix the car's defects.

What should you do? How do you make this important decision? Do you want to facilitate or discourage this car's immediate development? How do you weigh the benefits of the car versus fact that the car will encounter major problems in only four years? It is right to give consumers full information about a product they buy. It is also right to reduce environmental pollution. It is right to have a viable business. What should you do? To make matters worse, you need to formulate a rapid decision about whether you will coax the components through testing and rewrite the report.

The first fact we should note about the preceding example is that the right course of action is not altogether clear. Ethical conversation is less about finding the one and only right thing to do than it is about finding the better thing to do. Whatever you choose to do, real people will be hurt and others will benefit. Similarly, any decision you make will be both potentially risky and potentially beneficial for the firm.

Second, one of the best ways to help yourself make a tough decision such as this one is to relax, which will help you think better. Of course, you are anxious. But remembering that you are not alone in struggling with such issues can reduce your anxiety about ethical dilemmas a little. We all face them to varying degrees. How we respond to them is one of the most important character tests we face.

Finally, remember that you already know some things that can help. Use what you have learned so far. Make a list of the value priorities that would move you toward sharing more information about the car with the consumers. Considering different roles and their accompanying interests might help you as you formulate value priorities. Now consider the value priorities that would lead you to withhold the information. Then ask yourself, "Given my sense of who I should be in terms of my personal values, which of these value priorities would I typically align myself with?" You might also consider whether you would support these same value priorities with your firm's financial health on the line. Are there any significant facts that might change your desire to act according to that value emphasis?

In this chapter, we want to offer you positive steps that would lead toward a more thoughtful ethical decision. Bright and good people have struggled with such decisions long before you and I started taking our turn at business ethics. Their hard work and thought has been distilled into a few general, classical guidelines that move us toward our goal of more ethical business decisions.

Before we describe these powerful and generally dependable guidelines, we want to be certain that you do not think they are a substitute for reasoning about ethics. They take us quite a distance, but in some instances, they fall short of a strong conclusion. Our objective here is to help you reason better about business ethics. But you and your value priorities, as influenced by the value structure of your organization, are the ultimate glue that pastes these steps together.

## THE GOLDEN RULE

When you were a child, you probably heard your mother or father say, "Don't hit your sister! How would you like it if she hit you?" This interaction might have been the first time you encountered the Golden Rule. Alternatively, you might have heard about the Golden Rule in church. "Do unto others as you would have them do unto you." Confucius and Aristotle offered similar messages.

Many different interpretations and variations of the Golden Rule have been offered. For example, one scholar has identified six ways the Golden Rule can be interpreted.

1. Do to others as you want them to gratify you.
2. Be considerate of others' feelings as you want them to be considerate of your feelings.
3. Treat others as persons of rational dignity like yourself.
4. Extend brotherly or sisterly love to others, as you would want them to do to you.
5. Treat others according to moral insight, as you would have others treat you.
6. Do to others as God wants you to do to them.[2]

What these suggestions share is a reminder that ethics requires awareness that other humans matter. We are pretty certain that we matter, and because we see ourselves in others, we should strive to think long and hard about the effects of our actions on both those we see and also those we cannot directly see, but who matter as human beings nevertheless.

We matter; our families matter; other citizens matter; all those with whom we live have interests and needs that should matter in our thinking. When our thinking about others translates into action, we take actions similar to those of Coca-Cola Co., which is now providing costly HIV and AIDS drugs for its employees in Africa.[3]

This may be a good place to point out that obedience to the Golden Rule gives us a good feeling about ourselves. When we try to follow it, we become more than just a solitary human in a social jungle. We feel a justifiable pride when we recognize that important interests exist outside our personal space. Just imagine what a damning image we would see in the mirror if a glance revealed someone glaring back at us who believed that "only I matter!"

Let's return to the example at the beginning of the chapter. Using the Golden Rule as your ethical guideline, how you would you behave? Would you hide the information, or would you disclose the information? Put yourself in the consumer's shoes. As a consumer, would you want to know that a car's environmental features would last only four years? Are there other stakeholders in the organization whose interests should be the focus of your application of the Golden Rule?

Consider the Enron Corporation, once a multibillion-dollar energy trading company that filed for bankruptcy on December 2, 2001. Let's suppose you are an executive for the Enron Corporation, at one time labeled the "world's greatest corporation." You receive millions of dollars from complex business partnerships arranged with Andrew Fastow, the former chief financial officer. However, these partnerships allow your company to hide debt, and you tell your employees to buy more company stock. Meanwhile, you sell your stock and receive several million dollars.

As the value of Enron's stock plummets, numerous employees are losing most of their investments in their 401(k) plans. For instance, a North Dakota Enron employee invested $330,000 in Enron stock, which dwindled to $1700 after the company's collapse. If you were an ethical executive for Enron, would you engage in similar practices using the Golden Rule as your guideline? Would you want to be one of the Enron employees who lost their life savings while you, one of the company's executives, collect millions of dollars from complex business partnerships?

**CRITICAL THINKING BOX**
Although the Golden Rule is a powerful ethical tool, it could in some circumstances have results we would want to avoid. Can you think of an example?

Some contemporary business leaders engage in action that shows a belief in the Golden Rule. James E. Burke is one leader who shows respect for classical ethical guidelines, especially the Golden Rule.

As you read the following information, ask yourself: Which of Burke's actions show his respect for the Golden Rule? Which of the six interpretations of the Golden Rule fits Burke's actions best? Don't forget the work of James E. Burke as you read the rest of the chapter. His actions show his respect for more than one classical ethical guideline.

## PUBLIC DISCLOSURE TEST

Let's go back to the new car dilemma from the beginning of the chapter. If the Golden Rule test did not seem to help you think through the dilemma, a second tool available is the Public Disclosure Test. That is, choose a course of action and imagine what would happen if your actions were made public. For example, suppose you decide to hide the car's important flaw from its prospective consumers. Now suppose that your decision to hide the flaw were to be printed in the newspaper. How would the public react? How would you feel about the public's having full knowledge of what you intend to do?

You probably recognize immediately the worth of this second classical guideline. We care about what others think about us. We should especially care about what virtuous, thoughtful people think about us. Such people provide a special light that helps us see with improved vision the effects and implications of our decisions. They give us perspective we might miss because of the personal ties we have to alternative options and their results.

To see how this test could prevent unethical behavior, stop for a moment and think of examples of corporations that failed to apply the public disclosure test. In other words, think of examples of corporate actions that have generated negative reactions from the public. Could the business have anticipated the public's reaction?

Another way to think of the public disclosure test is to view it as making our actions transparent—as providing sunshine that makes our actions open to the scrutiny of others. The premise of this classical guideline is that ethics is hard work, labor that we might resist if we did not have frequent reminders that we live in a community. As a member of that community, our self-concept is tied, at least in part, to how we are perceived by that community.

Consider whether Bernard Ebbers, the former CEO of WorldCom, would have acted differently if he had used the public disclosure test. Ebbers used WorldCom's funds to grant himself a $366 million personal loan when a different company he managed was financially troubled.

### MEET THE LEADER: JAMES E. BURKE

The work James E. Burke is doing today is impressive. In his retirement years, he acts as chairman of the Partnership for a Drug-Free America. In this capacity he is leading an organization that has undertaken a significant public service media campaign to help stop drug abuse. Burke's work shows his commitment to relationships based upon trust. He believes that "every relationship that works is based on trust, and you don't develop trust without moral behavior."

What makes James Burke's life work more impressive is that he had a long, distinguished career at Johnson & Johnson prior to his retirement work. In his 40 years with Johnson & Johnson, 15 as the company's leader, Burke earned a reputation for remaining true to the company's corporate mission, especially during tough times. The Johnson & Johnson Credo states that "Johnson & Johnson's first responsibility is to the people who use its products and services; the second responsibility is to its employees; the third to the community and environment; and the fourth to the stockholders." Additionally, Johnson & Johnson believes that stockholder interests will be served naturally as an outcome of the company's pursuit of the first three goals.

Burke's commitment to the Credo and emphasis on relationships built on trust was highlighted by the "Tylenol scare" in the 1980s, when consumers ingested Tylenol capsules tainted with cyanide. Burke took quick action and made sure the product was pulled from the shelves. Eventually, Johnson & Johnson stopped making Tylenol in capsule form because it could not ensure customer safety in spite of modifications to the product's packaging. In the short run, the decision was a financial setback. However, consumers regained confidence in the product.

When Princeton University in 1977 awarded Burke with an honorary degree, Doctor of Law, it summed Burke's accomplishments well: "[w]hen Tylenol fell victim to terror, [Burke] put compassion before cost to maintain the public's confidence in a company synonymous with baby powder and Band-Aids. Having brought comfort and reassurance to a nation suddenly fearful of drugs that heal, he now leads a coalition of corporate citizens to focus our attention on drugs that kill."

*References:*
David Bollier, *Aiming Higher: 25 Stories of How Companies Prosper By Combining Sound Management and Social Vision* (New York: AMACOM, 1996), VII, VIII.
www.princeton.edu/~compub/news/97/q2/0603honorary.html
www.jnj.com/who_is_jnj/hist_index.html

**CRITICAL THINKING BOX**
Under what circumstances could the public disclosure test lead to especially unethical conduct?

If Ebbers had thought about how his friends, employees, and shareholders would react, do you think he would have hesitated to take the money?

One potential problem with the public disclosure test is its requirement that we can actually determine how the public would react. For example, would consumers want the information about the car if they understood the positive impact on air pollution of large-scale purchases of the car? Say you decide to withhold the information because you believe you know what the public thinks, even though you have never asked "the public." Now, how do you think the public will react if they discover that you acted in a certain way because you believed you knew what they thought?

As the critical thinking box suggests, a second drawback to this ethical theory is that the effect of this ethical guideline depends quite a lot on the social norms of the public itself. In a community of thieves, public disclosure of my theft of a firm's assets would hardly serve as an inhibitor to my plans to steal. For example, consider the effects of the social norms of Taiwanese business culture on the public disclosure test discussed in the Global Box.

Does this potential problem of variable social norms mean that the public disclosure test is not helpful as an ethical guideline? Not at all!

### GLOBAL BOX

#### TAIWAN

Taiwan is a country of scarce resources. For generations, the Taiwanese have struggled to satisfy their needs. This scarcity fostered a culture of individualism and a desire for success. Taiwanese attitudes toward the role of business in society reflect their passion for success. In Taiwan, the goal of businesses is similar to that of most U.S. enterprises: to make a profit. A survey of more than 1,000 Taiwanese managers found that productivity, efficiency, and profit were the most important business goals. Such a strong emphasis can be placed on profit maximizing because the accumulation of wealth is a socially acceptable goal. At the New Year holiday, for example, Taiwanese salutations include, "I wish you a great fortune in the coming year!"

The emphasis on profit making may, however, have negative implications for Taiwanese business. A significant percentage of respondents said that ethics were irrelevant to real business. Talk of ethics, the respondents noted, was a public relations ploy. They also expressed a willingness to act scrupulously if it would increase a company's profits. When coupled together, individualism and a desire to achieve can result in reduced attention to the ethical implications.

*Source:*
Carol Yeh-Yun Lin, "A Comparison of Perceptions about Business Ethics in Four Countries," *Journal of Psychology* 133 no. 6 (1999): 641–655.

A constant theme in our book is ethical improvement, rather than ethical perfection. The public disclosure test definitely forces us to think about considerations that deserve our attention. Hence, the test makes our decision more robust because we become more sensitive to the interests of those diverse groups affected by the ethical dilemma.

### Universalization Test

If neither of these tests helps you in an ethical dilemma, a third classical guideline might shed new light on the situation. This test shares with the other two a focus on the many people whom our actions affect. The universalization test asks us to consider what the world would be like were our decision copied by everyone else. Applying the universalization test causes us to wonder aloud, "Is what I am about to do the kind of action that, *were others to follow my example*, makes the world a better place for me and those I love?" We ask: What if everyone did that?

Think about the actions of the Enron executives. Reports about the financial condition of the company overestimated the company's profits by almost $1 billion in the year before the company's collapse. This misrepresentation of the company's equity misled stockholders and Enron employees, who consequently made unsafe investments in the company. When Enron collapsed, these stakeholders were adversely affected while the executives profited. Using the universalization test as an ethical guideline, do you think the world would be a better place if others followed the Enron executives' actions?

Unlike Enron, other corporations have wondered, "If other companies were to follow our example, would the world be a better place?" One company that has worked hard to answer this question positively is Merck & Co. Merck's actions regarding river blindness not only improved the lives of individuals, but also inspired other companies to duplicate Merck's generosity in their own businesses. As you read the Values in Action Box, ask yourself: How did company leaders apply this test with regard to river blindness? Does the universalization test work the same way with regard to drugs that respond to AIDS? Does Merck show respect for other classical ethical guidelines, in addition to its respect for universalization?

When you reflect about the work of companies like Johnson & Johnson and Merck & Co., remember the purpose for applying ethical tests. All three classical guidelines should make us more aware of the tight connection between ethics and our inescapable ties to one another. The ethical focus forces us to be empathetic to the needs of others. Like James E. Burke and Merck's leaders, we can act on that concern by paying attention to the three classical guidelines.

## VALUES IN ACTION
### Merck and Co.

Merck & Co., Inc. is a pharmaceutical company that uses its research abilities to help citizens throughout the world combat disease. The company's reputation for high scientific standards and good global citizenship was shaped in large part by a mission it undertook over 20 years ago.

In the late 1970s, Merck researchers discovered that a drug they were testing for heartworm in dogs, ivermectin, might be a miracle cure for river blindness in humans. At the time, river blindness plagued millions of impoverished citizens in Africa and Latin America. A parasitic worm causes river blindness. This worm causes unbearable itching, so unbearable that victims often want to commit suicide. When the worms invade the eyes, they often blind their victims.[1]

The company's dilemma was that, in addition to the development project's large expense, the project was unlikely to generate revenue for the company. But the company's challenges went well beyond development. The company would also have to test the drug and distribute it to remote locations. Ultimately, Merck decided to go ahead and fund, develop, and distribute its new drug, Mectizan.[2]

Through Merck's Mectizan Donation Program, 25 million people per year are treated for river blindness. Merck has worked with public groups to make its program the largest, most successful public/private health care partnership in the developing world.[3] The United Nations estimates that river blindness may be eradicated by 2007.[4]

A more recent example of Merck's respect for the universalization test is illustrated by Merck's response to the issue of AIDS treatment. The company was faced with the issue of whether to drop prices for AIDS drugs and work with nonprofit groups to fight this epidemic, which has taken an especially heavy toll on citizens in sub-Saharan Africa.[5] In many ways, Merck's dilemma regarding the AIDS epidemic was more complex than the earlier dilemma concerning river blindness. For example, people with river blindness need to take just one Mectizan pill per year, whereas people with HIV/AIDS must take a cocktail of pills several times a day.[6] Also, the AIDS epidemic is more widespread than river blindness.

Early in the new millennium, Merck affirmed its commitment to improving global health by becoming the first pharmaceutical company to sell its HIV/AIDS medicines without profit in certain developing countries. The company joined the Bill and Melinda Gates Foundation and the government of Botswana in a five-year commitment to seek a way to treat HIV/AIDS in devastated countries. The coalition's goal is to help countries with weak infrastructures develop a health system that will support an effective response to the HIV/AIDS epidemic.[7]

The driving force behind Merck's efforts to improve global health is the commitment of the company's founder, George W. Merck, to help people. In 1950, Merck stated, "We try never to forget that medicine is for the people. It is not for the profits. The profits follow, and if we have remembered that, they have never failed to appear."[8]

*Sources:*

[1] David Bollier for The Business Enterprise Trust, "Merck & Co.: Quandaries in Developing a Wonder Drug for the Third World," in *Aiming Higher: 25 Stories of How Companies*

*(continues on the next page)*

(continued)

*Prosper By Combining Sound Management And Social Vision* (1996), 280, 28–282 [hereinafter *Aiming Higher*].

[2] Ibid.

[3] "Merck: Practicing Good Citizenship Worldwide," *9 Metropolitan Corporate Counsel*, December 2001, 1 (col. 2) [hereinafter Good Citizenship Worldwide]. This article is an interview with Kenneth C. Frazier, Senior Vice President and General Counsel at Merck & Co., Inc.

[4] Karen Lowry Miller, Anna Kuchment, Mac Margolis, and Tom Masland, "The Pill Machine: How Much Money Should Big Drug Firms Have to Lose to Treat the World's Poorest Patients?" *Newsweek International* (November 19, 2001), available at 2001 WL 19100026.

[5] Good Citizenship Worldwide.

[6] Ibid.

[7] Ibid.

[8] Ibid.

## CRITICAL THINKING QUESTIONS

1. How can any of us use the universalization test to guide our decisions when we never have the necessary evidence to know for certain what the world would be like if everyone made one of the decisions we are considering?

2. Does the use across cultures of some version of the Golden Rule provide convincing evidence that this particular classical guideline provides reliable guidance for business ethics?

# APPENDIX A

# Ethical Theories

Until now, you've been learning many *practical* ways to think about ethical behavior. We hope the guidelines we have given you will be useful when you are faced with difficult decisions in the "real world" of business. But perhaps you're wondering about the source of these practical ideas. As much as we would like to claim credit for such guidelines ourselves, we must refer you to other philosophers who, long before we were thinking about ethics, proposed the ideas from which we drew our guidelines.

This appendix is an attempt to briefly introduce you to those *ethical theories* (theories that tell us how we *should* behave) that have influenced the practical ideas in this book. A warning: these ideas are complicated. Much of the reason we chose to omit these theories from the body of our book was that we felt these theories were often too complicated to put into practice in the business world. You will often be asked to make quick decisions that will impact the lives of hundreds of people. Our guess is that you won't have time to pull out your philosophy textbook with its complicated explanations of ethical theories. And even if you did have time to reference the book, these theories don't give you much help unless you have large amounts of time to think about them!

Nonetheless, we *do* feel that these theories, as complicated as they are, contain very important insights relevant to doing good work. It is our guess that before you picked up this book you had some idea of what it meant to be "ethical." Additionally, we bet that you were not shocked by any of the guidelines we have proposed, even though you may have been unaware of such useful tools. This basic, consistent expectation of what it means to be ethical is because most of us, in one form or another, subscribe to one of three general ethical theories. All three of these general ethical theories are represented in the ethical guidelines of this text—hence the general consistency among our suggestions and your previous conceptions of the right.

Does everyone subscribe to one of these ethical theories? Not at all! However, *in general*, most of us think of "the ethical" as some variation of one of these themes, which, as you may have already guessed, were introduced by major philosophers long ago.

We will begin with the youngest ethical theory and work our way back in time. First, we will learn about the ethical theory of **Utilitarianism,** proposed by Jeremy Bentham and John Stuart Mill. This theory argues that we should decide what actions are ethical based solely on the *consequences* of the actions. We will then move on to the **Deontological** ethical theory of Immanuel Kant. Although Kant has much to say about morality, the primary idea we will focus on in this appendix is his idea that ethical behavior simply results from doing one's *duty*. We will finish our appendix with an overview of one of the oldest ethical theories—Aristotle's **Virtue** ethics. According to this theory, an ethical individual is not one who behaves in certain ways, but rather one who possesses certain *virtues*.

## UTILITARIANISM: THE ETHICS OF CONSEQUENCES

Suppose you are a middle manager at an insurance company. One day, while going through one of your employee's account ledgers, you notice $100 missing. You approach the employee, and after initially pleading ignorance, she confesses to taking the money to pay last month's rent. She is a single mother and has been struggling to pay the bills and keep food on the table for her three children. She promises that she will pay it back next month. You sympathize with her, but wander back to your desk confused about what to do next.

Before you can decide the best action to take, your boss approaches you and asks you if you know anything about $100 shortage in your accounts. It turns out that your boss does not have enough information to discover who might have taken the $100. If you do not tell him, he will never know. What should you do?

You already have multiple tools that you can use to help with your decision here. If you were your boss, how would you like to be treated? What if everyone did what you choose to do? Would you want the public to know what you are about to do? All of these tools from chapter 4 are particularly useful in thinking about this issue because they get you to think about *consequences*.

Consequences are at the very center of a Utilitarian ethical theory. In fact, what distinguishes Utilitarians from almost all other ethical theorists is that they believe that consequences are *all* that matters when making an ethical decision. In our preceding example, Utilitarians would say that the *only* thing that should count when you are making the decision about what to do should be the consequences of your action. For example, you shouldn't worry about whether you've been taught that lying is wrong because, according to Utilitarians, lying is only wrong when it leads to bad consequences.

Utilitarianism is only one of multiple *consequentialist ethical theories*. It stands out from other consequentialist theories because it argues that we are to be concerned with the consequences of our actions on *everyone*. In other words, when thinking about our decisions we are to be *impartial*. We must not favor our friends or relatives over others. In the example, you must treat your employee and your boss as if they were of equal worth.

So, how do we decide which consequences are best? Two of the most common answers to this question can be found in the writings of Jeremy Bentham and John Stuart Mill. The original Utilitarian, Jeremy Bentham, argued that the best consequences are those that lead to the greatest amount of *pleasure* over pain. This type of Utilitarianism is referred to as *Hedonistic Utilitarianism* and is most specifically directed toward increasing the amount of sensate and short-term pleasure in the world.

However, Bentham's predecessor, John Stuart Mill, argued that the best consequences are those that lead to the greatest amount of *happiness*. This form of Utilitarianism is often referred to as *Eudaimonistic Utilitarianism* (eudaimonia is the Greek word for "happiness"). This form of Utilitarianism is more specifically directed toward increasing the amount of reflective and long-term happiness in the world.

As you might have already guessed, there are numerous practical problems with this approach to ethical decision making. Although the theory may seem intuitively correct to most of us, it becomes quite difficult to put into practice. As we saw earlier, there is much controversy over what yardstick we should use to evaluate the consequences of an action. Should we take those actions that will lead to the most amount of pleasure? Happiness? Money? You get the idea.

The second, and perhaps more damning, problem with Utilitarianism is that it is incredibly difficult to measure and compare the benefits and costs of each consequence. Even if we decide that we want to do only those actions that produce the greatest pleasure, how do we decide which actions will produce more pleasure than others? The preceding example is somewhat oversimplified so that you will be able to see the differences between the three different ethical systems we discuss in this appendix. However, in the business world you will often face ethical dilemmas that will cause harm *no matter what you decide*. When this happens, Utilitarians argue that you should determine which action would lead to the least harm. Yet, they never give us a tool for this calculation. This and other important criticisms of Utilitarianism have led many to accept the ethical theory of one of the two following philosophers.

## DEONTOLOGY: THE ETHICS OF DUTY

Perhaps you're thinking that a consequentialist perspective is seriously flawed because there are many situations, including the preceding scenario, in which the perspective of Utilitarianism requires one to lie. You may think that lying is wrong—period—not just because it will lead to negative consequences.

Or perhaps you've noticed that considering *only* the consequences of an action may lead one to take actions that end up using people as *mere* means to certain ends. For example, according to the Utilitarian ethic, it might be ethical for us to kill one innocent and healthy human being so that we can give her organs away to five individuals who will die without them. If we think about *only* the consequences here, this action seems to be the right thing to do. One dead and five alive is a better consequence than five dead and one alive!

If you're thinking to yourself that an ethical theory should urge us to consider something beyond consequences, you might be a proponent of a **Deontological** ethical theory. In fact, you may even be saying that consequences should *never* matter when making an ethical decision. If you are in this camp, you agree with the *extreme deontology* proposed by the philosopher Immanuel Kant. Deontological ethical theories urge us to consider our *duty* when making ethical decisions (Deon is the Greek word for "duty"). Some Deontologists claim that we should consider duty *and* consequences, whereas Kant claims that we should *never* consider consequences.

The only characteristic that makes an action right, according to Kant, is whether it was done for the sake of duty to some ethical law. It is important to note that, unlike Bentham and Mill, Kant is concerned with ethical motivation. He doesn't want you to act only in accordance with your duty—he wants you to act for the sake of duty. In other words,

Kant doesn't want you to tell your boss about the stolen money because you could be fired if you don't. He wants you to tell your boss about the stolen money because you are intrinsically motivated to do the right thing—to tell the truth.

So, you might be asking how we know which duties we have and which we don't. Things get really complicated here with Kant, but for our purposes, we will focus on his two most important contributions to ethical thought.

The first contribution is one you have already seen before, but in a different form. He argues that it is our duty to act in accordance with principles that can be willed into universal laws. This is another form of the universalization test to which we referred in chapter 4. If you decide that you are going to lie to your boss, you might be acting on the principle "Lie whenever it is possible to lie without getting caught." Kant would argue that there is a severe problem with the universal law "*Always* lie whenever it is beneficial to lie." Therefore, he would argue that in our initial scenario you should tell your boss the truth.

The second major contribution Kant makes to moral theory is his belief that it is our duty to treat people as ends in themselves and never as *mere* means. In other words, we can never reduce people to the status of being nothing more than things, tools, or conveniences; instead, we must see them as valuable in their own right. This point is important for ethical decisions because it bars us from acting in ways that ignore the value of personhood. Remember the example of killing the one innocent individual for the sake of the five? Kant would find such an action ethically depraved because you are treating the innocent individual as a mere means and therefore not respecting his worth as a human being.

It is important to note, before moving on, the differences between Kant's theory of duty and others. Not all Deontological ethical theories hold that we have a duty to respect persons as ends in themselves or a duty to act in accordance with universalization. Other Deontological theories hold that we have different duties. What makes the theories similar is that they are all committed to acting for the sake of duties.

As you might imagine, the fundamental problem with deontological systems is how one determines which duties they are obligated to follow. Many Utilitarians, for example, argue that Deontological theories encourage us to follow rules that don't actually exist.

## VIRTUE: THE ETHICS OF CHARACTER

You've now been acquainted with two seemingly different ethical theories. Utilitarianism argues that you should do that which leads to the best consequences and Deontological ethical systems argue that you should do that which you are motivated to do for the sake of duty. Utilitarianism is interested in the consequences of your actions, whereas Deontological theories are interested in the motivation behind your actions.

What do both of these theories have in common that this third theory does not? They are fundamentally concerned with *action*, whereas virtue ethicists are mostly concerned with *character*. In other words, Utilitarians and Deontologists are interested in the question, "What should I do?" Virtue ethicists are interested in the question, "Who should I be?"

The emphasis on character in ethics is by no means new. Hundreds of years before Bentham, Mill, or Kant, Aristotle was speaking about the importance of character. In modern philosophy, there has also been a renewed interest in ethical theories of character similar to the original **Virtue** ethics of Aristotle (see Kennedy's cardinal virtues in chapter 3). According to Aristotle, to be classified as one with strong character, you must possess certain *virtues*. Virtues are simply those character traits that are habitual and good for people to have because they lead to successful human living.

There are a couple of important ideas within this definition that we should be sure to highlight. First, virtues are *habitual*. To possess the virtue of honesty, one must practice honesty on a consistent basis—as if it were simply a habit. Next, we note that virtues are those habits that are *good* for people to have. This distinction is important, because according to Aristotle, vices are habitual too. The only difference between a virtue and a vice is that one leads to human flourishing whereas the other does not. How does one decide which habits will lead to human flourishing? Good question!

Many individuals have different answers to this question, but Aristotle believed that the best path to successful human living was to always take the middle ground. In other words, a virtue to Aristotle was that habit that was not too extreme in one direction or the other. Let's look at some examples. Aristotle spoke often about the importance of courage as a virtue. He understood courage to be a "middle-ground" type habit because if one is courageous they are neither cowardly nor overconfident and foolhardy. Another example is the virtue of generosity. Aristotle also saw this virtue as middle ground because one could be either stingy or extravagant in their giving to others.

How would a virtue ethicist respond to our original scenario? In many ways it is hard to tell because we have ended our scenario with the question, "What should you *do*?" Yet, it seems that Aristotle might respond by saying that you should do what is in alignment with the type of person you wish to become. In other words, if you believe that a virtuous person is one who does not lie, then you should not lie.

As you may have already noticed, virtue ethicists have been known to talk about actions from time to time. In fact, many virtue ethicists simply argue that their theory is meant to *complete* our standard ethical theories that speak about action without character. However, there are also virtue ethicists who hold that actions *never* matter. This theory, however, seems to suffer from the same incompleteness of which they accuse other theories. Is it possible to speak about character without speaking about action? It seems that actions *do* matter at times, for how can we decide which habits are worthy of being virtues if we don't also look to the *consequences* of such actions?

| Ethical Theory | Ethical Guideline |
|---|---|
| Utilitarianism (Jeremy Bentham & John Stuart Mill) | Do that which leads to the best consequences for everyone involved. |
| Deontology (Immanuel Kant) | Do that which you are motivated to do for the sake of duty. |
| Virtue Ethics (Aristotle) | Do that which is consistent with the type of person you wish to become. |

## ENDNOTES

[1] Facts for this chapter opener come from Kermit Vandivier, "Why Should My Conscience Bother Me?" in *In the Name of Profit*, edited by Robert Heilbroner (Garden City, NY: Doubleday, 1972). After Vandivier blew this whistle on his company, he worked as a newspaper reporter.

[2] Jeffrey Wattles, "Levels of Meaning in the Golden Rule," *Journal of Religious Ethics* 15, (1987): 106–29, quoted in W. Patrick Cunningham, "The Golden Rule as Universal Ethical Norm," *Journal of Business Ethics* 17 (1998): 105–09.

[3] Nann Carrns, "Coke Is Helping African Bottlers Add AIDS Care to Health Benefits," *Wall Street Journal*, 27 September 2002.

# CHAPTER 5

# Moral Mentors in American Corporations and Organizations: The Models for Good Work

**THE FOCUS:**
How can you spot a moral mentor—someone who models good work and brings out the moral best in others?

Some people have more experience and skill than you and I have in thinking through ethical issues in business. Consequently, it makes sense to attempt to identify those business leaders who can serve as mentors for us as we struggle with ethical questions at work. As you read the following scenario, ask yourself how you would have identified those in the organization that could serve as a moral mentor.

You have worked in the same job for the past three years. Your job has many desirable traits—it provides opportunities for you to travel to interesting places, you've interacted with higher-level employees who have taught you some key business skills, and you are making a substantial salary. In some ways you are content with your job, but you know it is time to move on, either to a new department or to a new company. Although you would never announce this reason at work, your primary motivation for wanting to move on is that your current boss's behavior turns your stomach.

Your current boss is exactly the kind of person you read about in chapter 2, the type that sociologist Robert Jackall would describe as a "promotable" person. Your boss is a woman who will do virtually anything to climb the corporate ladder. She jumps on command, and she expects her employees to do the same. In addition, your boss loves her power. One of her greatest joys is "sticking it" to other people.

Another of your boss's key traits is that she demonstrates the "can-do" positive exterior you know your company likes. But underneath it all, she is at best amoral. At worst, her moral code could be summed up as, "I'll do whatever the CEO wants me to do." Recently, you told your mother, "The biggest difference between my boss and Enron executives is that my boss has not yet gotten caught."

Over time, the culture your boss has created in your division has generated a great deal of daily stress for you. You are having panic attacks in the night, and you seriously wonder if your company is the next Enron. In addition to these major concerns, small things are eating away at you. It is increasingly difficult for you to be your best moral self at work.

You recall some incidents that have bothered you. You turned in an inflated expense report, something you know other managers do all the time. You yelled at a subordinate in a shamefully harsh tone and then discovered that your boss saw this incident as demonstrative of your leadership potential. You also described a recent project you led as "highly successful" when it was mediocre. Other people accepted your self-generated "success" label without question. As a result of such incidents, you are starting to see yourself as "promotable," and your promotable self is someone you do not like.

You've decided to interview to see whether you can find a new job. You are not sure what you are looking for in a new boss, except that you know you want to work in a place where it will be *easy* to be your best moral self. You wonder how you would recognize a "moral mentor" if you met one.

You ask yourself many questions, "Are there any moral mentors in corporations and organizations today? What would an ideal moral mentor look like? How can I avoid the charismatic–tyrant boss, the opposite of a moral mentor? If I cannot find an ideal moral mentor, can I at least find a pretty good moral mentor—a boss who creates a culture I find acceptable in terms of moral standards?"

The overriding goal of this chapter is to equip you with ways to answer the preceding questions so that you can identify moral mentors— those who do good work and who bring out the best in others. The chapter assumes that we need more than words for ethical training; we need people. We need to see that ethics is not just a blackboard phenomenon, but that doing good work is something real people have done and are doing.

We will begin our search for these real-life people by describing the ideal model mentor—that boss you may be lucky enough to have, at least once in your working life, who does more than good work. The ideal mentor engages in morally terrific work. The chapter then describes the opposite of an ideal moral mentor—that boss who seems appealing initially. However, the more you get to know this person, the more you realize he or she will not help you create the kind of moral partnership you aspire to create. We'll refer to this kind of boss as a charismatic tyrant, and if you are searching for a moral model, this is the kind of boss you will want to identify and then avoid. In fact, the charismatic tyrant is so morally flawed that he or she is often proud to engage in morally questionable work.

We recognize that life is not perfect. Not all bosses are ideal moral mentors. Thankfully, they are not all charismatic tyrants either. Therefore, the last part of the chapter addresses the search for the "pretty good" moral mentor. This pretty good moral mentor is striving to be an ideal moral mentor, but constraints, often beyond their control, make it impossible for them to be terrific. Throughout the chapter, you should be thinking about not only finding models for yourself but also becoming either an ideal or pretty good moral mentor yourself. You have the potential to be someone other people, if they place a high priority on engaging in morally good work, would want as a boss.

## THE IDEAL MORAL MENTOR

A **moral mentor** is someone who models good work and brings out the moral best in others. A mentor makes personal investments in bringing out high-quality, other-oriented traits of their employees. In serving as a mentor, this individual moves in and out of leadership roles, serves as a resource, and gives employees the opportunity to make discoveries for themselves. Employees who want to do good work admire the moral mentor; they want to be like them. An **ideal** moral mentor is terrific. The ideal mentor is an individual who:

1. Demonstrates the utmost **integrity.** Integrity means "the courage of our convictions, the willingness to act and speak in behalf of what we know to be right."[1] In particular, a person with integrity can: "(1) discern what is right and wrong, (2) act on what they discerned, even at a personal cost, and (3) say openly that they are acting on their understanding of right and wrong."[2]

   In other words, the person who demonstrates integrity engages in responsible reflection.[3] This reflection yields self-understanding about beliefs. These beliefs are rooted in the classical ethical guidelines you learned about in the last chapter. When facing a moral dilemma, the moral mentor acts on his or her beliefs, even if doing so will not lead to the next promotion. Finally, the person must be willing to announce the basis of their actions. The person must be willing to make it clear to others that they are willing to "walk their talk."

2. Acts on **values** that **show the highest regard for others.** The ideal moral mentor's value priorities are likely to include several of the following: honesty, justice, caring, and community. A good example

of a CEO acting on his values and showing high regard for others is Joseph Neubauer of Aramark.[4] In 1984 corporate raiders tried to take over his company. Though Neubauer would have received a large financial windfall from the takeover, he fought against it. In fact, the CEO mortgaged his home and took out a personal loan to fend off the raiders. His efforts resulted in a successful management buyout that most likely saved thousands of jobs. Neubauer explains, "I felt obligated to the people who worked with me."

3. Can **facilitate moral excellence in others** by **encouraging conversation.** In chapter 1 we introduced the importance of conversation about ethics. For individuals to develop moral maturity, they must interact with peers.[5] This interaction raises the opportunity for a person to hear what others believe, then reconsider their own beliefs. When the moral mentor encourages conversation, he or she makes it possible for people to challenge others' views. An additional way that the ideal moral mentor encourages ethics is that, as a manager, he or she is careful about what behavior to reward and punish.

4. **Welcomes dissent.** Instead of asking everyone to be "yes-men"[6] who obey the king, the king wants a jester,[7] someone willing to poke fun at the ruler in order to expose potential weaknesses in action plans.

5. Demonstrates behavior that **can stand the test of time.** Too often, "talented" individuals, also known as corporate stars,[8] show that their primary strength is putting on a good show. They can start or follow the latest corporate fad. Whether the fad is to "empower employees" or "think outside the box," the star shines. But corporate fads about behavior come and go, and stars cannot always maintain their image. The ideal moral mentor's behavior never goes out of style, at least not in the eyes of those who are trying to be their best moral selves.

Perhaps you are thinking that these characteristics are too demanding—nobody could ever be such a good model. However, ideal moral mentors exist. One example is Aaron Feuerstein, leader of the textile company Malden Mills. As you read the following Values in Action Box, think about the characteristics of an ideal moral mentor. Also, if you are a regular news reader and know that Malden Mills filed for bankruptcy in 2002, be patient! We know about the company's plans to reorganize. We will discuss the implications of Malden Mills' financial development on Feuerstein's credibility as an ethical model later in this section. For now, we will say that we still give Aaron Feurstein high marks as a moral mentor.

Remember, the ideal moral mentor models good work and brings out the moral best in others and, as an ideal, excels at (1) demonstrating integrity, (2) acting on values that show the highest regard for others, (3) facilitating moral excellence in others, (4) welcoming dissent, and (5) demonstrating behavior that can stand the test of time.

---

**VALUES IN ACTION**

**Aaron Feuerstein and Malden Mills**

A devastating fire on a December night in 1995 gave America the chance to watch values in action as Malden Mills and its owner, Aaron Feuerstein, made decisions about the company's future.

Malden Mills, located in Lawrence, Massachusetts, produces Polartec and Polarfleece, which are synthetic materials used in outdoor clothing. Its customers include several catalog companies (e.g., L.L. Bean) and the Department of Defense.

During Christmas season 1995, an explosion and fire destroyed three of the plant's critical buildings. Malden Mills and Aaron Feuerstein had to decide whether to rebuild in Lawrence or take the insurance money and move to a location with cheaper labor costs. Mr. Feuerstein decided to rebuild in Lawrence, the community that had supported the privately held company over the years and had supplied the company's top-notch workforce.

Mr. Feuerstein celebrated the opening of the new manufacturing plant in September 1997 by reciting a prayer. He said, "I thank you, majestic God of the universe, for restoring to Malden Mills and its employees, our life and soul." The workers celebrated because Mr. Feuerstein had gone beyond his commitment to workers by rebuilding and rehiring his employees. In addition, he continued to pay workers who were unemployed because of the fire.

At the dedication of the new plant, Jay Mazur, national president of Unite!, a garment workers' union, praised Mr. Feuerstein for "taking the high road to make the product better instead of the low road of cheapening the product, downsizing workers and running away to another location." Mr. Feuerstein explained to the crowd, "There was no way that I was going to take 3,000 people and throw them into the street. And there was no way I was going to condemn Lawrence to economic oblivion. No."

As of 1997, economists praised Mr. Feuerstein for his brilliant business skills. They have pointed out that at the time of the fire, Feuerstein had refined a high-quality product, demonstrated good customer service, and trained workers so well that they were hard to replace.

In the late 1990s, the company was enjoying increased sales and higher productivity. The fire gave Feuerstein and the company the chance to affirm its value priorities. The company did an especially good job of showing its emphasis on the values of **community** and **security** for employees.

*Reference:*
*"Promise Is Kept: Mill Reopens," New York Times*, September 16, 1997.

---

Aaron Feuerstein gets especially high marks with regard to our first two criteria. He is terrific in that he demonstrates the utmost integrity and acts on values that show the highest regard for others. For Feuerstein, a sense of right and wrong comes from his religious faith. For guidance, he relies on the Torah, which is the book of Jewish law.[9] In newspaper and television interviews, he has expressed his belief that businesses should "do the right thing" by looking out for the long-run interests of their employees and communities.[10] Also he cares highly about his employees and sees them as assets.[11]

Feuerstein has criticized companies like Enron as "terrible" for "sacrific[ing] everything for the immediate gain."[12] He points out that ". . . the god of money has taken over to an extreme" in modern America.[13] Although some of his creditors are currently unhappy with him,[14] and some want to oust him from his leadership role,[15] Feuerstein has not wavered in his commitment to employees and the Lawrence, Massachusetts, community.

It is difficult to know the extent to which Feuerstein fulfills the third and fourth characteristics, facilitating moral excellence in others and welcoming dissent, because interviews do not focus on Malden Mills' internal corporate culture. We do not know what the company rewards and punishes or what kinds of conversations take place within the company. Companies that are on the right track with regard to these two criteria may reward moral excellence in the employee evaluation process. They may also welcome dissent by establishing a mechanism that allows employees to bring bad news to the attention of bosses with no fear of punishment. Managers and executives who are on the right track want to learn about problems while there is still time for repair.

We do know, however, that employees of Malden Mills respect their boss. The company has a union that has never gone on strike.[16] Employees are loyal to Feuerstein because he is tenacious, and he looks out for them.[17] Employee loyalty is usually consistent with companies that facilitate moral excellence and welcome dissent.

Whether Feuerstein's behavior stands the test of time requires some reflection. Malden Mills is currently reorganizing under bankruptcy laws. It is possible that by the time this textbook is in print, Feuerstein will be a symbolic leader of the company, stripped of his decision-making power.[18] Some writers have already questioned whether Feurstein is a good model of business ethics and have lumped him in the same "failure" category as Enron and WorldCom executives, even though Feuerstein is a "good guy."[19] Some people might say, "What good is Feuerstein's other-oriented decision making if, financially, the company can't survive?"

In particular, commentators have criticized Feuerstein for looking out for "nebulous stakeholders,"[20] spending too much money on building an environment- and worker-friendly plant after the fire,[21] and miscalculating how much insurance money would support the company's rebuilding efforts.[22] Some people are willing to throw up their hands and say, "What good is Aaron Feuerstein if he ends up in trouble financially?"

For us, the question of whether Malden Mills ends up as a financial success is separate from whether Feurstein is an ideal moral mentor. Consider this analogy. We would still call a person a "hero" if they ran into a burning building to save someone, even if the person the hero carried out of the building died from their injuries.[23] Similarly, with regard to ideal moral mentors, we need to focus on the person's intent and behavior, rather than the ultimate financial outcome

The more appropriate question regarding the fifth criterion is, "Has Feuerstein's behavior gone out of style in the eyes of those who strive to be their best moral selves?" Some may argue that it is immoral to make creditors unhappy in the short run. However, we are not willing to make this judgment because the process by which Feuerstein has made his decisions is nothing like the lying, fraudulent behavior of Enron executives. We believe Feuerstein's other-oriented behavior will never go out of style. Complying with a moral duty to employees and a community is not a fad. As his reorganization plans show, Feuerstein intends to look out for all stakeholders, including creditors.

One lasting lesson of the Malden Mills case is that even in America, where religion is usually separate from business, some companies do engage in good work influenced by the religious beliefs of the men and women who run them. In the following Global Box, ask yourself about the extent to which Feurstein's religiously influenced beliefs are consistent with Buddhist principles. Also, as you read the Meet the Leader Box, note that Rosanne Haggerty's work with the homeless began when she was an employee of a nonprofit organization, Catholic Charities, in New York City.

## THE CHARISMATIC TYRANT

The opposite of an ideal moral mentor is a charismatic tyrant. Charismatic tyrants do not model good work, and they do not bring out the moral best in others. Before we move on, we should clarify what we mean when we say "charismatic tyrant." By charismatic, we mean magnetic. People are drawn to them. By tyrant, we mean bully.

A charismatic tyrant manages to draw employees into their circle and then gets them to follow their lead down a path of engaging in morally bad work. Followers are often like abused spouses. They know they should get out of the relationship, but for a complex set of reasons (especially financial ones), they believe they are stuck. Charismatic tyrants are the opposite of ideal moral mentors. That is, they (1) fail to demonstrate integrity, (2) act on values that show little regard for others, (3) bring out the worst in others, (4) prohibit dissent, and (5) demonstrate behavior that cannot stand the test of time.

Thomas O'Boyle, in his book *At Any Cost*, portrays Jack Welch, the former CEO of General Electric, as a charismatic tyrant.[24] Although Welch was widely admired as a master strategist and manager by other firms, he engaged in many questionable ethical practices. For example,

**GLOBAL BOX**

## BUDDHISM

If you were asked to describe the attributes of a person who practices Buddhism, you are not likely to include "shrewd businessperson" as part of the description. This may be a reasonable assumption, but it should not lead to the conclusion that Buddhism does not say anything about business. In fact, Buddhism does provide ethical direction specifically for business practitioners.

Buddhist teachings include the "Noble Eightfold Path." This set of teachings prescribes factors needed to lead an enlightened life. One of the eight factors is "Right Livelihood." Right Livelihood applies Buddhist ethics to work. There are five Buddhist principles that cannot be broken while working: (1) one cannot cause harm to another, (2) one may not cheat, (3) one may not lie, (4) one cannot promote intoxication, and (5) one cannot engage in sexual exploitation. Buddhist teachings do allow the pursuit of profits and wealth. However, greed and the hording of wealth and profits are not tolerated. As a result, businesses and persons who acquire wealth are encouraged to share these gains with employees and the community.

You may be thinking that these principles are great in the abstract, but impossible to implement in the real business world. Yet, there is a network of businesses committed to proving this hypothesis wrong. British-based Windhorse Trading is an example of a company based on Buddhist ethics. Windhorse is an importer and wholesaler of goods for the gift market. The company's goal is to maintain a spiritual and cooperative working environment that is loyal to Buddhism while remaining profitable. Often the methods for achieving the first goal appear to conflict with achievement of the second goal. For instance, all employees are given at least two months off to attend retreats—a perk that would make many profit-seeking businesspersons cringe. Windhorse also sponsors many activities that take employees away from their tasks during the workday, such as meditations, prayer circles, and time for spiritual reflection.

Windhorse management insists that the business can remain profitable while remaining attentive to Buddhist traditions. The employees willingly accept their low pay for the opportunity to enrich their spiritual lives. They also support the company's charitable giveaways. A few years ago, when Windhorse was struggling financially, the company decided to cut back on plans to expand the business. They chose to cut back rather than compromise employee benefits and programs dedicated to enriching spiritual life. The successful goal of making a profit is secondary to Windhorse's desire to maintain a company that follows the teachings of Buddha.

*Source:*
Bodhipaksa, "Reinventing the Wheel: A Buddhist Approach to Ethical Work" in *Spiritual Goods: Faith Traditions and the Practice of Business*, edited by Stewart W. Herman (Bowling Green, OH: Philosophy Documentation Center, 2001), 33–54.

## MEET THE LEADER: ROSANNE HAGGERTY, FOUNDER AND EXECUTIVE DIRECTOR OF COMMON GROUND COMMUNITY

Rosanne Haggerty is a moral mentor and leader who engages in partnerships with organizations and corporations to empower homeless Americans. In 1990, she founded Common Ground Community, a nonprofit organization in New York City. The organization "works to end homelessness through the creation of innovative programs designed to promote **stability** and **independence** for the individuals it serves."[1]

The organization's overriding goal is to help people who were formerly homeless stay housed, and to further this goal, its first project was to renovate the Times Square Hotel. To make this project happen, Haggerty enlisted the help of The Center for Urban Community Services, which provides an on-site, comprehensive support system for tenants. Haggerty also enlisted the support of corporations, including Starbuck's and Ben & Jerry's, which provided franchises within the building that offer jobs to tenants. Other corporate partners include Marriott, the Gap, and the Home Depot.[2] Haggerty says, "What's perhaps been most unusual about our particular journey is the role of the business community . . . [Business has been] an extraordinary potential partner in accomplishing some of these very vital goals of moving people back into opportunity in the mainstream, and stable lives again."[3]

In the properties Haggerty manages, tenants include elderly, ill, formerly homeless, and low-income working people. Tenants learn to be responsible for themselves and to be good neighbors. Her recent projects have focused on creating housing opportunities for especially challenging populations: young people leaving foster care, homeless who are transitioning from hospitals, and long-term street people.[4]

Several organizations have honored Haggerty for her work. For instance, in 1998, the Peter F. Drucker Foundation for Nonprofit Management honored her with their annual award for nonprofit innovation. In October 2001, Haggerty was named as a recipient of a prestigious MacArthur Fellowship, an award that is worth $500,000 over five years.[5] The MacArthur Fellows program described Haggerty as "a committed social service champion and determined leader."[6] The program awards give recipients an opportunity for even greater achievement.

Haggerty demonstrates the traits we used to describe an ideal moral mentor. She acts on her value priorities of innovation and compassion, and these values show her orientation toward others. She facilitates excellence in her tenants. Her behavior has stood the test of time. She continues her work, taking on new housing projects that apply her time-tested strategies for success. Some might even call Haggerty a hero because she "open[s] us to new possibilities of what might be," acts on a "positive moral imagination," and cares about people less fortunate than herself.[7]

*(continues on the next page)*

*(continued)*

*Source:*

[1] This mission statement comes from Common Ground Community, Inc., HDFC's Web site, at www.commonground.org

[2] This information comes from a transcript of a videotape in which the organization presents the award to Haggerty/Common Ground Community. See www.pfdf.org/award/winners/1998.

[3] Ibid.

[4] Kristen Sterling, "Housing Advocate and Columbia Graduate Student, Rosanne Haggerty, Receives Prestigious MacArthur Fellowship," *Columbia News*, at www.columbia.edu/cu/news/01/10/macArthur_fellowship.html (retrieved August 19, 2002).

[5] Ibid.

[6] Ibid.

[7] Dick Keyes, "America Must Rediscover Heroism," in *American Values: Opposing Viewpoints*, edited by David L. Bender, 81, 87 (San Diego, CA: Greenhaven Press, 1989).

O'Boyle chronicles how Welch orchestrated massive layoffs and created an atmosphere conducive to illegal, fraudulent behaviors and the firing of potential whistle-blowers. Welch also demanded rewards, including a lavish compensation package.[25] GE now pays for his $15 million apartment in Manhattan, his Mercedes, and his limousine, in addition to security, satellite television, and computers for each of his six homes. Although financially successful, Jack Welch appears to have been a charismatic tyrant.

Although some charismatic tyrants are proud to be "bad boys,"[26] most do not advertise themselves as the opposite of a moral mentor. Instead, to know whether you are working for a charismatic tyrant, you will usually need to look for warning signs. The charismatic tyrant:

1. Often expresses herself in **simple and absolute terms.** The charismatic tyrant's messages about how to behave usually show little reflection. They speak using one-liners, which are rooted in the amoral tradition of pure self-interest. Also, when the charismatic tyrant speaks, she is usually sure she is right. Even when engaging in decision making about complex matters, the tough charismatic tyrant believes expressions of confusion or uncertainty are wimpy.

2. Is a **narcissist,** and his special strain of narcissism is "off the deep end."[27] For some leaders, self-love provides a driving engine toward productive, important work.[28] In contrast, the charismatic tyrant's narcissism has reached a point of dysfunction. As you read the traits of a dysfunctional or reactive narcissist in the following section, note that this label could serve as an umbrella for other items on our list of warning signs.

3. **Treats other people poorly.** The charismatic tyrant is the boss who screams at others and fails to treat them with dignity. This person is like a spouse abuser, only in the form of a boss.
4. **Demands conformity** at all times. To encourage agreement, the charismatic tyrant punishes dissenters loudly.
5. **Lacks key business skills,** yet sees herself as uniquely talented. Unfortunately, followers find out too late that the charismatic tyrant's business skills are lacking. This boss is good enough at presenting herself as talented that it takes a while for followers to see reality.

### Dysfunctional or "Reactive" Narcissists

Dr. Manfred Ket de Vries describes dysfunctional or reactive narcissists as individuals who "continually try to boost a defective sense of self-esteem and are preoccupied with emotions such as envy, spite, and vindictive triumph over others."[29] Although Ket de Vries' background is in the fields of psychoanalysis and economics, he sounds a lot like Hotchkiss, the licensed clinical social worker the text introduced in chapter 2. Ket de Vries explains that indicators of a narcissistic personality disorder are that these individuals:

- Tend to have a grandiose sense of self-importance
- Habitually take advantage of others in order to achieve their own ends
- Live under the illusion that they are special, that their problems are unique
- Feel a sense of entitlement—they believe they deserve special treatment and that the rules outlined for others do not apply to them
- Can never get enough compliments
- Lack empathy—they cannot experience how others feel
- Often demonstrate rage when they do not get their way.[30]

You should be cautious if a potential boss fits any of the characteristics of a charismatic tyrant because, unfortunately, charismatic tyrants exist. Albert Dunlap, former CEO of the Sunbeam Corporation is just one example. Before we take a careful look at Al Dunlap and the five warning signs that alert you to the possibility you are working for or with a charismatic tyrant, you need to know some basic facts about his leadership role at the Sunbeam Corporation (see Values in Action Box).

How does Albert Dunlap measure up against our five characteristics of a charismatic tyrant? While at Sunbeam and other corporations, Dunlap fulfilled all five. He (1) expressed himself in simple and absolute terms, (2) demonstrated "off-the-deep-end" narcissism, (3) treated others poorly, (4) demanded conformity, and (5) lacked essential business skills.

## VALUES IN ACTION

### Albert Dunlap (aka. "Chainsaw Al" and "Rambo in Pinstripes") and the Sunbeam Corporation

Usually, our Values in Action Boxes show the positive side of values. Here, however, we will focus on the dark side of one particular value: **efficiency.** Recall from chapter 3 that one definition of efficiency is *to minimize costs.* If a leader values short-run efficiency above all other values, sometimes many stakeholders end up suffering the consequences. This is especially true if, on top of minimizing costs, the company leader is not willing to follow the law.

Between 1996 and 1998, Albert Dunlap's actions changed the Sunbeam Corporation forever. When Sunbeam's board of directors hired Chainsaw Al in 1996, they did so because they thought the company needed Dunlap's special talent. He promised to make the company lean and mean. People in the business world praised him for bringing new life to the idea that the business of business is to maximize profits for shareholders.

Within months of joining Sunbeam, Dunlap fired thousands of employees. He was so proud of this tactic that he named it after himself; he called it "Dunlapping." [1] This act sent the stock price soaring because, at the time, Wall Street analysts were infatuated with corporate leaders who applied lean-mean turnaround strategies. [2] Dunlap's lean-mean tactics became more aggressive with time. In hindsight, stakeholders (especially shareholders) learned Dunlap's true formula for "success." As one former employee put it, "He worked to a formula: you come in, you cut everything to the bone, take the accruals, which you later turn into earnings, and then you sprinkle a little money around so it looks like you're doing something, and then you package it up and sell it before you do anything about future growth." [3]

Dunlap's formula failed at Sunbeam because he could not outrun his strategy. Before he could sell the company and get out, stock options fully realized, federal regulators caught him and his handpicked right-hand men engaging in several unethical and allegedly illegal business practices. For example, executives allegedly manipulated sales figures, misstated revenue expectations, and used fraudulent accounting methods.

When analysts found out that the company was not really poised for a turnaround, the stock price fell to virtually worthlessness, and investors lost billions. Sunbeam Corporation never recovered from its Dunlapping. The company was so lean that it could not succeed at developing and manufacturing new products. As a result, Sunbeam was bankrupt by 2001.

On January 11, 2002, Dunlap settled a civil class-action lawsuit with shareholders. He agreed to pay $15 million as his share in the settlement of the lawsuit. [4] On August 11, 2002, Sunbeam settled a civil class-action suit brought by more than 10,000 investors for $141 million. The basis of the suit was fraud. [5]

In addition to the class-action lawsuits, the Securities and Exchange Commission charged Dunlap and five others (four former Sunbeam executives and an Arthur Andersen partner) of engaging in massive fraud and manipulating accounting rules to present the company as financially healthy when it was not. The Arthur Andersen partner, Phillip E. Harlow, was the auditor in charge of Sunbeam's audit.

*(continues on the next page)*

(continued)

In September 2002, Dunlap settled with the SEC by agreeing to pay a $500,000 fine and to accept a ban that will prevent him from ever serving as an officer or director of a publicly traded company.[6] Trial against former Sunbeam executives Robert J. Gluck, Donald R. Uzzi, and Lee B. Griffith and for Harlow is scheduled for early 2003.[7]

Before this incident, the SEC had already settled civil charges with the two companies involved. The SEC had previously settled with Sunbeam by issuing a cease-and-desist order.[8] Arthur Andersen settled with the SEC for $110 million. Additionally, the company's chief financial officer, Russell A. Kersh, had previously settled with the SEC for a $200,000 fine. He had also agreed to pay $250,000 to settle a civil lawsuit.

The Justice Department began a criminal investigation of the management of the Sunbeam Corporation during Dunlap's reign.[9] At this point, it appears that Dunlap's legal problems are ongoing.

*Sources:*

[1] Albert Dunlap, *Mean Business: How I Save Bad Companies and Make Good Companies Great* (New York: Times Business, 1997) [hereinafter *Mean Business*].

[2] Pamela Williams, "Al Dunlap's Disgrace," *Australian Financial Review*, August 21, 2001, 2001 WL 21622134 [hereinafter "Dunlap's Disgrace"].

[3] Ibid.

[4] John A. Byrne: "Why Chainsaw Al Opened His Wallet," *Business Week*, January 28, 2002, 2002 WL 9359665. Byrne writes that Dunlap feared a jury would find him guilty of fraud, and that would hurt his pending civil case with the SEC.

[5] Jenni Bergal, "Class Action against Boca-Raton, Fla.-Based Sunbeam Corp. Is Settled," *Knight-Ridder Tribune Business News*, 2002, WL 25436580.

[6] Floyd Norris, "Former Sunbeam Chief Agrees to Ban and a Fine of $500,000," *New York Times*, at www.nytimes.com, September 5, 2002.

[7] Ibid.

[8] Floyd Norris, "Justice Dept. Starts Inquiry at Sunbeam," *New York Times*, at www.nytimes.com, September 9, 2002.

[9] Ibid.

Dunlap's message at Sunbeam was simple and absolute. His message was: **maximize profits for the shareholders.**[31] At times, when someone suggested he look out for stakeholders other than shareholders (e.g., employees and local communities), he would quip, "Business is not a charity." His world was black and white. Corporations exist for shareholders, and any action other than cost cutting was charity. Additionally, Dunlap was a business leader who made decisions quickly and with little information. In fact, a read of his memoir, *Mean Business*,[32] suggests that he got angry when anyone wanted him to consider all the facts relevant to a decision. He prided himself on making instant decisions—no matter how little he knew.

Second, Dunlap demonstrated "off-the-deep-end" narcissism. His self-love was evident to everyone around him. Additionally, we can see by his willingness to flout several laws that he believes rules that apply to everyone else do not apply to him. High-level employees referred to him as a "power-monger" and a "control freak."[33] Another employee points out that "Dunlap took great pleasure in sacking people and thinning the ranks."[34] One additional comment is that, "At the time, working for Al Dunlap was a living hell. I disagreed with his management style and culture. We disagreed on just about everything. He would very much liked to have sacked me, but he couldn't [because of contracts and so forth].... He showed me how a totally dysfunctional leader operates."[35]

Dunlap, consistent with unhealthy narcissism, does not see himself the way others see him. He speaks now through a lawyer, Frank C. Razzano. This lawyer presents Dunlap as a victim. He says, "For whatever reason, [Dunlap] has become a lightning rod for unfounded accusations and vilification in the press."[36]

A third and overlapping warning sign that a person may demonstrate the traits of a charismatic tyrant is that they make a habit of treating others poorly. Dunlap was famous for his brutal exchanges with managers.[37] He was proud of his special skills of yelling at people and demeaning them. One former employee commented, "He just doesn't care about the human element. And he's got . . . one of the biggest egos in the U.S., if not the world. And he puts on so much pressure, and bullies people into the sort of things they know are wrong."[38]

Dunlap also meets our fourth characteristic of a charismatic tyrant: he demanded conformity. Dissenters were always the first to go. Reading *Mean Business* makes it clear that Dunlap did not listen to anyone but himself and a few "yes-men" advisors. Not only did he fire anyone who questioned his judgment, he was proud to put that firing on display for all to see and hear.[39]

Finally, Dunlap lacked essential business skills. He said that he could make Sunbeam lean and mean, that he could turn the company around and maximize profits for the shareholders. Some people have referred to Dunlap as a "one- trick pony," but he failed at his one-trick.[40] His mass firings made the company so lean that it could not engage in enough work to ensure its long-term survival.

**CRITICAL THINKING BOX**
What traits would you like to see in a moral mentor? Can you use your work experience to add to our description?

# GLOBAL BOX

## JAPAN

Competitiveness is entrenched in many aspects of American culture. The business environment is especially laden with competition. Thus, it may be difficult for Americans to imagine a culture that is uncomfortable with the idea of competition. If our imaginations do not stretch this far, we need only look to a common business partner, Japan, for a example of such a country.

The notion of competition is relatively new in Japan. Until the late 1800s, the Japanese did not even have a word for competition. The renowned Japanese enlightenment thinker, Yukichi Fukuzawa (1835–1901), is credited with introducing and legitimizing the idea of competition in Japan. Fukuzawa created a word for *competition* by combining the Japanese symbols for struggle and rivalry. Competition was particularly appealing to the Japanese during the late 1800s. At this time, Japan was ruled by a feudal system in which one could not advance without having a social or political connection. Competition offered the opportunity of advancement based on one's efforts and abilities.

Competition also appealed to Fukuzawa because he saw in it the potential to foster a society based on high levels of trust. Fukuzawa believed that although competitive firms would be operating at arm's length, they would also need to cooperate to achieve their respective objectives. Because the relationship would not be personal, the firms would have to trust each other to perform satisfactorily.

Americans, however, generally prefer not to risk relations with other companies without the insurance of formal contracts. Thus, American businesses regularly create and enter into contracts that specify the terms of the relationships. When the Japanese and Americans first began doing business, the Japanese did not understand the need for the use of contracts. The Japanese assumed that the firms just trusted each other. Hence, contracts represented a lack of trust in the eyes of the Japanese.

Although more and more Japanese businesses are using contracts for international business purposes, many still consider it disrespectful and, on some level, unethical to use them. Even Japanese businesspeople who do use contracts believe that the terms should be flexible. They consider it unethical to not allow parties to deviate from contracts when circumstances demand changes to the original terms.

Despite these changes in business thought, the Japanese are still averse to admitting that they are in competition with other businesses or other persons. Employees who try to outdo their coworkers or work against the interests of the group to advance their own careers, such as Albert Dunlap, will not be rewarded in Japan as they would be in the United States.

*Sources:*
Yuichi Shionoya, "Trust as a Virtue" in *Competition, Trust, and Cooperation: A Comparative Study,* edited by Yuichi Shionoya and Kiichiro Yagi, 3–19 (Berlin: Springer, 2001).
Boye Lafayette De Mente, *Japanese Etiquette and Ethics in Business* 6th ed., (Lincoln wood, IL: NTC Business Books, 1994).

### A Few Words about Al Dunlap by a Respected Business Writer

In his 1999 book, *Chainsaw: The Notorious Career of Al Dunlap in the Era of Profit-at-Any Price*, author John Byrne, a senior writer for *Business Week*, offers his opinion about Al Dunlap and his role in America business. In the book's Epilogue, Byrne writes that "Al Dunlap sucked the very life and soul out of companies and people. He stole dignity, purpose, and sense out of organizations and replaced those ideals with fear, intimidation, and pirates' wages.... The leadership style he practiced was inconsistent with good business, thoughtful management, a strong economy, even a civilized society."[41]

The extent to which we categorize someone as fulfilling the warning signs of a charismatic tyrant (or even the extent to which we agree with the validity of these characteristics in the first place) may be influenced by cultural norms. Ultimately, many Americans were offended by the behavior of Al Dunlap. But, for a few important years, Wall Street analysts and many others loved him. When investors found out that Dunlap was taking on a leadership role at Sunbeam, they raced to buy the company's stock. No one (except employees) seemed to care about Dunlap's harsh management style. If Dunlap had worked in Japan, people probably would have questioned his behavior much sooner, given different cultural norms about the value of competitiveness.

## THE PRETTY GOOD MORAL MENTOR

So far we have learned how to identify both charismatic tyrants (so that you can avoid them) and ideal moral mentors (so that you can imitate them). However, when you are considering people for potential moral models, we realize that you will be interacting with others in today's messy, less-than-perfect reality. It is unlikely that your current boss is an ideal mentor who demonstrates the integrity and other-oriented, time-tested behavior of Aaron Feuerstein or Rosanne Haggerty. Moreover, you may not have a boss who welcomes dissent and makes facilitating moral excellence in others the top priority. On the other hand, you are also unlikely to work for a boss whose behavior is a series of temper tantrums and who expresses a deceptively simple message that leads employees down a path to behaviors that may culminate in an ethical disaster.

Instead of having a boss who fits a moral dichotomy, you probably work or will work for managers whose behavior falls in between the two

| The Moral Mentor Spectrum | | |
| --- | --- | --- |
| Charismatic Tyrants | The Pretty Good Moral Mentor | The Ideal Moral Mentor |

extremes. Hopefully, you will find a pretty good moral mentor. This boss is much closer to the Aaron Feuersteins of the business world than the Al Dunlaps, but constraints make it difficult for this boss to be terrific.

If we think through our criteria for the ideal moral mentor, the pretty good moral mentor should do a "pretty good" job of demonstrating integrity, acting on values that show regard for others, facilitating excellence in others, welcoming dissent, and demonstrating behavior that can stand the test of time.

You may be asking, "Why can't everyone have a boss like Aaron Feuerstein?" This question is important. It is tempting to say that we should all aim high and keep looking for the ideal moral mentor. However, aiming too high starts us down a disappointing road ending in cynicism. Hardly anyone will meet our standards for an ideal mentor, and it will be tempting to say all people in business are deplorable. We will want to quit. Additionally, individuals who pin all their hopes and dreams onto a particular kind of boss or leader show their own immaturity and narcissism. We should all practice saying, "I'm not that special. I'm not entitled to the perfect job, the perfect boss, or the ideal moral mentor." It is unrealistic to keep searching for the ideal moral mentor.

For one thing, we must consider to whom the moral mentor answers. Most people's bosses answer to their own boss, who may or may not value what your boss values. A boss has to please someone higher up or face the possibility of losing his or her job. Aaron Feuerstein is the CEO of a closely held company, not a publicly traded one. He is at the top of a hierarchy. He answers to investors, but they are likely to be patient with him.[42] Most of the people he answers to invested in Malden Mills in part because they like his worldview, including his emphasis on employees, the community, and long-term commercial success.

But Aaron Feuerstein's position is not typical of most managers. Because your boss is probably not a CEO or high-level management, she is not so far up in the organization that her values priorities can fully shape the company's culture and vision. Your boss can act on his or her value priorities, but only to the extent they mesh with the company's

**CRITICAL THINKING BOX**
Under what circumstances could the public disclosure test lead to especially unethical conduct?

We have not given examples of pretty good moral mentors. From reading this section, can you see why not? In our culture, we tend to glorify celebrities and other famous people. How might pretty good moral mentors be different from celebrities? Why are they unlikely to be famous?

## The PGMM (Pretty Good Moral Mentor) Scorecard

Are you a PGMM? Use our scorecard to find out. Feel free to modify the scorecard and use it to assess your current boss. Additionally, you may want to ask your coworkers and subordinates to rate you, in case your perceptions of yourself do not match their experience of working with you.

Write "+1" or "−2" on the lines to the left.

_____ I know myself (e.g., I can articulate my beliefs regarding right and wrong). **Plus one point.**

_____ I am willing to act on my beliefs and value priorities. **Plus one point.**

_____ I am willing to let people know I am acting on my beliefs, even if letting people know brings about a personal cost. **Plus one point.**

_____ My value priorities include values that show a high regard for others (e.g., compassion, justice, and honesty). **Plus one point.**

_____ As a person who helps shape my organization's culture, I tell the kinds of stories that could improve the culture. **Plus one point.**

_____ The way I speak and act at work helps bring out the moral best in others. **Plus one point.**

_____ I am mature enough to hear bad news and welcome dissent, as long as that dissent reflects thought and a certain amount of respect. **Plus one point.**

_____ If asked, my coworkers and/or subordinates would say it is easy for them to be their best moral selves when working with or for me. **Plus one point.**

_____ I am the same basic person everyday, and my behavior can stand the test of time. **Plus one point.**

_____ I feel comfortable expressing uncertainty and confusion at times; I do not view the world as simple and absolute. **Plus one point.**

_____ I am very other-oriented; no one could see me in those lists about off-the-deep-end or unhealthy narcissism. **Plus one point.**

_____ My business skills are solid. **Plus one point.**

_____ I realize that, in assessing myself, I might be thinking too highly of myself. **Plus one point.**

_____ I have occasional temper tantrums when I do not get my way. **Minus two points.**

_____ I see other people as overly moralistic and invested in ethics whereas I feel certain that ethics does not pay. **Minus two points.**

_____ I usually see "ethical dilemmas" as simple, and I am usually sure I am right. **Minus two points.**

_____ I am pretty sure that talking about ethics is a waste of time. **Minus two points.**

_____ In my heart of hearts, I believe I am really special in a number of ways (e.g., I am a great businessperson and a really great human being). More people should be like me. **Minus two points.**

_____ My coworkers probably see me as "golden" (e.g., favored by higher level executives) and, in labeling me this way, they are showing their envy. **Minus two points.**

_____ I believe that this textbook's emphasis on the fact that "other people count" is too idealistic. Business is not a charity. I have a strong belief in survival of the fittest, and I am really fit. **Minus two points.**

_____ **Total Score** To be a pretty good moral mentor, you must have a minimum score of plus 10 points.

**CRITICAL THINKING BOX**
The PGMM Scorecard might not work to reveal to charismatic tyrants or off-the-deep-end narcissists the error of their ways. Why not? Hint: If Albert Dunlap were to rate himself on the PBMM Scorecard, would he be likely to give himself a high or a low score? If he rated himself low, would he care?

mission. By contrast, Aaron Feuerstein can easily be himself at work because his value priorities can define the company's culture.

As you consider the possible role that others can play in your ethical development, don't forget that you can also affect your coworkers for the better. *You* can strive to be an ideal moral mentor, to the extent that you have the power to demonstrate the utmost integrity, act on other-oriented values, facilitate moral excellence, welcome dissent, and demonstrate behavior that will stand the test of time. This is a noble goal. If you cannot be an ideal moral mentor, you can at least be a pretty good one. A pretty good moral mentor creates an environment in which "employees want to act responsibly and find it easy to do so."[43] The **pretty good moral mentor** *reinforces the basic ethical standards individuals bring with them to the workplace.* To aid you with your development as a pretty good moral mentor, we have developed a scorecard that will help you evaluate yourself and highlight areas that need improvement. But first, we will briefly discuss one way that you can begin to reinforce morals and values in the workplace.

### Pretty Good Moral Mentors Tell Certain Kinds of Stories

One action to take that will help you on your path toward pretty good moral mentorship is to tell stories that improve the moral environment of your workplace. The stories we tell say a lot about who we are.

Robert G. Kennedy, author *Virtue and Corporate Culture: The Ethical Formation of Baby Wolverines*,[44] writes about how important it is for managers to recognize good behavior publicly. One way to do that is to tell stories about good behavior. He writes that "[e]very organization has stories, even legends, about outstanding accomplishments."[45] He points out that stories "help. . . communicate standards of behavior in ways that volumes of policy statements never could."[46]

> What stories or legends exist within the corporation or organization that employs you?
> What do these stories say about what your company values?
> What stories do you tell? What do these stories say about you?

## Moral Mentors Wrap-up

In the opening of chapter 5, we presented a scenario in which a person was thinking about what to look for in a boss. Now that you have read chapter 5, you know that, if you want to create a moral partnership with the firm that employs you, it is essential that you find a boss who makes it easy for you to be your best moral self. Ideally, you want a boss who demonstrates integrity, acts on values that show the highest regard for others, facilitates moral excellence in others, welcomes dissent, and demonstrates behavior that stands the test of time. Additionally, as you move up the hierarchy in the organization that employs you, you should try to become an ideal or pretty good moral mentor yourself. Pretty good moral mentors can help create the kind of moral partnership we believe is possible in today's business world.

## CRITICAL THINKING QUESTIONS

1. What assumptions are being made about the nature of human beings when we seek guidance from pretty good moral mentors, rather than utterly spectacular moral mentors? Would it be fair to say that we cast our vision too low when we are pleased to find a pretty good moral mentor?.

2. Aaron Feuerstein may be a moral mentor that we should follow. But would we want to call someone a business leader in the moral domain unless the decisions he or she made provided at least some financial success? In other words, if the decisions a businessperson makes are not at least minimally successful from a profit perspective, would we still want to call the person a moral mentor?

## ENDNOTES

[1] Stephen L. Carter, *Integrity* (New York: Basic Books, 1996), 7.

[2] Ibid.

[3] Christopher Stone, *Where the Law Ends: The Social Control of Corporate Behavior* (New York: Harper & Row, 1975).

[4] Nanette Byrne, "The Good CEO," *Business Week*, September 23, 2002, 80–88.

[5] Kohlberg's moral development theory asserts that individuals must interact with peers for them to question their strongly held views.

[6] John A. Byrne, "How to Fix Corporate Governance," *Business Week*, May 6, 2002, 2002 WL 9361003. Byron writes: "the best insurance against crossing the ethical divide is a room full of skeptics . . . CEOs must actively encourage dissent among senior managers . . . "At too many companies, the performance review system encourages a 'yes-man culture' that subverts the organization's checks and balances."

[7] Manfred Ket de Vries, "Leaders Who Go off the Deep End: Narcissism and Hubris," in *Life and Death in the American Fast Lane* 229 (1995) (He cites George Bernard Shaw, "Every despot must have one disloyal subject to keep him sane.) [hereinafter "Off the Deep End"].

[8] For a good article on talent, corporate starts, and narcissism, see Malcolm Gladwell, "The Talent Myth: Are Smart People Overrated?" *The New Yorker*, July 22, 2002, 28, 31.

[9] CBS News, *60 Minutes*, 8/11/02, manuscript available as a Westlaw document, 2002 WL 8424881 [hereinafter *60 Minutes* Interview].

[10] See, e.g., Steven Syre, "This CEO Puts Ethics Before Profits," *Boston Globe*, June 30, 2002, G1, 2002 WL 4136036 [hereinafter "Ethics Before Profits"].

[11] Mark Shields, "Two Extremes of Corporate Leadership," *Seattle Post-Intelligencer*, December 3, 2001, B3, *citing* an interview of Feuerstein from PBS's *NewsHour*.

[12] "Profile: Malden Mills CEO Coming under Fire from His Creditors for Putting His Employees Before Earnings," *CBS News: Morning News*, Thursday, August 15, 2002, 2002 WL 3294609.

[13] *60 Minutes* Interview.

[14] See Ibid.

[15] Ross Kerber, "Malden Mills Asks Creditors to Give It Time," *Boston Globe*, August 21, 2002, C1, 2002 WL 4144612.

[16] Ibid.

[17] *60 Minutes* Interview, *supra* note 9.

[18] Ibid.

[19] Marianne Jennings, "Remembering the 'Business' in Business Ethics," *Washington Post*, August 25, 2002, B07, 2002 WL 25998598.

[20] Ibid.

[21] *60 Minutes* Interview, *supra* note 9.

[22] "Ethics Before Profits," *supra* note 10.

[23] Comment by Craig Barkacs at the Palm Springs Academy of Legal Studies in Business conference in February 2002.

[24] Thomas F. O'Boyle, *At Any Cost* (New York: Knopf, 1998).

[25] Daniel McGinn and Geoffrey Gagnon, "Jack Is Paying for This," *Newsweek*, September 16, 2002, 42.

[26] And "bad girls," of course.

[27] "Off the Deep End", *supra* note 7.

[28] Ibid.

[29] Off the Deep End, *supra* note 5, at 223. The list of indicators is taken nearly verbatim from page 223.

[30] Ibid.

[31] Apparently, he was applying Milton Friedman's agency view of social responsibility, which emphasizes maximizing profits while complying with legal rules and ethical custom. Unfortunately, Dunlap understood the first part, but not the second.

[32] Albert Dunlap, Mean Business: How I Save Bad Companies and Make Good Companies Great (New York: Times Business, 1997) [hereinafter Mean Business].

[33] Pamela Williams, "Al Dunlap's Disgrace," Australian Financial Review, August 21, 2001, 2001 WL 21622134 [hereinafter "Dunlap's Disgrace"].

[34] Ibid.

[35] Ibid.

[36] Ibid.

[37] Ibid.

[38] Ibid.

[39] *Mean Business, supra* note 32.

[40] *Chainsaw, supra* note 41.

[41] John A. Byrne, *Chainsaw: The Notorious Career of Al Dunlap in the Era of Profit-at-Any Price* (New York: Harper Business, 1999), 351–354 [hereinafter *Chainsaw*].

[42] Of course, Malden Mills' creditors are not as patient, and he does answer to them.

[43] Joanne B. Ciulla, "Messages from the Environment: The Influence of Policies and Practices on Employee Responsibility," in *The Leader's Companion: Insights On Leadership Through The Ages*, edited by J. Thomas Wren, 492, 499 (New York: The Free Press, 1995).

[44] *St. John's Review of Business*, Winter 1995/1996, 14, 15.

[45] Ibid., 15.

[46] Ibid.

# Part Two • Application

## CHAPTER 6
# Getting the Facts Necessary for Good Work

**THE FOCUS:**
What are the facts shaping this particular ethical dilemma?

Four women worked in a bonding and coating department of a plant.[1] Their job responsibilities were to (1) prepare and assemble tubing components for the factory's product and (2) perform light cleanup of their immediate work areas.

One day, the supervisor asked three of the four women to conduct an extensive cleanup of the work area. They were to wash the walls that extended 12 to 15 feet from the floor, clean the light fixtures in the work area, and scrape the floor to remove hard deposits, which were by-products from the production. These three women were African American. The fourth woman who typically worked in this area was excused from this difficult cleaning task. She was white.

The women protested, arguing that heavy cleanup was not in their job description. In response, the supervisor indicated that they had to do the work "or else." Because they failed to conduct the cleanup tasks, the supervisor took the three women to the plant manager's office. Suppose that you are plant manager. What would you do?

As plant manager, you are not well prepared to make a decision if you do not know the relevant facts. Facts shape ethical dilemmas. Certain sets of facts create or extinguish ethical dilemmas. They provide the environment or context in which an ethical decision must be made. Consequently, your first task in any moral predicament is to identify the facts that are necessary for doing good work.

But what exactly is a fact? A fact is a building block or piece of information. It is a statement about the way the world is. For example, a fact may be a statistic or a testimonial.

When you encounter a potential ethical dilemma, you should identify the facts that shape that dilemma. Here are some of the facts shaping the beginning work-assignment example.

1. Four women worked in a factory.
2. A supervisor asked three of the four women to conduct heavy-duty cleanup work.
3. These three women were black.
4. One white woman was not asked to do the extensive cleanup work.

Given this set of facts, you may be somewhat troubled by the supervisor's selection of the three black women to do the extensive cleanup work. However, given the small number of workers involved, you might wish to collect more facts from the supervisor to investigate the intent for this particular work assignment.

Through talking with the supervisor, suppose you find out:

FACT A: Only three workers were needed to perform the cleanup work, so the supervisor randomly selected three of the four workers to perform the work by putting all four names in a hat and randomly pulling out three names.

By adding this fact to the list you created earlier, you might evaluate the supervisor's work assignment less harshly. Why? This new fact seems to hint that the supervisor wasn't unfairly using race to select workers to perform an unpleasant task.

Instead, suppose the supervisor tells you the following:

FACT B: The supervisor excused the white woman from the cleaning work but brought in another black woman from another department to join the three black women to engage in the cleanup work.[2]

This fact makes the supervisor's work assignment much more questionable. You are probably much more likely to infer that the supervisor was selecting the workers based on their race.

Finally, suppose the supervisor gave you the following fact:

FACT C: The supervisor told the women that "colored people should stay in their places."[3]

This fact provides strong support for the conclusion that the supervisor was making work assignments based on the workers' race. Your evaluation of the supervisor's behavior has change immensely, given this one particular fact. Consequently, your behavior in response to this fact would be very different compared with the alternative response if the supervisor randomly selected the workers. Thus, you see the importance of identifying the relevant facts of an ethical dilemma.

## LEGAL REASONING AND FACTS

As we mentioned in chapter 1, law is one tool available for our evaluation of ethical dilemmas. In a few chapters, we will discuss the interaction of law and doing good work, but for now we will focus on the important role that relevant facts play in legal reasoning.

When a judge is faced with deciding a case, he or she first identifies the relevant facts of a particular case. Second, the judge identifies any relevant laws triggered by the facts of the case. She then identifies other cases that have addressed similar fact patterns. Finally, the judge considers how those fact patterns and resulting decisions fit with the facts of the current case. One of the strengths of legal reasoning is that it recognizes how different facts lead to different conclusions.

To further clarify the interaction of law and facts, consider the following constructive discharge case, *Casenas v. Fujisawa USA*.[4] Bernadine Casenas was a sales representative for a pharmaceutical products company. After her first year of work, she received an 8 percent raise and was rated highly commendable. The next year, she was again rated highly commendable and received a 7 percent raise. However, she was unhappy with her evaluation, and she requested that her supervisor increase her merit raise. The supervisor changed her evaluation but did not increase her merit raise. Casenas then accused her former supervisor of sexual harassment, arguing that her rejection of his sexual advances led to her lower performance evaluation.

Casenas identifies several instances of harassment: (1) her supervisor said she could buy a pair of shorts and wear them when they were in Palm Springs on a business trip, (2) he frequently raised the topics of penile implants at work, (3) he requested her to make X-rated movies available on her satellite system, and (4) he asked her whether she got aroused watching X-rated movies.

Company officials conducted an investigation and reprimanded Casenas's alleged harasser by written warning. He was to have no contact Casenas, and he was to refrain from making comments about penile implants and X-rated movies to female employees. Despite this formal reprimand, Casenas was unhappy. She sent several memos to company officials, arguing that she should have received a raise and should have been considered for a district manager position. Company officials tried to meet in person with her several times to discuss her complaints, but Casenas refused in-person meetings. Finally, she met with the officials for five hours to discuss all of her complaints.

She eventually "involuntarily resigned" from her job, arguing that she had no chance of career advancement. In response to her resignation, company officials sent her a letter expressing their commitment to her career advancement. Casenas sued the company for sexual harassment and sought lost wage damages because she believed she was constructively discharged. Constructive discharge is a theory that asserts that an employer made an employee's job so difficult that the employee had no reasonable choice but to quit.

These facts shape the problem for the court: Did the company's activities in response to Casenas's sexual harassment claims constitute constructive discharge? The court says that an earlier case, *Turner v. Anheuser-Busch,*[5] provides everything that the court needs to know to decide Casenas's case. The facts in *Turner* were quite different from Casenas's case. Turner worked for a brewery for six years. For four years, he had "good" ratings on his performance reviews; however, after he complained of the brewery's violation of federal and state law, internal company policies, and the employer's collective bargaining agreement, he was subject to harassment and received "needs improvement" ratings. His supervisors then told him that his job performance had been deteriorating. In response, Turner resigned and claimed he had been constructively discharged.

The *Turner* court set forth a three-part test for constructive discharge: (1) the employee was subject to intolerable working conditions, (2) the reasonable person faced with the intolerable conditions would have no reasonable alternative but to quit, and (3) the employer must knowingly increase the intolerable working conditions.

The court then compared the two cases and stated that Casenas's employer was a "textbook example" of how to respond to an employee's claim of harassment. The court determined there were no intolerable conditions, and the company officials' response was "exemplary." Consequently, the facts regarding the officials' response were particularly important: if they had not been so willing to talk with Casenas about her claims, the court might have found evidence of intolerable working conditions.

**CRITICAL THINKING BOX**

Think about the facts in Casenas's case. We noted that the company's willingness to respond and meet with Casenas had persuaded the court that she was not subject to intolerable working conditions. Can you identify any other facts that, if varied, might change the court's conclusion? Explain why these particular facts are important.

## COLLECTING FACTS

You can clearly see from previous examples that many facts shape an issue. However, only *certain* facts are pertinent in evaluating a dilemma. If we return to the industrial work assignment problem at the beginning of the chapter, we can see that identifying the process through which the products are made in the factory does not help you to evaluate whether the women have been treated fairly. Furthermore, the fact that Bernadine Casenas talked derogatorily about her alleged harasser does not help you decide whether her working conditions were intolerable. Consequently, good decision making about ethical dilemmas requires you to sift through the available facts and give weight only to those facts that affect the problem at hand.

In addition to cutting out irrelevant facts, you will sometimes need to do a little work to add to your list of available, pertinent facts. Your initial list may not be inclusive; there may be other facts relevant to your decision of which you are not yet aware. That is, there may be some missing information.

How do you know whether you have all the facts? Generally, you will *never* have every fact that would be helpful when you make a decision. Your ability to collect facts will be constrained by time and availability of information. For example, in many cases where businesspeople have to make decisions regarding ethical dilemmas, they must make the decision within a matter of minutes or hours. Given this short amount of time, they will not be able to find *every* potentially relevant fact.

Furthermore, certain information may not be available to you. You might want to know how your supervisors would perceive your actions but do not have the opportunity to approach them. Alternatively, you might like to know more about the intent of the people involved in the dilemma. Yet, depending on your relationship with these people, you may not be able to ask them about their intent. Thus, you need to identify as many possible facts within a unique set of time and information constraints.

There are some questions you might ask yourself to help ensure that you have as many facts available to you as possible. Generally, you might want to ask yourself the "W" questions: Who? What? When? Where? and Why?

First, consider *who* is involved in the dilemma. For example, in the industrial example, the people involved include the three black workers, the white worker, and the supervisor. Who else is involved or affected by the decision? One of your responsibilities as plant manager is to evaluate the behavior of all the plant's supervisors. Thus, other supervisors may be more likely to engage in certain behavior depending on your response to this incident. Finally, industrial shareholders may be affected by this incident. If the media finds out that a supervisor was allegedly making racist comments, the shareholders might lose confidence in the company. Due to the potential number of people who could be affect by your decision, your decision is important. Thinking broadly about those groups of people affected by the decision is a good step toward making a wise choice.

Second, you need to figure out, as best you can, what has happened, when, and where it occurred. A good place to start would be to talk to the parties involved, if possible. Then, you could try to find some kind of evidence (additional facts) that supports the facts you collected from the involved parties. For example, suppose Casenas claimed that her supervisor had been making harassing phone calls to her home. Checking his phone records is one way of gathering evidence to support a set of facts.

Obviously, you may not have time to do such a thorough job of fact gathering. However, you need to know enough about a situation so that you will feel confident in moving through the FILOP process (see chapter 1 for an overview of FILOP). In the following Values in Action Box, you will see how Douglas Durand, a vice president at a pharmaceutical company, learned of several troublesome facts that forced him to take action against his employer, TAP Pharmaceuticals. Note that one of the important facts that shaped Durand's action was his concern over his own criminal liability for the company's action. We encourage you to give weight to such facts; you are part of an ethical dilemma, and you should be concerned about how you will be affected by this dilemma.

Now that you've seen the reactions of others to sets of facts, it is your turn. In the following section, you will get a chance to evaluate some facts. When you are reading, think about what other facts would be useful in making a decision.

## SILICON VALLEY LAW FIRM DILEMMAS

In August 2002, the national unemployment rate increased to 5.7 percent.[6] However, in Silicon Valley—the hub of technology development—the numbers were much grimmer: 7 percent unemployment.[7] Approximately 180,000 jobs in the San Francisco Bay Area have disappeared since 1999.[8] These jobs span the engineering, computer science, and legal fields.

During the technology boom of the 1990s, the ranks of several Silicon Valley law firms had swelled in responce to the demand for dot-com corporate work. However, once the dot-com boom subsided, law firms discovered they had too many attorneys with too little work. Furthermore, many of the dot-com clients were unable to pay their legal bills. Less work and unpaid bills meant that partnership committees, those responsible for law firm management, had to reduce their attorney

## VALUES IN ACTION
### Douglas Durand[1]

Douglas Durand worked as a pharmaceutical salesman for Merck for twenty years. In 1995, he left Merck to become a vice president of sales at TAP Pharmaceuticals. His major responsibility was to promote a prostate cancer drug called Lupron.

However, soon after he began working at TAP, Durand was troubled by some disturbing facts. First, he discovered that his sales representatives could not account for up to 50 percent of their samples of Lupron. Durand knew that failure to account for even one drug sample could lead to company fines of up to $1 million. When Durand tried to implement a program to reward those sales representatives who were able to account for all their samples, the company cut the program, claiming that Durand simply did not understand company culture. Furthermore, Durand learned that the company was encouraging doctors to sell the free samples of Lupron and charge Medicaid the full price.

Later, during a sales trip to a urologist's office, Durand noticed a big-screen television in the urologist's waiting room. Attached to the television was a plaque that stated, "This presented as a service to medicine by TAP Pharmaceuticals." Further investigation by Durand revealed that TAP had offered every urologist in the country a television. In some instances, TAP also presented urologists with computers, fax machines, and golf and ski vacations.

Third, Durand was troubled to learn that TAP had no internal legal department, which could have provided helpful legal counsel in ethical dilemmas. According to Durand, TAP viewed an internal legal department as a "sales prevention department."[2]

Finally, when Durand participated in a conference call among his sales staff, he learned that they were discussing ways to bribe urologists. The sales staff suggested that TAP give a 2 percent "administration fee" to any urologist who would prescribe Lupron instead of a competing cancer drug. When one of the sales representatives voiced a concern about getting caught, another sales representative joked, "How do you think Doug would look in stripes?"[3] Durand realized that, given his management position, he would likely be blamed for the bribery.

When Durand considered the accumulation of these troublesome facts, he knew that he had to take action. He began to document the Medicare and Medicaid fraud and turned this information over to the government. Furthermore, he took a lower-paying job at a different pharmaceutical company and filed a whistle-blower suit under the False Claims Act.

Eventually, TAP paid $875 million in criminal and civil penalties, and fourteen TAP employees were indicted. Durand received $78 million as the allotted percentage under the whistle-blowing act.

*References:*
Lisa Biank Fasig, "Exposing Medicaid Fraud at TAP Pharmaceutical Changes Whistle-Blower's Life," *Providence Journal*, September 14, 2002.
Bruce Japsen, "'Cowboy' Culture Blamed in TAP's Fall," *Chicago Tribune*, April 26, 2002, 1.
[1] Charles Haddad, "A Whistle-Blower Rocks an Industry", *Business Week*, June 24, 2002, 126.
[2] Ibid.
[3] Ibid..

workforce. At what point do you think the partnership committee should tell the lower-level attorneys and staff about the staff problems that will eventually lead to the layoffs?

There are several ways to reduce a workforce. First, the firm may offer a severance package and ask for workers to voluntarily leave. Or the firm may lay off workers and provide them with several weeks' pay.[9] A third option is that the firm may engage in performance-related firings.[10]

Attorneys who have been downsized by performance-based reviews argue that Silicon Valley firms are not being honest about their financial health. These attorneys argue that their professional reputations are harmed by the stigma associated with performance-based terminations when, in fact, the real reason for their termination was the sluggish economy combined with the firm's financial health.

Suppose you are in a management position at a Silicon Valley law firm, and the partnership committee has been discussing the need to decrease the firm workforce. The committee is debating whether to publicly lay off workers or terminate them through performance reviews. If you had to vote on one action, would you support layoffs or performance terminations?

Additional information may change your vote. You know that two other large firms in the area that conducted layoffs received an enormous amount of negative publicity. Second, one of these firms lost a notable client, presumably because the infamous layoffs undermined the client's confidence in the firm's financial health. Given these facts, how would you vote? Could additional information change your mind?

You should also know that there was an article in the area's legal paper recently about attorneys who have been terminated through performance reviews. These attorneys have struggled to find new jobs, compared with those attorneys who have been terminated through layoffs. Furthermore, law students looking for jobs report that they are less likely to work for firms that have conducted performance terminations rather than layoffs. Do these facts change your initial vote? What additional information would you like to know to help you come to a conclusion about your vote?

## CRITICAL THINKING QUESTIONS

1. This book has tried to emphasize that the law is only a starting point for thinking about business ethics. Yet the examples in this chapter are legal examples. Return to any of the opening scenarios at the start of chapters 2 through 5 and make a determination of what facts you would need to know before you made a decision in that particular instance. Remember not to request facts that would take longer to generate than you would have to make the business decision.

2. To what extent is this chapter based on an unrealistic assumption about the meaning of a fact? Are the things that we know as facts universally accepted or primarily accepted from a particular perspective? If the latter concept of a fact is correct, what must an ethical businessperson think about as she or he gathers the facts?

## ENDNOTES

[1] These facts are from *Slack v. Havens*, 522 F.2d 1091 (9th Cir. 1975).

[2] Ibid.

[3] Ibid.

[4] 58 Cal. App. 4th 101 (1997).

[5] 7 Cal. 4th 1238 (1994).

[6] Department of Labor Current Population Survey, http://www.bls.gov/cps/home.htm.

[7] Byron Acohido, "2003 May Be a Better Year," *USA Today*, August 19, 2002, 3B.

[8] Sam Zuckerman, *"Job Market Collapse has People Packing," San Francisco Chronicle*, September 22, 2002, A2.

[9] Renee Deger, "Wilson Proceeds as Planned with Layoffs of 100 Staffers," *The Recorder*, August 21, 2002. "Laid off staff members were given four weeks salary plus one week for every year of employment with the firm. [The company] also will offer health benefits through October plus emergency child care and outplacement assistance."

[12] Ibid., "[T]he firm has quietly shed at least 168 associates through performance-related firings."

# CHAPTER 7

# Determining the Issue That Requires Good Work

After reading chapter 6, you are ready and able to identify facts relevant to an ethical dilemma. You are probably familiar with the fact-finding process as a result of research papers from high school and college classes. Recall that in your papers, you did not merely copy a list of facts and then turn in the paper. Instead, you, the researcher and writer, had to organize the facts into a meaningful structure. The organization of your paper was centered on your thesis statement.

A similar approach will help you as you encounter ethical dilemmas. As you read the following example, first try to create an organized list of the facts. Then, sort the available facts so that they are meaningful to you. Now, pause and review your work. Why did you organize the facts the way that you did? What specific question were you to answer? This question is the issue that you have identified for the ethical dilemma.

You are responsible for environmental compliance for your company's factories. Part of your company's manufacturing process involves the discharge of a certain level of air and water pollutants along with a certain amount of hazardous waste. You are particularly proud of your company's environmental compliance record over the past two years; you have had no violations.

Unfortunately, your company is starting to have economic difficulties, and the CEO and CFO have both indicated that layoffs are a real possibility. Moreover, they have been emphasizing the need for cost-cutting measures.

As you sit in your office looking over your monthly compliance reports, you are surprised at how low your hazardous waste production and emissions have been for the past month. Your company recently implemented a new but expensive environmental monitoring program. Given your company's concern about economic problems, you wonder whether you might be able to reduce some costs by slightly increasing your emissions for a short time. By increasing the factories' air and water pollutant emissions for just a few months, you might be able to "create" $100,000 for your company.

How do you respond to this problem? Are the increased emissions worth $100,000? As the previous chapter suggested, it seems you need to know more facts. For example, suppose the emissions are particularly hazardous to human health in even minute quantities. Here, your dilemma would seem to be whether $100,000 was worth hazards to human health.

However, suppose you knew that an increase in emissions would have no noticeable effect on human health, but you would surpass the legal emission limits imposed by the law. Alternatively, suppose you could increase the emissions and still be under the legal limits imposed on your company. You feel a little uncomfortable with allowing emissions to increase, given that you have spent a lot of time emphasizing the importance of environmental compliance to the CEO and the CFO. But you also realize the importance of saving money. Now what do you do?

These three alternative facts about the ethical problems involved in your situation address different ethical problems. In one case, your actions could create a human health threat. In the second, your actions would likely violate the law. In the third, your behavior may be legally permissible, but you have a feeling that something associated with your behavior could be wrong. How can you frame or define the ethical dilemma so that you can begin to address the issue?

In each case, there is a different type of problem. In the previous chapter, you learned how facts shape ethical dilemmas. This chapter suggests how to arrange the facts, transforming them into a statement of your problem. This statement is called the **ethical issue.**

## ISSUE: CONFLICT AS A QUESTION

An issue is a statement of your dilemma in question form. Examples of issues include

- Should I take or borrow company property (e.g., floppy disks) for my own personal use?
- Should I take sole credit for an idea produced by collaborative effort?
- Should I look the other way when my employer discriminates against minorities?

Glance back to chapter 2. The "Everyday Ethical Dilemma" chart provides more examples of ethical issues.

Stating the conflict as a brief question is beneficial for several reasons. First, you are forced to identify the problem in a few brief words. Stating the problem succinctly keeps you focused. Second, stating the problem in the form of a question emphasizes that you need to take action: you need to find an answer to your problem. Finally, questions frequently have more than one answer; thus, when you state your dilemma as a question, you are encouraging a search for alternative answers.

## ALTERNATIVE WAYS TO STATE THE ISSUE

Thus, once you gather the facts, you should state the problem in the form of a question. However, there will almost certainly be several ways to state this question. The way in which you frame the question may help you to think more carefully about the problem.

For example, suppose you are an accountant, and you are looking at various ways of moving liabilities off your company's balance sheet. Suppose, like Enron, your company is considering borrowing money through a special-purpose entity it would create simply so it can keep the loan transaction off its own balance sheet. One way to state the issue in this example is

ISSUE 1: *Should my company create a special-purpose entity?*

This question is brief and focused, and it suggests that you need an answer to a problem. However, the preceding phrasing is not particularly helpful if we want to carefully reflect about the problem. To think more carefully about the ethical dilemma, we would need to ask additional questions about what it means to create a special-purpose entity. Your goal in stating the issue as a question is to help you to think about the problem in a clear and concise manner, but this particular phrasing simply creates more questions. Instead, suppose you state the issue in the following way.

ISSUE 2: *Should my company hide its liabilities from its balance sheet to make it appear more profitable?*

Again, the question is focused and prompts you to find an answer. And this time, the question better expresses the dilemma associated with hiding liabilities.

Once you have identified the crux of the dilemma, you can reword your issue according to the level of abstraction you want to answer. For example, consider the following ways to restate Issue 2. Notice that as you go down the list, the questions become less specific to your company and balance sheets.

ISSUE 3: *Should my company mislead its investors through its accounting techniques?*

ISSUE 4: *Should companies use creative accounting techniques to describe their financial health?*

ISSUE 5: *Is misuse of accounting techniques a form of lying?*

ISSUE 6: *Should generating profits be a company's highest concern?*

For your purposes, you will probably want to try to generate more specific questions, like Issue 2. These specific questions will help you focus on the actions you personally need to consider. But realizing that the specific issue is part of a family of issues can provide you with the larger perspective that others may be considering when thinking about this same situation.

## FRAMING THE ISSUE

You now know the importance of stating the issue as a question, and you realize that there are alternative ways to state an issue. But how do you translate your particular set of facts into a question when there are so many ways to phrase the question? Phrasing the question is important because it shapes the way you will respond to the dilemma, such as deciding which values are involved and which ethical guideline is most applicable.

One way to make this task easier is to think about general categories of issues that frequently arise in the business context. To help you get started, this section lays out some of these categories.

First, you might encounter a *human health question*. You, or others, could be physically harmed by the dilemma. Examples of these human health issues include Ford's exploding Pinto or Bridgestone/Firestone's tire tread separation problems, which led to more than 203 deaths.[1]

Within the category of human health, certainty, the degree of harm, and the length of time before the harm may all vary. For example, perhaps you are aware that if an employee works in your company's manufacturing plant *over a period of years*, her health is likely to deteriorate as a result of hazardous chemicals in your plant. Moreover, like the H. B. Fuller glue-sniffing case presented in chapter 1 and discussed further in chapter 11, a particular product may not necessarily be deadly but could still cause some very serious health problems if used improperly by customers. Alternatively, as a manager, you might have studies suggesting that your product has caused cancer in laboratory animals, but you have no evidence to suggest that it is harmful to humans.

At the stage of issue identification, when you have evidence of harm to human health, you do not need to be *certain* about the probability, degree, or length of time associated with harm before you act to prevent the harm. Given the serious societal repercussions associated with harm to human health, you might wish to assume the worst when you formulate your issue. In any case, you should note that harm to human health issues is a special category of business ethics dilemmas that deserves your most careful attention.

Alternatively, an ethical issue could be about a *need for public disclosure*. Your dilemma may involve an issue that affects the public's decisions about the company or the company's products. Suppose you discover that your company is engaging in deceptive advertising regarding your line of organic products. You know that some of your customers would not be purchasing your products if they did not see "NATURAL" on the label. However, they don't realize that these natural components are present in every company's line of these products. What should you do?

Other examples of business dilemmas that may stimulate the need for public disclosure include

- Approving false financial statements
- Bribery
- Sharing insider information
- Stealing information from another company

Perhaps your ethical dilemma does not harm human health, nor does the potential transgression affect the general public in some other pressing way. However, you still feel *discomfort* when you consider the situation. Frequently, this discomfort may be associated when a proposed course of action conflicts with a need for honesty. For example, are you comfortable with bluffing in a negotiation? Should you embellish the truth when you are interviewing for a job to ensure that you get the offer? Other types of issues that may fall under the discomfort category include

- Disregarding company procedures
- Responding dishonestly on psychological tests
- Telling lies to cover for difficult or failed projects
- Discrimination and harassment
- Using company expense accounts inappropriately
- Conflicts of interest
- Patient/client confidentiality
- Billing inaccuracy

By dividing these issues into categories, we do not necessarily mean that when an issue falls into a discomfort category, your response to this issue is not as important as it would be if it were an issue in the harm-to-human-health category. Clearly, violations of some of the discomfort issues can have serious ethical and legal consequences. Rather, you should think of these categories as organizational tools to help you think about how to frame an issue.

## YOU SHAPE THE ISSUE

In addition to recognizing that issues typically fall into one of the three categories, you should realize that your own value preferences affect how you phrase an issue. For example, if you prefer justice over efficiency when these two values conflict, you are going to be more likely to phrase and respond to certain issues. When you read the Meet the Leader Box, note how Mary Kay Ash's previous instance with a specific issue about fairness and background experience in sales influenced ethical issues in her own business plans.

You shape the issues not only because you phrase the question, but also because you are the one who identifies the moral conflict in the first place. If you are extrasensitive to honesty conflicts, you might be more likely than others to frame a problem as an ethical dilemma.

## MARKETING CREDIT CARDS: PRACTICE IDENTIFYING THE ISSUE

Now, try to apply what you have learned, especially in chapters 6 and 7, to identify an issue in the following example. You work in the marketing department for a large national banking corporation developing plans for reaching targeted groups in creative ways. You most recently worked on an advertising campaign to encourage thirty-something singles to use your credit card. You were particularly proud of your idea to link your marketing campaign to the TV show *Sex in the City*. When a particular New York City restaurant would be featured on the show, your credit card company would sponsor mixer parties at this restaurant or club. Outside New York City, your company would sponsor similar parties with *Sex in the City* themes. At these parties, attendees would pay a cover charge with their credit cards.

Your manager was thrilled with the results from this campaign; consequently, you received a $10,000 bonus. When you get into your office after taking a much-needed vacation, you find an e-mail from your senior manager regarding your next project. This campaign needs to be aimed at college and high school students. At the end of the message, your manager tells you that if you can repeat your success in your new assignment, you will likely be promoted, which would mean a salary increase of more than $20,000.

Attached to the e-mail is a background report summarizing what work your company has done thus far to attract college students. Along

---

### MEET THE LEADER: MARY KAY ASH

Mary Kay Ash could not afford to go to college, so she began working two jobs: secretary and home salesperson for Stanley Home Products. When she first started selling Stanley Home Products in the mid-1940s, she was not very successful; she averaged approximately $2 per hour in net income from her home sales shows. Because Ash believed that she could make money selling these products, she concluded that her sales techniques were problematic. She attended a sales conference, paid attention, and was the "Queen of Sales" the very next year.

Mary Kay began recruiting other women to become independent contractors for Stanley Home Products. Recruiting someone to become a Stanley salesperson meant that the recruiter would get a percentage of the recruitee's sales. After she recruited 150 women in the Houston area, Stanley Home Products insisted that she move to Dallas to develop that area as well. The company refused, however, to allow her to continue to receive commissions on her Houston recruits. Mary Kay believed this refusal was extremely unfair, and she made sure that when she later started her own company, Mary Kay Cosmetics, it did not repeat this particular practice.

Mary Kay Cosmetics is a direct sales company that specializes in skin cream and makeup. Salespeople, called beauty consultants, are independent contractors who buy Mary Kay products for 50 percent of the price. They create an inventory of beauty supplies and sell them at Mary Kay parties. At the parties, the beauty consultants focus on teaching attendees about the products. Mary Kay believed that this process helped give women who may have never worked before a sense of self-confidence.

Mary Kay set the corporate culture for her company. Explicit in the Mary Kay corporate code was the idea that the Golden Rule was a practical guide for business affairs. Moreover, she believed that everyone should seek to improve themselves while enjoying their work.

*Source:*
Laureate: Mary Kay Ash: American National Business Hall of Fame http://www.anbhf.org/laureates/mkash.html.

---

with other credit card companies, your company has been targeting this highly profitable market for some time. Eighty-three percent of undergraduate students have at least one credit card,[2] whereas half have four or more credit cards.[3] Sixty percent of college freshmen report having credit cards,[4] and many of these students first got these cards in high school. Approximately two-thirds of undergraduate students have used one credit card to pay for another.[5]

In the past, your company has contracted with college campuses for the exclusive right to blanket the campus with offers for credit cards. Several company representatives would set up stands on campuses and give away promotional materials to those students who would apply for credit cards. Some of these promotional materials include cups,

T-shirts, sweatshirts, sunglasses, candy, key chains, and water bottles. Your company has found that college students are easily attracted to free items, and future campaigns will likely be successful if they are associated with free products.

The main reason that your company targets college students is because of students' tendency to spend. In 2001, the average credit card debt of students was $2327, and approximately 10 percent of these students have more than $7000 of credit card debt.[6] Not only do college students spend a lot, but they are often late with monthly payments. In fact, students are three times more likely to be at least 90 days late in making payments to credit cards. As a result, they are much more likely to pay late fees and over-the-limit fees.[7] Moreover, the interest rate on these accounts is usually at least 18.99%. Add these habits together, and credit card companies like yours make a significant amount of money from the fees associated with college students' credit accounts.

Amid all this seeming good news for your company, one part of the report about college student spending troubles you. The report indicates that young people under the age of 25 are the fastest growing age group seeking bankruptcy protection.[8] This factor is disturbing because your company wants the students to spend, but they don't want the spending to increase to the extent that the students will file for bankruptcy. Typically, your company has found that a student's family (usually the parents) will pay the amount owed if the student gets into serious problems.

Even though most students can and do turn to their families to bail them out of trouble, not all students have this option. In particular, your company is slightly concerned about some recent publicity about a student who hung herself in her dorm room amidst her credit card bills.[9] As a result, several congressional leaders have proposed that credit card companies be banned from college campuses. These leaders express concern that students may not be able to finish their studies due to excessive debt. Moreover, these leaders argue that by racking up large amounts of debt, students suffer long-term consequences to their careers, marriages, and opportunities for home ownership, savings accounts, and investment opportunities. Your company's official response is that these students are consumers and are capable of making their own choices.

You finish reading the report and feel a little uneasy. What's wrong? You were comfortable with your previous campaign. How is this situation different? When tackling these questions, you should start by identifying the facts in this scenario. Don't forget to note the facts that affect your own position in the company. After you have identified the facts, try to identify the issue, using what you learned in this chapter. You might want to start forming the issue by thinking about the categories of issues. And don't forget, there is more than one way to state the issue.

*Remember:* You can do good work only after you have taken care to frame the issue in a fashion that both highlights the ethical questions at issue and also directs your attention to the actions you can take in response.

## CRITICAL THINKING QUESTIONS

1. How would you respond to someone who presented you with an ethical dilemma in the form of a statement of his or her position? In other words, how would you explain to them the importance of realizing that an ethical dilemma is just that: a group of options that needs to be approached with curiosity?

2. Chapters 1–5 provided background for making ethical decisions. Which of those chapters seems particularly important in getting the issue straight?

## ENDNOTES

[1] Timothy Aeppel, "Firestone Milestone Brings Dilemma," *Wall Street Journal*, August 18, 2000, B8.

[2] Andi Baca, "Legislation Needed to Prevent Harmful Credit Card Use on Campuses," *University Wire*, September 23, 2002.

[3] John J. LaFalce, "Credit Cards: A Big Problem for Young People," *Buffalo News*, September 22, 2002, at H5.

[4] Ibid.

[5] Ibid.

[6] Jon Chavez, "College Students Used Credit Cards Less This Year," *The Blade*, September 15, 2002.

[7] Ibid.

[8] John LaFalce, "Credit Cards a Big Problem for Young People," *Buffalo News*, September 22, 2002, H5.

[9] Jan Galletta, "Drowning in Debt," *Chattanooga Times*, October 13, 2002, E2.

# CHAPTER 8

# Locating the Relevant Law: The Framework for Doing Good Work

**THE FOCUS:**
What laws are relevant to this ethical dilemma?

Once you have established the facts and issue of a business dilemma, you may feel confused about where to go next. Does applying what you have read thus far to a particular business dilemma seem a bit daunting? If so, don't worry. We know that you've learned about business culture, values and value preferences, classical ethical guidelines, and moral mentors, and all this new information can be difficult to sort through. We suggest that, after you understand the dilemma as best you can, you should check current laws. As you read the chapter, ponder the following questions: How would familiarity with current laws help me in an ethical dilemma? What should I do if I cannot find a law pertaining to my dilemma?

You are the sales manager of a relatively new company. You oversee twenty salespeople who take telephone orders from customers. When your customers call you to place their orders, your sales representatives ask several customer preference questions. These questions change monthly. Although some customers choose to not answer these questions, approximately 60 percent do respond. Consequently, your company has generated a fairly extensive customer profile.

As sales manager, you are responsible for developing new ideas that would cut costs and generate revenue. In your last performance reviews, the CEO mentioned that you needed to be more proactive in putting forth such ideas, and she has hinted that she is thinking about replacing you.

One day, when you overhear one of your sales representatives asking the customer preference questions, it occurs to you this preference information might be useful to other companies. Moreover, your company might be able to profit from the sale of this information.

You type in "selling customer information" in Yahoo's search engine and find an article that describes how some companies claim their collections of customer data as assets.[1] One specific company, Toysmart, has sold or has tried to sell customer information such as phone numbers, home addresses, and statistics regarding the customers' shopping habits.[2] However, this article explains that many consumer groups have complained about Toysmart's attempt to sell customer information because the information was collected under the assumption that it would not be shared.

Another article argues that, because companies are simply going to use customer information for their own profit, consumers should be less willing to trust companies that sell such information. One of your company's stated values is to build customer trust, and if you put yourself in your customer's situation, you would probably prefer that a company not share your own personal information. Therefore, you are concerned about advocating ideas that could potentially harm the company–customer relationship.

Furthermore, you feel there might be something a little shady in selling your customers' personal information to the highest bidder. Not only are you possibly hurting your trust relationship with the costumer, but you also suspect that, given the customers' assumption when they call, selling the information is rather dishonest. However, when you think about the precarious nature of your job, you decide to draft a proposal to the CEO to suggest selling customer information. But you wonder, are there any ethical problems associated with selling your customers' information?

After a few more Internet searches, you are surprised to discover an article describing several bills that have recently been proposed in Congress to regulate companies' use of their customers' personal information. It never occurred to you that it might be *illegal* to sell the customer information. You wonder whether there are any laws that are currently in effect that regulate the use of customer information.

## LAW: THE STARTING POINT IN EVALUATING AN ETHICAL DILEMMA

Having read chapters 6 and 7, you realize the importance of identifying the facts and stating the issue as a question. The first step in answering the issue is to identify the relevant law. The law generally sets a baseline for your behavior that you should not venture below. In other words, unless you, and possibly the company, wish to be punished and expose the company to the resulting negative publicity, you need to behave in accordance with the law.

**CRITICAL THINKING BOX**
Throughout much of this chapter, we assume that we should obey the law. Is this assumption valid? Can you think of an instance in which a businessperson might be ethically justified in disobeying the law?

But how should you behave if you are not sure exactly what the law is regarding your dilemma? You have several options. First, you can simply claim ignorance of the law and choose one course of action. This choice is a problem because your ignorance of the law will not be a successful defense in court to a violation of the law.

If your company has in-house counsel, your second option is to talk to the company's attorney about the applicable law. However, there may be some reasons why you would not wish to speak to your company's attorneys.

- The attorneys themselves might be involved in the wrongdoing.
- They might wish to "solve" the problem by firing you.
- You may wish to keep the dilemma to yourself until you collect more information.
- You wish to be informed about the law before you talk to them.
- You don't think they will be able to spare the time to consider your problem.
- You think your problem is too inconsequential to put before the in-house counsel.

However, given the size of your company, you may not have in-house legal counsel. Although you could consult an attorney on your own, legal advice is extremely expensive. If you are a new company, you will need some kind of legal advice about federal requirements regarding employees. For example, federal laws regulate working conditions, workplace safety, payment of wages, and discriminatory behavior. Plus, you need to do all of this information gathering quickly.

In the next section, we will discuss a third option available to you: finding the law on your own. But first we want to emphasize what appears obvious but is sometimes forgotten in the middle of making a difficult business decision: Ethical dilemmas almost always have legal implications. For example, as CEO of your company, should you misstate numbers in an accounting report to make your profits look higher? The Sarbanes-Oxley Act of 2002 requires the CEO and CFO to prepare a statement certifying that the company's financial reports fairly present the conditions of the company. Consequently, under the new act, you could be liable for misrepresenting the company's financial conditions. As a business manager, you should have some basic knowledge about how to navigate through basic business law. The following sections will help you find the relevant law on your own.

If you cannot ask your organization's attorneys about the issues you suspect are legal issues, remember you may get started in your quest to find the law by: (1) asking a friend or relative with a law degree to answer your legal questions, (2) contacting a regulatory agency that may be able to answer your legal questions, and/or (3) educating yourself using a legal environment of business textbook. If you choose the third option, make sure you locate a book that aims to teach business students, not law students, about law. Legal environment of business textbooks get to the essence of legal rules.

In many ways, finding an attorney to identify and respond to legal issues is the most efficient way to complete the "L" step of the FILOP process. Law students spend approximately one year learning the basics with regard to finding the law. Unfortunately, though, you are in a hurry and probably do not want to go to law school to figure out how to find the law. With some guidance, though, you may be able to find some relevant law yourself.

Now you know that finding law is a difficult task! However, you are not necessarily being asked to find the actual law. Instead, your goal in fulfilling the "L" step in FILOP is to educate yourself about the general legal issues that may inform your decision. We believe you can do this by engaging in careful searches on the Internet. In the next section, you will see how to use law Web sites to find articles or summaries to shape your thinking about the law. Read the appendix to this chapter if you want to search the way a lawyer or law student would search. This appendix teaches you about how different sources of law are created and how to conduct a more sophisticated search for law.

Notice that the focus on the law in this chapter is an American perspective that is not necessarily shared by businesspeople in other parts of the globe. As the following global box reveals, the law as a guide to ethical business actions may be a less valuable tool in other jurisdictions.

## FINDING THE LAW WITH A CAREFUL INTERNET SEARCH

Remember, your goal is to learn a *little* about the law to help guide your decisions. Thus, the Internet is a great resource for gaining a little knowledge about the laws that affect your behavior. Before you go to the Internet, though, it might be a good idea to review a legal environment of business textbook to get a sense of your subject matter, as a lawyer might see it. For example, your boss might be hassling you, asking for sex in exchange for a promotion. A quick review of a legal environment of business textbook will refine your description of what is happening, and you will know to search for law related to "quid pro quo sexual harassment."

**GLOBAL BOX**

**GREAT BRITAIN**

Many countries respond to ethical problems in business by passing laws. Great Britain is an exception to this tendency. Great Britain takes more of an antilegalistic approach to business ethics. This approach may be due, in part, to widespread distrust of the effectiveness of legal remedies. A paper produced by the Institute for Business Ethics in London stated, "Rigid control can sometimes be worse than the abuse which it tries to eliminate."

Although Britons may be reluctant to remedy scrupulous business behavior through laws, they recognize that some remedy is often necessary. Rather than saddling the government with the burden, the responsibility shifts onto the shoulders of businesses themselves—at least in theory. The practicality of this ideal is debatable, however. The Institute of Business Ethics reports that barely 50 percent of British companies have adopted internal codes of ethical conduct for their employees. This is a small percentage when compared with the 84 percent of U.S. companies that have adopted such codes.

*Source:*
Fred Seidel, "Business Ethics in Three European Countries: A Comparative Approach" in *Working Across Cultures: Ethical Perspectives for Intercultural Management*, ed. Heiko Lange, et al., 235–261 (Dordrecht, Netherlands: Kluwer Academic Publishers), 1998.

Once you have some basic understanding of words attorneys might use to describe the issue you are facing, you should start your search at Findlaw, *http://findlaw.com*. When you get to this Web site, you will see you have two ways to go about finding law. First, you can read categories of information Findlaw presents, similar to the way a textbook presents information. Findlaw contains a large amount of information for businesses. For example, under "Business Resources" on the home page, you can access information about contracts, debts and bankruptcy, employee and employer rights, intellectual property, small business legal concerns, and business deductions. Second, you can type in a string of words to search for information about your precise legal question. At the top of the Findlaw page, you will see two boxes. The one on the left allows you to type in a string or words, or **search.** For example, you may type in "boss wants sex." The box on the right allows you to decide where to look. Click on "Article Library" to articles that explain law.

Let's practice using Findlaw. Suppose you are considering breaking a supply contract because you think it would be cheaper for your company to break the contract than comply with the agreement. You go to Findlaw and locate an article under "Small Business Concerns" called "Top Ten Reasons to Avoid Breaching a Contract."[3] Here, you learn that you would likely be sued for breach of contract, and you would have additional costs that you might not have considered: damage to your reputation, legal fees, damages awarded in the lawsuit, and time away from your business. You could also conduct a search, typing in the words "breach of contract," and searching in the article library.

Suppose you are interviewing candidates for an open position at your company. The employee who formerly worked in this particular position was frequently absent from work because of a disability. Obviously, you want to find the best candidate to fill this position: someone who is well qualified, articulate, and personable. You also are interested in hiring a healthy employee. Are there restrictions on the types of questions you can ask in your interview?

You go to Findlaw and do a keyword search for "interview questions." You pull up two articles: "Illegal Job Interview Questions" and "How to Comply with the Americans with Disabilities Act When Hiring New Employees." In these articles, you learn that you are not permitted to ask specific questions about a candidate's disabilities. Instead, you should ask questions about the candidate's abilities. You also learn that asking questions about disabilities is a violation of the Americans with Disabilities Act.

In addition to Findlaw, there are several other good legal Web sites that provide summaries or links to short articles about particular legal topics.

| At this Web site: | You will find: |
| --- | --- |
| Findlaw<br>*http://findlaw.com/* | **Articles that discuss:**<br>a) **Business resources** (debt, contracts, starting a business)<br>b) **Public and consumer resources**<br>c) **Cases, Constitution, legal subjects** |
| Legal Information Institute<br>*http://www.law.cornell.edu/* | a) **Law by topics** (e.g., First Amendment Rights, Employment law, Contracts)<br>b) **Constitution**<br>c) **Cases** |
| Catalaw<br>*http://www.catalaw.com/* | A **catalog** of Web sites of worldwide law. Search by subject, such as environmental law, tax law, alternative dispute resolution, and contract and remedy law. You may narrow your search by country. |
| Megalaw<br>*http://www.megalaw.com/*<br>*top/top.php* | Search by topic: such as labor and employment, unfair competition, media law, consumer law, damages, libel law, antitrust law, bankruptcy law. |
| Yahoo<br>*http://www.yahoo.com* | Try a general search for your topic in the search engine. You might come across a useful news article about the legal issue. |

You should now know how to find some general information about the law. But how do you know which laws you should be concerned about? This section provides a brief overview of some illustrative laws that should affect your thinking about doing good work.

### Example One: Applying the Law of Sexual Harassment

Sexual harassment has been defined as "unwelcome sexual advances, requests for sexual favors, and other verbal or physical conduct of a sexual nature ... [that] explicitly or implicitly affects an individual's employment, unreasonably interferes with an individual's work performance, or creates an intimidating, hostile or offensive work environment."[4] As a business manager, you should be concerned about sexual harassment in the workplace by both supervisors and coworkers.

Title VII of the Civil Rights Act of 1964 prohibits discrimination with respect to terms and conditions of employment in the workplace on the basis of race, color, sex, religion, or national origin. Sexual harassment is prohibited under Title VII because it is a form of discrimination that alters the "terms and conditions of employment" on the basis of sex. Thus, under statutory law, if an employer allows sexual harassment to alter the terms and conditions of employment, the employer may be liable to the harassed employee.

The statute is silent about how the harassed employee must demonstrate her case; thus, the courts have laid out what elements a plaintiff must demonstrate. The Supreme Court recently decided two cases, which lawyers refer to as *Faragher*[5] and *Ellerth*.[6] These cases consider exactly when an employer will be liable for harassment. First, the courts recognize two general types of harassment: quid pro quo harassment and hostile work environment harassment. If a supervisor tells an employee that she must offer sexual favors or suffer a job detriment, the supervisor has engaged in quid pro quo harassment. If the employee actually suffers a job detriment, both the supervisor and the employer are liable to the employee. The employer is liable to the harassed employee because, under agency theory, the employer is liable for the acts of its agents, and a supervisor is an agent of an employer.

The second type of harassment courts recognize is called **hostile work environment harassment.** This form occurs when the harassing conduct is based on sex and is so severe and pervasive that it alters an employee's working conditions Hostile work environment harassment typically occurs over an extended period of time. For example, if a coworker repeatedly makes sexual innuendoes to or touches another employee, this coworker may be engaging in hostile work environment harassment.

The Supreme Court makes a distinction between a coworker or a supervisor creating the hostile work environment. If a coworker is the harasser, the employer is liable if it knew or should have known about the harassment. In other words, if the harassed employee complains about the harassment, the employer has notice of the harassment and should then take steps to remedy the harassment. If the employer knows and does not take action, it will be liable to the employee.

However, if a supervisor creates the hostile work environment, the employer will automatically be liable for the supervisor's harassment *unless* the employer can show two defenses: (1) the employer exercised reasonable care to prevent or correct the harassing behavior, *and* (2) the employee failed to take advantage of preventative or corrective opportunities. Given this standard of liability, it is particularly important for an employer, and you as a business manager, to take an employee's report of sexual harassment very seriously.

Courts vary on what is considered to be "severe and pervasive" conduct. Thus, if you are concerned about what the courts consider severe and pervasive and how this would affect your company, you could search for hostile work environment cases in the circuit courts that govern your company.

### Example Two: Applying the Law That Governs Financial Transparency and Corporate Accountability

Starting with the fall of Enron in December 2001, state and federal legislators passed legislation that imposes duties on directors, officers, employees, auditors, and accountants of corporations with regard to financial transparency. For instance, the corporate laws of many states require directors and officers to act in the primary interest of the shareholders. All of the decisions made by these officials should serve the interests of shareholders. Corporate officials were also subject to securities regulations, tax laws, and other government mandates. However, these obligations have become more numerous with the passage of the Sarbanes-Oxley Act of 2002, a new federal statute passed as a result of a wave of corporate accounting scandals that became apparent in 2001 and 2002.

The act significantly enhances the obligations of corporate directors and officers. It requires corporate officers to sign quarterly and annual filings submitted to the Securities and Exchange Commission (SEC). The officers' signatures indicate that they have reviewed the filings and found them to be true and complete representations of the company's financial status.

In addition to requiring directors and officers to certify company filings, the act forbids them from accepting personal loans from the company unless the loans are also available to outsiders. The act also prohibits officers and directors from buying or selling shares of equity security during a "blackout period." A blackout period occurs when individual shareholders are barred from conducting any trading. Now, if a company wants to impose such a period, it must give 30 days notice before declaring the blackout.

Although many provisions of the Sarbanes-Oxley Act (SarbOx) affect only boards of directors and corporate executives, there have been important changes to the U.S. Criminal Code that affect all levels of employees. Congress made it a crime for any person to knowingly make, alter, destroy, or conceal a false entry to any business record if the entry is made with the intent to impede, obstruct, or influence an investigation or the contemplation of such a matter. This new provision means that even if an investigation has not been launched, businesspersons could still commit a crime if they knowingly destroy a document that they think could be used in an investigation. Businesspersons will have to be more vigilant about their record keeping because this crime is punishable by up to 20 years in prison.

The Sarbanes-Oxley Act also makes it a crime to retaliate against any person who provides authorities with information about the potential commission of a federal offense. The act makes it clear that retaliation against whistle-blowers will not be permitted if the victim has provided truthful information. This provision represents an important constraint on managers because they ordinarily have the power to sanction subordinates.

SarbOx and other new corporate accountability laws were passed with a stiff warning that companies will be expected to comply with their minimal requirements. Some companies, however, do not need a lecture about complying with the law. These companies, such as Timberland, not only comply with the law, but also go beyond it.

Sample Legal Questions You May Encounter as a Business Manager

| **Employer/Employee Concerns** | **Business Operations** |
| --- | --- |
| Disabled Workers | Accounting |
| *What does it mean to "reasonably accommodate" an employee?* | *Who regulates accountants?* |
| Drug Testing of Employees | Advertising |
| *Should the company engage in drug testing at the preemployment stage, or is it better to engage in random drug testing later?* | *What labeling requirements does the FDA impose on food manufacturers?* |
| | Bankruptcy |
| Employee E-mail Communication | *Which creditors have first dibs on company assets when a company declares bankruptcy?* |
| *Do employees have a right to privacy with regard to e-mail?* | Breach of Contract |
| Employee Records | *What remedies are available when someone breaches a lease agreement?* |
| *Do employees have a right to look at their company personnel files?* | Building Permits and Codes |
| | *Which local agency typically issues building permits?* |
| Employment Discrimination | Business Insurance |
| *Is it lawful for employers to prefer white employees if upper-level managers feel more comfortable around people like themselves?* | *Can a business insurer avoid paying a claim if the business engaged in intentional misconduct?* |

| **Employer/Employee Concerns** | **Business Operations** |
| --- | --- |
| Firing Employees | Consumer Protection |
| *Can a manager fire a subordinate because of a personality clash?* | *Does a government agency test all products made for infants before companies can market them?* |
| Hiring Alien Workers | Credit |
| *What paperwork must employers complete if they hire alien workers?* | *Has a particular lender been accused of engaging in race discrimination with regard to its lending practices?* |
| Noncompete Agreements | Cybersquatting |
| *In what circumstances is a court likely to throw out a noncompete agreement because it is too restrictive?* | *Who has the legal right to a particular Web address?* |
| | Debt Collection |
| Overtime Pay | *What rules govern the behavior of debt collectors?* |
| *Who decides whether a particular employee is really a manager exempt from federal requirements that employers provide overtime pay?* | Environmental Laws |
| | *How much pollution is a particular company allowed to emit?* |
| | Funding and Securities |
| Sexual Harassment | *What rules govern the extent to which a company must disclose "bad news" to potential investors?* |
| *Can a man file a sexual harassment claim when male colleagues are teasing him to the point that it is causing emotional distress?* | Illegal Contracts |
| | *If a person signs a contract to purchase marijuana and the seller breaches the contract, does the buyer have any rights?* |
| Whistle-blowers | Intellectual Property |
| *What legal protections do individual states offer to whistle-blowers? Does the federal government offer any protection?* | *What kinds of work can be copyrighted?* |
| | Leasing a Facility |
| | *How can a business get out of a lease it has signed?* |
| Workers' Compensation | Loans |
| *In what circumstances can an employee sue their employer for negligence?* | *What happens when a lender hides the truth about the interest rate that will apply to a particular loan?* |
| Workplace Safety | Product Liability |
| *Does federal law require employers to let their employees know the details of chemicals they handle?* | *When is a manufacturer strictly liable for a product it manufactures and markets?* |
| | Writing Bad Checks |
| | *How much can a business charge a customer who wrote a check that bounced?* |

# VALUES IN ACTION
## Timberland

Timberland, like other morally excellent companies portrayed in this book, is a company guided by its values. Timberland CEO Jeffrey Swartz explains that the company must do more than provide money for shareholders and outdoor gear for customers:

> No longer will it be enough to measure business by profit, efficiency, and market share. Citizens must also ask how the private sector will contribute to standards of social justice, environmental sustainability, the health and strength of community, and the values by which we choose to live.[1]

Because Timberland's ethical goals are so broad and ambitious, it does more than merely comply with the law. To achieve its vision of a better world, Timberland goes above and beyond what the government requires it to do.

Timberland treats its employees around the world far better than the law requires. The company contracts with a plethora of international suppliers to manufacture its outdoor gear. Although many other companies have come under fire for their treatment of workers in overseas plants, Timberland has actively sought to ensure that its subcontractors comply with both the law and Timberland's internal code of conduct.

In 2000–2001, a nonprofit firm audited all of Timberlands' facilities. The purpose of the audit was not merely to find out how the facilities were doing financially, but also to determine the noise level, the quality of lighting, and the air quality.[2] Timberland reports that the voluntary audits have improved employee compensation, overtime payments, nondiscrimination, break times, and employee health and safety. Although Timberland initially tries to improve working conditions in suppliers' factories, it has terminated contracts with several organizations that have not improved to the company's specifications.[3]

Timberland also holds training sessions for thousands of factory workers in China and the Dominican Republic. Local nongovernmental organizations gave educational sessions on human rights, local labor law, and Timberland's Code of Conduct. Timberland is not required by law to provide these training sessions, but the company sees them as integral to its success.

Timberland also treats its employees in the United States in an exemplary manner.[4] The company allows its full-time employees to spend 40 paid hours per year doing community service.[5] Timberland also provides financial and volunteer assistance to a myriad of community groups. Finally, the company has committed to reducing its impact on the environment. It has taken steps to decrease its carbon dioxide emissions, reduce energy consumption, and use recycled materials.[6]

Again, these policies go far beyond the requirements of corporate, labor, and environmental laws. Although Timberland is surely aware that the law does not require them to adopt these policies, the company does not feel limited by legal requirements. For Timberland, the law is a starting point for how they should treat employees and comply with regulations. The goals, values, and attitudes of the company help to shape the company's substantive policies. One outcome is clear: employees, communities, and the environment benefit when companies such as Timberland meet and exceed the standards set by law. In addition, Timberland enjoys sustained corporate success, as measured in both monetary and nonmonetary terms.

Sources:

[1]Community Service, http://www.timberland.com/cgi-bin/timberland/timberland/corporate/tim_about.jsp?c=Community%20Service

(continues on the next page)

*(continued)*

[2]Timberland: Global Business Alliances, http://www.timberland.com/cgi-bin/timberland/timberland/corporate/tim_about.jsp?c=Global%20Labor%20Standards

[3]Ibid.

[4]*Timberland 2001 Corporate Social Responsibility Report*

[5]CNN.com, Other Responsible Businesses. Posted on September 30, 2000, http://www.cnn.com/SPECIALS/2000/yourbusiness/stories/other.businesses/

[6]We've Got to be environmentally Responsible. http://www.timberland.com/cgi-bin/timberland/timberland/corporate/tim_about.jsp?c=Environment

This chapter has emphasized the importance of familiarizing oneself with the law as the first step in making tough business decisions. Although lawyers know best the answers to precise legal questions, you do not necessarily need a lawyer or even a law degree to find out what laws affect your business operations. The chapter has provided you with resources that can help you find applicable laws. The chapter also presented examples of how you should think about legal rules once you find them.

Think back to the customer information case at the start of the chapter. Consider what legal sources you would want to consult to familiarize yourself with the laws governing customer information. These laws might tell you that your company is permitted to sell customer information as long as it does so within certain guidelines. After finding out this information, you might feel as if the law has made your decision for you. However, even if the law does not prohibit selling customer information, would it be clear that you should advocate selling customer information? When you answer this question, make sure you consider both the short- and long-term consequences of the decision you make. How would a CEO of Timberland probably answer this question?

*Remember:* Even when the law is clear about what you are allowed to do, you should still carefully consider whether you should do what the law allows. You should keep in mind that the law is merely a starting point for those struggling with tough decisions. Although you should strive to comply with the law, ethical considerations might lead you to refrain from acting in the manner that the law allows. When attempting to manage a lawful business, you might want to do even more than the law requires.

## CRITICAL THINKING QUESTIONS

1. A common critical thinking problem occurs when you search for information, in this case about what the law is, only to find that there are disputes about the meaning of existing laws. What do you plan to do when you encounter differing portraits of the law? What guidelines would you use for determining whether particular sources are more reliable than others?

2. What are the ambiguous elements of the legal meaning of *hostile work environment*? In other words, which words need to be clarified to be able to apply the relevant law in this domain?

## APPENDIX

# Sophisticated Searches for the Law

If you want to find the law the way a lawyer or law student would conduct a legal search, you need to have a basic understanding of the structure of the legal system. There are four sources of law: the legislative branch, the executive branch, the judicial branch, and administrative agencies.

### LEGISLATIVE BRANCH

The legislative branch is responsible for creating laws. Both the federal and state Congresses create law by introducing a bill into either the House of Representatives or the Senate. If both houses of Congress vote affirmatively on the bill, the bill becomes law.

The legislative branch generally creates two types of statutes: criminal and civil law statutes. Criminal law governs the relationships between the individual and the state. Thus, the government is a party in a criminal case. The purpose of criminal law is to punish offenders and prevent wrongful conduct. This punishment typically takes the form of imprisonment or fines. In contrast, civil law governs the relationship between two private parties, such as two companies or a company and an employee. As a business manager, you will need to be concerned with both criminal and civil law.

You can find federal statutes in the United States Code (U. S. C.), whereas you will frequently find state statutes in a state code (e.g., California Code, Ohio Revised Code Annotated). Depending on your ethical dilemma, you may need to locate federal, state, or local laws. The process of finding the law looks a lot more complicated than it is. Use the Table 8.1 on next page as a guide.

Here is an example of a statute citation: 42 USC 2000e-2. The citation provides the title and section number of the United States Code. Thus, in this example, under Title 42, Section 2000e-2 of the United States Code, you would find the following statute:

(a) Employer practices
It shall be an unlawful employment practice for an employer
   (1) to fail or refuse to hire or to discharge any individual, or otherwise to discriminate against any individual with respect to his compensation, terms, conditions, or privileges of employment, because of such individual's race, color, religion, sex, or national origin.

This statute prohibits discrimination on the basis of race, color, religion, sex, or national origin. If you have a statute citation, you can retrieve the statute at *http://www.findlaw.com/casecode/uscodes/*.

**TABLE 8.1** Where to Find the Law

| Level of Government | Legislative Law | Executive Orders | Common Law/Judicial Interpretations | Administrative Regulations |
|---|---|---|---|---|
| **Federal** | United States Code (USC)<br><br>United States Code Annotated (USCA) | Title 3 of the Code of Federal Regulations<br><br>Codification of Presidential Proclamations and Executive Orders | United States Reports (U.S.)<br><br>Supreme Court Reporter (S.CT.)<br><br>Federal Reporter (F, F.2d, F.3d)<br><br>Regional Reporters<br>Federal Supplement (F. Supp.)<br>Federal Agency Reports, (titled by agency, e.g., F.C.C. Reports) | Code of Federal Regulations (C.F.R.)<br><br>Federal Register |
| **State** | State code or state statutes (e.g., Ohio Revised Code) | | State reports | State administrative code or state administrative regulations |
| **Local** | Municipal ordinances | | Varies; often difficult to find. Many municipalities do not publish case decisions but do preserve them on microfilm. Interested parties usually must contact the clerk's office at the local courthouse. | Municipality administrative regulations |

---

**Other Sites for Finding Statutes**

**FEDERAL STATUTES**
**Search by keyword:**
http://uscode.house.gov/usc.htm
http://www4.law.cornell.edu/uscode

**Browse by Title and Subject:**
http://resource.lawlinks.com/Content/Legal_Research/united_states_code.htm

**STATE STATUTES**
http://www.findlaw.com/11stategov/
http://www.leginfo.ca.gov.statute.html
http://www.law.cornell.edu/topics/state_statutes.html

**MUNICIPAL CODES**
http://www.generalcode.com/webcode.2.html#cali
http://www.municode.com/Resources/online_code.asp

---

Suppose you want to determine whether there are any statutes that address discrimination in the workplace, but you do not have a statute citation. You can use the same Findlaw site to search the text of statutes for any federal statute that mentions discrimination. Alternatively, you can browse the U.S. Code by popular name there.

Sometimes, you might wish to examine a proposed bill to see what types of requirements may be imposed on you or your company in the future. You can search for bills by citation or by keyword at *http://thomas.loc.gov*. A search for "privacy" bills returned the following bills: "Online Personal Privacy Act of 2002," "Consumer Privacy Protection Act of 2002," and the "Federal Privacy and Data Protection Policy Act of 2002."

## EXECUTIVE BRANCH

A second source of law is the executive branch. At the federal level, the president, his staff, and his cabinet constitute the executive branch. The federal executive branch creates law in two ways: (1) treaty making and (2) executive orders. At the state level, governors may issue executive orders.

As a business manager, you should be most concerned about compliance with executive orders. For example, President Johnson issued Executive Order 11246, which required government contractors to create affirmative action plans to hire and promote minorities and women.

You can find executive orders issued by President Bush at *http://www.whitehouse.gov/news/orders*.

## JUDICIAL BRANCH

Federal and state courts interpret the Constitution and the laws passed by the legislative branches. When two parties disagree about the meaning of a statute, they bring the disagreement before the court. On a case-by-case basis, the court examines the language of the statute, along with the legislative history of the statute, to resolve the disagreement. The court will also consider other earlier relevant case decisions, or **precedents.** Lower courts (e.g., trial courts) must follow the decisions or precedents of higher courts (appellate and supreme courts). The court's written decision is then printed in a **reporter.**

When parties initiate a lawsuit, they must file their case in either a state or federal trial court. At the federal level, the trial court is called the **district court.** There are 96 district courts in the United States, and a party brings a case in a district court with a corresponding geographical district court. When a party appeals a district court ruling, one of twelve federal **circuit courts of appeals** reviews the district court's decision. If a party appeals the circuit court of appeals decision, the U.S. Supreme Court decides whether to hear the case.

The location of a case in a reporter is called the "citation" of the case. For example, the Supreme Court recognized sexual harassment as a form of sex discrimination in *Meritor Savings Bank v. Vinson*, 477 U.S. 57 (1986). The citation provides the following information:

[volume number of the reporter][reporter name] [page number](year).

[477]                      [U.S.]                  [57]          (1986)

You will find U.S. Supreme Court cases in the "U.S." reporter.

Understanding how to read case citations is important to you for one reason: you should be most concerned about the cases decided by courts that might decide disputes in which your own business could be involved. For example, if your business is in California, you should pay close attention to Ninth Circuit court of appeals decisions, along with decisions in the northern, eastern, southern, and central districts of California. If your business is in Ohio, you should give special attention to Sixth Circuit court of appeals decisions, along with the northern and southern districts' courts of Ohio. Table 8.2 can help you determine which courts you should consider in your legal search.

You can find federal case law at *http://www.findlaw.com/casecode*.

TABLE 8.2 Classifications of United States Courts of Appeals

| First Circuit (1st) | Second Circuit (2nd) | Third Circuit (3rd) | Fourth Circuit (4th) | Fifth Circuit (5th) | Sixth Circuit (6th) |
|---|---|---|---|---|---|
| Maine | Connecticut | Pennsylvania | District of Columbia | Louisiana | Kentucky |
| Massachusetts | New York | Virgin Islands | Maryland | Mississippi | Michigan |
| New Hampshire | Vermont | | North Carolina | Texas | Ohio |
| Puerto Rico | | | South Carolina | | Tennessee |
| Rhode Island | | | Virginia | | |
| | | | West Virginia | | |

| Seventh Circuit (7th) | Eighth Circuit (8th) | Ninth Circuit (9th) | Tenth Circuit (10th) | Eleventh Circuit (11th) | Federal Circuit |
|---|---|---|---|---|---|
| Indiana | Arkansas | Alaska | Colorado | Alabama | |
| Illinois | Iowa | California | Kansas | Florida | |
| Wisconsin | Minnesota | Hawaii | New Mexico | Georgia | |
| | Missouri | Idaho | Oklahoma | | |
| | Nebraska | Montana | Utah | | |
| | North Dakota | Oregon | Wyoming | | |
| | South Dakota | Nevada | | | |
| | | Washington | | | |

## ADMINISTRATIVE REGULATIONS

Congress has delegated to federal regulatory agencies the authority to make rules governing the conduct of business. Examples of these agencies include the Securities and Exchange Commission, the Federal Trade Commission, the Equal Employment Opportunity Commission, and the Occupational Safety and Health Administration.

Federal agencies publish both proposed and final rules in the *Federal Register*. Final rules can also be found in the Code of Federal Regulations, whereas you will find the state and local rules in the state administrative code or the municipality administrative regulations. Should you need to find information from the *Federal Register*, you can locate it online at *http://www.access.gpo.gov/nara/index.html#pd*.

## ENDNOTES

[1] *Amazon Privacy Policy under Scrutiny: Are we Hearing the Music?* Center for Law, Commerce, & Technology, UW School of Law, http://www.law.washington.edu/lct/techlaw_archive/amazonpolicy.html.

[2] Greg Sandoval, *Failed Dot-Coms May Be Selling Your Private Information*, June 29, 2000, http://news.com/com/2100-1017-242649.html.

[3] http://biz.findlaw.com/business_commercial/legal/source/business_events/be8_5breaching.html

[4] See www.eeco.gov/facts/fs-sex.html.

[5] *Faragher v. City of Boca Raton*, 118 S. Ct. 2275 (1998).

[6] *Burlington Industries, Inc. v. Ellerth*, 118 S. Ct. 2257 (1998).

# CHAPTER 9

# Identifying the Alternative Options for Good Work

> **THE FOCUS:**
> How do I identify my options in response to an ethical dilemma?

When you are faced with a tough ethical dilemma, what thoughts cross your mind? Often, businesspeople fall into the habitual trap of thinking that they must consider "both" sides of the dilemma: usually, either go along with corporate pressures or resign. However, acknowledging only two options to a business problem is like trying to paint a black-and-white portrait without any shades of gray. The result? Details are lost, and frustration builds as artificial limits imposed on communication prohibit a clear exchange of ideas. As you read through the following example, consider how your decision-making abilities would be compromised if you considered only two extreme options.

You take a vice presidency position at a large company. After a few months of working there, you discover that even though the CEO has made over $300 million in the past three years, he has been using some questionable accounting and expense techniques for his own personal benefit.[1] Specifically, you discover that the CEO has been using an employee loan program to purchase home fitness equipment, art, furniture, yachts, and antiques. Additionally, he has been using the loan program to pay for home construction and remodeling costs as well as the salaries of domestic help.

The purpose of the employee loan program is to encourage employees to own company stock. Executives can borrow money through the loan program to pay the taxes on the company stock. You discover that over the past five years, the CEO has borrowed more than $270 million through this loan program, but only $30 million was used for paying tax liabilities.

Although you are new to the company, you realize that the CEO's behavior is problematic. Moreover, you are troubled because you believe that the company's board of directors is aware of the CEO's behavior. As an ethical businessperson, what should you do in this situation?

## RESISTING THE BLIND ALLEY OF LOOKING AT "BOTH" SIDES

Whatever you eventually decide to do in the preceding example will only be as strong as the number of options you permit yourself to consider. In other words, any business problem has a large array of possible solutions. We needlessly limit the potential wisdom of our responses to an ethical dilemma when we too quickly consider just a couple of the many available choices.

Why do we need to be reminded to "consider our options"? Scrolling mentally through your options is extremely important because you can thereby save yourself from the horrible feeling later that you acted prematurely. Like the rest of us, you do not want to choose a poor option simply because you were unaware of a better option. Because one of the best ways to avoid making a terrible choice is to acknowledge other options, we want to urge you to do so.

When you take a job, for instance, you are selecting a particular ethical space within which you must make important judgments that may affect the interests of many people. Normal insecurities will often cause us to see ourselves as having only two options; we feel compelled to choose between the job with the ethically mediocre company or unemployment.

Even though the thought of all the red flags your potential job raises makes you cringe, you might accept the position because it seems better than no job at all. Although we do not want to be glib here because we realize that acquiring a job in a timely fashion is a necessity, a one-week wait might have provided you with any number of other job possibilities. But an option such as this is no longer relevant once you made your choice from the artificially small list of "job or no job."

The point is simple but powerful. The quality of your ethical decisions can be only as good as the scope of the options that you consider before making your decision. Decisions, like ice cream, rarely come in only two flavors. Our tendency to dichotomize situations into the good and the bad, the right and the wrong, pro and con, and for and against stands in the way of a more robust understanding of the boundaries of good work.

Consider what would be lost to a businessperson if he or she were to consider only the two extreme options in the following table. Sometimes one of the extremes may be the best decision you can make, but recognizing the superiority of that particular option should occur only after you have compared it to a broad array of alternatives.

**CRITICAL THINKING BOX**
Our tendency to think that there are only two solutions to a problem could be a result of the limited information that we have when we first encounter a problem. How can missing information affect our ability to generate alternative solutions? How do we know when to stop trying to obtain additional information about our options? Could having too much information ever hinder our decision-making processes?

## OPTIONAL PATHS TO GOOD WORK

| Business Ethical Dilemma | "Both" Options | Alternative Paths |
| --- | --- | --- |
| You have worked at your new job for only a year, but in that time you have learned a great deal about the organization. Before your organization launches an advertising campaign you notice that the flyer already printed for the local newspaper is misleading. The flyer promotes "free" checking from the bank, but in actuality there are substantial hidden fees when the "free" checking account is opened. However, your organization has only enough money in the budget for one printing of the flyer. Because you are a relatively new employee, you do not have the authority to alter the company's ads. What should you do? | • Ignore the problem or pretend that you did not see the flyer. The flyer is someone else's job so you will not concern yourself with it. <br><br>• Resign your position if the flyer is not altered or prevented from running in the newspaper. | • Talk with a coworker about the flyer to find possible solutions. <br>• Tactfully inquire about the inaccuracy of the flyer with a manager. <br>• Use your position to explain to clients the full costs of opening a "free" account. <br>• Create several ideas for future advertisements that accurately spell out the special advantages for clients who use the services of your firm. <br>• Create and sponsor arguments for why your firm would benefit by offering the attributes it promised in the initial flyer. |

*(continues on the next page)*

*(continued)*

| Business Ethical Dilemma | "Both" Options | Alternative Paths |
|---|---|---|
| Your organization is entertaining guests from a non-Western culture. In this culture, it is common that a night of entertainment on business trips includes visiting a strip club. Your coworkers have entertained business guests by taking them to a strip club in the past. This time your boss has asked you to entertain the visitors, who are all of the same sex as yourself, by taking them to the club. You consider patronizing strip clubs to be morally wrong. What should you do? | • Go to the strip club with your guests.<br>• Resign from your position rather than compromise your morals by going to the strip club. | • Ask your guests about other entertainment options.<br>• Explain your reservations about going to the strip club to your boss. Have another coworker lined up to go in your place.<br>• Explain your reservations to the boss and offer to take the guests on another outing.<br>• Advocate arguments for why your firm would benefit from instituting a policy that prevents entertaining business guests at strip clubs. |
| You work in an insurance agent's office. Your boss (the agent) asks you to sign a document in a policyholder's name. The document waives the policyholder's uninsured motorist coverage. You know that forging the policyholder's name is illegal, but when you raise the issue with your boss she says, "It's not a big deal. We do it all the time. The policyholder would waive the coverage if he were here. We just forgot to give him the form." You're still uneasy about the situation. What should you do? | • Forge the policyholder's signature.<br>• Resign your position rather than forge the policyholder's signature. | • Call the policyholder to discuss waiving the coverage and signing the form.<br>• Indicate that you signed for the policyholder by including "S/B" for "signed by."<br>• Go to your boss's supervisor or another upper-level manager to discuss your boss's request.<br>• Ask your coworkers if they are opposed to this practice. If they are, then go to the boss as a group and explain that you are all bothered by the situation. |

## HINTS FOR GENERATING OPTIONS

When an ethical dilemma arises, we are often caught up in the "heat of the moment." At this time, our ability to reflect in a clear and rational manner is often compromised. For example, if you were asked to create an advertising strategy to convince college students to eat a type of bread that had been found in dependable tests to stimulate hunger, the request would probably stir your passions. You *are* a college student yourself; hence, you are upset by the request to mislead or hide important information from your own cohorts. Yet you are also excited at the prospect of fulfilling an assigned responsibility, and you are already anticipating the potential financial rewards. When the passions start flowing as they are in this example, we are often in too big a hurry to rush to extreme options.

But after we take a few deep breaths and have some time to reflect, our thinking becomes a bit clearer. We are able to consider the options available to us in the ethical dilemma, and we are more likely to establish a workable ethical partnership between the person we want to become and the business culture in which we are trying to thrive. It might also help to brainstorm with a friend or colleague about the situation to get more ideas for options. But once we wish to think about or talk through multiple solutions to an ethical dilemma, what do we do to uncover these potential answers? Several generative strategies come to mind.

- Try to think of potential allies inside the firm with whom you could organize to improve the questionable behavior of the firm.
- Familiarize yourself again with the Mission Statement of the firm, as well as its stated code of ethics. Whenever you speak to someone about the decision that troubles you, make explicit references to these ethical guidelines. Encouraging your employer to live up to the high-sounding nature of its public statements might be effective in certain situations.
- Remind yourself of the various interests that would be affected by particular options. Use these reminders to indicate the winners and losers of alternative responses to the ethical issue.
- See whether you can create alternative and more certain avenues to profit for the firm by suggesting an action that would be less ethically troublesome than the direction toward which your firm is currently leaning.
- Diplomatically suggest options that build on earlier ideas of your supervisors. When selling these options, explicitly use the language and reasoning that had been used earlier by those supervisors.
- Consider options by which you could secretly encourage public pressure that would prevent your employer from taking a course of action that you believe to be unethical.

Each of these strategies provides space in between quitting and burying your head in the sand. They are not necessarily better options just because they are somewhere in the middle of the two extremes. However, they do illustrate the rich variety of approaches each businessperson has when faced with an ethical dilemma.

The wisdom of particular options will vary depending on the specific business environment in which the selected action must be applied. An option may be irrelevant or completely unacceptable in some work environments. For example, consider the options that would be unavailable for business relationships guided by the Chinese concept of "guanxi", the focus of the Global Box on the next page.

## THE PROFIT MOTIVE AND WEIGHING THE OPTIONS[2]

### Weighing the Options

#### *Use Past Knowledge*

This chapter is primarily concerned with encouraging you to generate as many optional decisions as is practical before you commit yourself to a particular action. However, we want to pause for a moment and remind you that you have already learned a lot about what to do with the options after you have spelled them out. Chapters 2 through 5 all make suggestions about how to narrow your list of choices.

The key to doing good work is in the preparation; proper preparation does not include an unfinished checklist. Listing multiple options, as this chapter suggests, will be of little use if you stare at the list and repeatedly demand in tones of rising frustration, "Now what am I to do?" Once you have identified the facts and the issue and brainstormed a list of alternative courses of action, continue with the decision-making process. For example, be alert to the business culture where you are required to function. You should also reflect about the ethical expectations you have for yourself and help yourself achieve that goal by incorporating the classical guidelines into your everyday thinking. All of these suggestions from previous chapters will provide you with the necessary background to make a strong contribution of good work to your community.

#### *Considering the Profit Motive*

For the businessperson, the profit motive looms over all other factors and is considered during every step of an ethical decision. Suggesting the desirability of a particular decision is not likely to be successful in a business setting unless that option first makes its peace with the profit motive.

Due to the ambiguity of the profit motive, "keeping the peace" when a firm moves toward good work is easier than you might imagine. We

**GLOBAL BOX**

**CHINA**

The ancient practice of guanxi still affects business relations in China. Guanxi is a difficult concept to succinctly define. One author describes it as "a relationship . . . among individuals creating obligations for the continued exchange of favors" (Dunfee, p. 192). The groups of businesspersons connected through guanxi are often referred to as the "bamboo network." Guanxi relationships begin with a blood or social connection between two people (usually men): one person does a favor for the other. The types of favors exchanged in a guanxi relationship vary. For example, a person may invite executives on an expenses-paid trip, entertain them at lavish parties, or introduce them to another businessperson from whom they could benefit. Whatever the favor, it creates an obligation on behalf of the favor's recipient to return the help. The Chinese take the obligation to return the favor very seriously.

Guanxi is an appealing tradition if one values trust and duty. Trust is an essential ingredient to a successful guanxi relationship. No formal contracts or written agreements are used because of the high level of trust between business partners. Presumably, businesspersons also feel a duty to help other colleagues in their network. This sense of duty can mean fulfilling obligations or going out of one's way to help another.

Although these characteristics may be appealing, guanxi has also come under ethical scrutiny. Guanxi may be ethically questionable in the sense that it diminishes equal opportunity to participate in the business world. Because it is built on blood or social relationship, guanxi excludes those who don't have access to business circles. The persistence of this practice may make it difficult for an ordinary Chinese person to advance, or even enter, the business world. Additional ethical problems may arise because the guanxi obligation is taken so seriously. For instance, a businessperson may be willing to act contrary to any number of important values if it were necessary to fulfill an obligation.

*Sources:*
Thomas W. Dunfee and Danielle E. Warren, "Is Guanxi Ethical? A Normative Analysis of Doing Business in China," *Journal of Business Ethics* 32, (2001): 191–204.
Darrly Crawford, "Globalisation and *Guanxi:* The Ethos of Hong Kong Finance," *New Political Economy* 6, no.1 (2001): 45–65.
Jinn-Yuh Hsu and AnnaLee Saxenian, "The Limits of Guanxi Capitalism: Transnational Collaboration Between Taiwan and the USA," *Environment and Planning*, 32, no.11 (2000): 1991–2005.

often take for granted that certain business options will bubble to the top because they can be successfully aligned with profitability. However, we sometimes forget that the "alignment" is not always obvious or guaranteed; profit projections are a risky business.

First, we must choose between short-run and long-run profitability. Because we can project results better over short periods of time, there is a temptation to pursue only those courses of action that enhance the immediate profit picture and, hence, the current management cadre. But a firm wants to be viable for the long haul, and in order to ensure the firm's continued existence, long-run profitability cannot be sacrificed to short-run gains that threaten the eventual financial health of the firm.

Aligning business decisions with long-run profits is a complicated game of risk. Companies are still trying to decide which computer program can capture the future well enough to predict the five- or fifteen-year effect of today's business decision. Some models certainly perform better than others, but extrapolating long-run profits necessarily encounters a large dose of indeterminacy.

This indeterminacy allows us enough latitude to make well-reasoned arguments that the more ethical decision is also more profitable. Good work may well be the best form of business because it provides both a better community and a more successful firm in the long-run. The "Values in Action" box presents facts that highlight the possibility that when company leaders realize that other people matter, this realization may lead to long-term financial success.

---

### VALUES IN ACTION
#### S. Truett Cathy and Chick-fil-A

In 1967, S. Truett Cathy founded Chick-fil-A Inc., a fast-food chicken restaurant.[1] Although he had no college education, Cathy's hard work and commitment to developing employee and customer loyalty led to Chick-fil-A's status as the United States' third-largest fast-food chicken restaurant. Although turnover is extremely high in the franchise industry in general, fewer than 5 percent of Chick-fil-A franchise operators leave the restaurant chain each year.

Cathy has made several decisions that have helped to develop this strong sense of loyalty. First, he insists that all Chick-fil-A stores close on Sundays so his employees can spend time with their families. Also, when other fast-food restaurants started serving chicken in 1982, Chick-fil-A sales were in danger. In response to the company's potential economic problems, Cathy could have behaved several ways. For example, he could have cut his employees' salaries or thinned the ranks through layoffs. Instead, he decided to pay himself no salary that year. Cathy appears to value **loyalty**, as he seems devoted to employees, who are key stakeholders in his company. He also has an understanding of **security**. He apparently wants his employees to enjoy the psychological comfort that comes from knowing they will receive a particular salary.

Chick-fil-A has enjoyed much business success. No one can say for sure why Chick-fil-A has had the success it has had. But a strong argument can be made that S. Truett Cathy's business decisions are as profitable as they are ethical.

*Source:*
[1] This information is from Sarah Z. Sleeper, "His Principles Served Him Well," *Investor's Business Daily*, October 14, 2002.

**CRITICAL THINKING BOX**
Cathy's strategy of cutting his own salary was intended to help Chick-fil-A's financial performance. Do you think this strategy had any other consequences? How do you think the company's decisions affected franchise owners and employees? If you were an investor in Chick-fil-A, would Cathy's move make you glad that you had invested in this company or nervous about your investment's prospects?

## Options Wrap-up

Unlike Cathy, some of us might have only seen two extreme options when our company's finances were jeopardized, such as either (1) lie about the financial condition of the company through manipulated balance sheets or (2) admit a downturn in expected profits and decrease employee salaries to make up the lost money. This chapter issues a warning against oft-committed, heat-of-the-moment mistakes such as this one. "What mistake is that?" you might ask. The mistake occurs when we assume that there are only two choices available to us. Worse, we assume those two choices are extreme ones, usually along the lines of either go along with the unethical action or quit the job. This tendency to dichotomize our options limits the quality of our ethical decision making.

An important lesson to take from this chapter is that there are rarely just two options. The chapter has provided you with suggestions and examples of how to generate alternative choices. When you are faced with an ethical dilemma, be sure to relax and reflect on options and how they align with your values. Don't rush into a quick decision; generating and evaluating options requires enough reflection time to think in a way that is both creative and critical.

The complexity of business decisions and need for clear-headed analysis is reflected in this chapter's section on profit motive. It is often unclear whether a strategy will or will not boost profits. We do know, however, that sometimes companies make the mistake of looking out for their short-run interest in boosting their stock price, without regard for other goals. This kind of simplistic decision making highlights the need for making business decisions after reflecting on all available options. To solve this dilemma, you will need to consider the available options and their possible effects. As you consider your choices, you may decide that your options are too limited or they are all unsatisfactory. In either case, you will need to generate more alternative solutions to the dilemma, such as decreasing expenses in an ethical way. After reading this chapter, you should now have a better understanding of how to expand the number of options available to you and, as a result, improve the quality of your decision-making process.

## CRITICAL THINKING QUESTIONS

1. Suppose that you are presented with two different product lines as possible areas of growth for your firm. Make as complete a list of options as you can that should shape your eventual decision. Why is the mandate to "make a profit" less helpful in making your decision than it might seem to be at first glance? How would your primary value priorities shape your consideration of the options?

2. Business decisions are often rushed. They must move at a faster clip than if the decision were one you could make after months of reflection. How can you move beyond simple consideration of two options when you are so frequently in a hurry? What did you learn in this chapter that would encourage you to try to take a little more time than ordinary pressures would permit?

## ENDNOTES

[1] These facts are adapted from the charges alleged against former Tyco International CEO Dennis Kozlowski. See Jeffry Krasner et al., "Tyco Alleges Kozlowski Misused $100 Million Ex-CEO Used Firm's Funds for Lavish Lifestyle, Lawsuit Accuses," *Boston Globe*, September 13, 2002, C1.

[2] Thanks to Jeff Hale of the University of Arizona for his analysis of profitability indeterminacy that resulted in this section.

# CHAPTER 10

# Applying Personal Ethical Principles to Doing Good Work

THE FOCUS:
How does my sense of who I want to become shape my behavior as a businessperson?

As you have grown into adulthood, you have joined thousands of youths past and present in a personal quest for identity. During this time of maturation and exploration, you grew taller, discovered strange foods, learned new skills, and may have even adopted a different style of clothing. Another characteristic, more important and less visible than these others, may have also begun (and hopefully continues) to evolve. We are referring to your image of your ideal self. A good way to think about this personal goal is by answering the question: How do I want people to describe me after I am gone? As you read the following situation, imagine how you would react so that you move closer to the image of who you want to become. How has this image changed over time, and how would these changes affect your behavior in the following business dilemma?

As a top-level manager of Union Oil Company, a financial grenade in the form of your daily newspaper arrives at your desk one morning. The newspaper contains a devastating report about a joint-business venture between your company and a foreign government. A few years ago, your firm partnered with the Cambodian government to build a $1.2 billion pipeline from the local gas fields to Thailand. Initially, your company was concerned about forming the joint venture. Certainly no one would confuse the Cambodian government with an active democracy. However, the government had the organizational strength to get the job done, and Union Oil had high hopes of healthy profits when the agreement was finally reached. In addition to your company's benefit, the pipeline would assist the Cambodian people by providing employment and development possibilities.

So far, the venture has looked promising. In particular, the construction of the pipeline has stayed on schedule. In fact, you wish some of your American contractors were as punctual in moving a project forward. But if the newspaper report today is correct, the techniques used by the Cambodian government to build a pipeline in a timely manner will create a nightmare for Union Oil.

The newspaper's reports from Cambodia, in the form of dozens of personal stories from villagers, remind you of previous corporate scandals resulting from unintended methods of operation. The villagers told the reporter chilling tales of being dragged from their villages by the Cambodian military, who organized them into chain gangs to build sections of the pipeline and beat them if they resisted. The article is accompanied by graphic pictures of scars and wounds allegedly caused by brutal soldiers committed to finishing the pipeline as promised.

You have just finished reading the article when your phone rings; the editor of the newspaper at the local university wishes to interview you. He wants to know what Union Oil intends to do about these atrocities. Before you can answer, an assistant shows you a fax from the legal department. The fax reminds you of the legal doctrine of "vicarious liability," by which joint-venture partners are legally responsible for each other's actions, and you cringe at the obvious implications. To make matters even more serious, you glance out your office window to see a growing picket line from Earth Rights International (ERI) protesting the treatment of ordinary Cambodian villagers coerced into building the pipeline that ERI has opposed since the project's first draft.

What will you say to the newspaper editor and legal department? How will you decide on a course of action? Notice especially that, in both this example and many real-life situations, businesspeople cannot take huge amounts of time to first brainstorm more than two extreme options and then study the ethical ins and outs each option. Perhaps you can buy an hour or two to make the decision, but you must often answer the metaphorical newspaper editor before his deadline. Like the preceding example illustrates, businesspeople must act quickly.

## THE ETHICAL DECISION IS YOURS

### Your Role in an Ethical Partnership

Another theme present in the beginning example and throughout this book is the emphasis on partnership. Business decisions arise from a partnership between you and the businesses with which you interact as an employee, manager, or leader (in addition to companies you associate with as a customer or investor). Sometimes it may be hard for you to see the partnership opportunities because the business firm with which you interact is, in a sense, bigger than you; it existed before you came into the picture, bringing a long history and established culture with it to its encounters with you. It also may function long after you have moved on.

Yet, the ethical partnership between you and the business firm can exist. You are a significant player in business ethics. Firms need you; they cannot function without your cooperation. Therefore, you cannot escape responsibility for your part in the ethical partnership. Although knowledge of the institutional culture at work is crucial to your understanding of the pressures and incentives to behave in particular ways, you must ultimately choose if you will follow in the encouraged behavior. You have to live with yourself after you take a stance in an ethical situation where you must responsibly influence a business firm, such as Union Oil and its actions concerning the villagers of Cambodia.

Imagine the various interests in a firm as pulling and tugging you toward their preferred solution to a business dilemma. You can allow yourself to be persuaded, or you can push back and resist the indicated direction. Of course, some people are in what seems to be a better position to push back. For example, the CEO of Texaco, Peter Bijur, assumed leadership at a time when Texaco was in the middle of a lawsuit alleging that the company had engaged in across-the-board racial discrimination in the areas of pay, performance evaluations, and promotions. He could have allowed himself to be pulled by internal corporate interests, which seemed to prefer a stance of denying that problems existed within the firm. However, as a strong leader with a moral vision that included an eye toward increased fairness for all employees, Bijur pushed back against company insiders. He quickly agreed to a settlement that compensated African-American employees for the discrimination they had experienced. Additionally, he made hiring and firing decisions— changes that brought in a new leadership team who shared his vision for justice.

Bijur also agreed to accept the help of a task force of outsiders, whose job was to review and revise the company's human resources policies.[1] As a consequence of Bijur's willingness to push back, the company was able to change its culture to make it fair for all employees. Today, Texaco is a model for workplace diversity. Increased diversity has made the company stronger and more able to withstand competitive pressures within the industry.

As CEO, Bijur was able to take a strong stand; he was able to act on his moral principles. However, taking strong stands is not easy. Even top executives cannot completely ignore outside influences; they still have to consider the immediate social and financial circumstances of the corporation. Certainly, Bijur faced serious financial risks and opposition from other company managers, who feared that a settlement would harm the company's image.

Similarly, business managers in subordinate positions try to reconcile both external pressures from the corporate environment and the pressure they place on themselves to act as responsible moral citizens. They often do so in the context of uncertainty about the consequences of a certain course of action. From the newly hired employee to the CEO, each ethical decision is a wrestling match among external pressures and an individual ideal of the ethical self. So, how do you sort out a seeming ethical free-for-all? What will you do if your boss asks you to inflate earnings statements for the next shareholders' report? You have already learned a variety of techniques to help you decide. In preparation for putting this knowledge to use, it would be a good idea to check on your personal beliefs about the relative weight of honesty and status as guiding values.

## Your Ideal World

Your beliefs about values are important, but how do you sort through them so that you can represent yourself effectively and ethically in your mental negotiations at the workplace? How do you balance the various interests and responsibilities, from coworkers to the environment, that are increasingly influencing business decisions? We have a suggestion, but first you should notice that a key part of our suggestion is not "how" to sort your beliefs but "when." Here's our suggestion: *Before* the ethical dilemma occurs, sit down by yourself or with friends and figure out what kind of ideal world you want to be part of and contribute toward creating. Describe that world as fully as you can.

For example, those of you who have had an economics course have experienced one such perspective of "heaven on earth." Economists invite us into a world in which life is at its best when we are consuming goods and resources. All the graphs you study and the economic "truths" you learned are only as good as that view of the purpose of human life. Do you agree with that perspective? Throughout this chapter, we will urge you to think about questions like this one. Your resulting image of an ideal world will give you a reflective portrait of just what kind of human being you wish to become.

You are surely aware that even a thoughtful, reflective view of the good life will not require and include the same things as another person's version. In chapter 1, we warned you that "thoughtful people disagree about value priorities, as their varying visions of a better world predict they would." Let's think together about another group's version of the ideal world. Some people see the building and sustaining of relationships with family and friends as much more important to doing good work than economists' goal of how often they get to purchase goods and services. To be glib, trips to the mall are, for these people, something one must do now and again and are not the route to a better world. Do you agree with this view?

Once you have a vision of your ideal world, you can use what you have learned so far in this book to prepare yourself *before* the ethical dilemma arises so that, when the time comes, you can quickly apply that vision to doing good work. Here are some practical steps.

- Highlight the values that drive your vision of the ideal world.
- Think about the values that habitually conflict with those values.
- Recognize that a core element of your character consists of a preference for certain values over others.
- Remember that violating these value preferences may be a violation of your image of yourself.

## MORAL PRINCIPLES AND YOU

### Identifying Your Moral Principles

Before we work through an example requiring you to have first reflected about the world you wish to help create, let's define a key term that will help as you work through the preparatory steps for doing good work. Recall that values are the basis of our moral or ethical perspective. They are the most basic unit with which we think about business ethics. Recall that what differentiates one businessperson from another from an ethical perspective is the set of common value preferences that creates her or his behavior.

A **moral principle** is a developed habit of mind that we bring to every ethical challenge; it is the defining group of value preferences that distinguishes us from one another. When we refer to someone as this kind of person and not that other kind, we are calling attention to the person's moral principles.

Those making decisions at work are persistently faced with choices that require them to take implicit stances with respect to value conflicts such as the following.

- Material success versus honesty
- Individual responsibility versus collective responsibility
- Competition versus cooperation
- Loyalty versus efficiency
- Compassion versus institutional security

Whatever significant value preferences you tend to bring to business dilemmas, such as compassion over institutional security, are your **moral principles**.

**CRITICAL THINKING BOX**
Under what conditions would businesspeople ever want to violate their moral principles? In other words, would any conceivable scenario force us to consider violating those moral principles?

To be self-aware about your moral principles, review the chapter about values. Which of these values would best describe your vision of an ideal world?

For instance, suppose you are the manager of a small wallpaper business. The foreman of the installation crew for your business, Ted, has been a loyal employee for twenty years. Ted's skills in interacting with customers and in ensuring quality wallpaper hanging have been impeccable for a long time. However, over the last ten months, he has gained about 85 pounds. You're not sure about the cause of this recent development, but Ted's number of recent sick days and the increase in customer complaints are hurting your business. If you hired someone in good physical shape (and you know of several competent people who would love to have his job), wallpaper installation jobs for your company would be completed quicker and with better costumer satisfaction. But what would happen to Ted if he were fired?

Imagine that, as a significant part of your ideal world, people who are persistent and dedicated to a job would be rewarded for their loyalty regardless of their ability level. You realize that this belief is centered on the key values of trust and goodwill. Because you wish to increase the role of these values in the human community, you are impelled to see loyalty as a higher priority than efficiency. In this case, retaining a long-faithful employee would be in line with the moral principles you had before Ted's employment was ever a concern. But then you wonder, "What about loyalty to the customers who keep me in business and loyalty to the other workers on the installation crew who must now work harder to compensate for Ted's shortcomings?" Even though your moral principles give you a starting point for making a decision, you will still have to think about how other factors in this dilemma (such as facts, the issue, relevant laws, and available options) interact with your habitual value preferences.

**Growing and Developing Your Moral Principles**

Although each of us brings to business decisions a particular set of moral principles, there are many influences that helped shape those mental habits. For instance, religion is often the most powerful starting point for the formation of moral principles. The Global Box provides one

GLOBAL BOX

## MIDDLE EASTERN COUNTRIES
## AND MORAL PRINCIPLES

Although some Muslims still strictly adhere to the tenets of Islamic law when conducting business, Western values and economic practices have infiltrated Middle Eastern society. To some extent, the mixing of cultures diminishes Islam's influence on business. A good illustration of this change is the practice of charging interest, or *riba*.

Islam prohibits the charging, taking, or paying of interest. The reasons for this prohibition are debated, but in general, interest payments are seen as contrary to Islamic social justice goals. The rule is also embedded in Islam's belief that no one should take advantage of the poor.

As one can imagine, this belief creates many difficulties in the modern business world. Consequently, various contemporary views on *riba* have developed. One view is that collecting or paying interest is permissible if the transfer of ownership of the goods takes place immediately. Such a transaction is referred to as *riba al-fadl*, or immediate credit. Another view holds that if the goods being exchanged are of the same quantity and kind, then interest is permitted. The most controversial perspectives are those related to interest on loans. Islamic law strictly prohibits the collecting or paying of interest on a loan. Some Muslims argue that this is unavoidable in the modern world; others adamantly maintain it is possible to avoid interest payments.

The issue of whether to charge or pay interest is a very serious one for modern Muslims. Muslims are concerned with corrupting their moral principles. They fear that one immoral act will corrupt the conscience and lead to more immoral behavior. The decision to collect or pay interest appears to start one down this perilous path. Nonetheless, modern business pressures many Muslims to take that "first step" by charging interest.

*Source:*
Abdulaziz Sachedina, "The Issue of Riba in Islamic Faith and Law" in *Spiritual Goods: Faith Traditions and the Practice of Business*, ed. Stewart W. Herman, 325–343 (Bowling Green, OH: Philosophy Documentation Center, 2001).

example of the formative influence of religion in shaping our understanding of the self we wish to become.

There is nothing about moral principles that, once acquired, requires them to be written in concrete in your mind. Part of what we mean by human growth is the evolution of our moral ideals. So, don't hesitate to modify your moral principles; after all, they are yours to use and manage. By all means, listen to the advice and counsel of those you respect. But when the ethical moment arises during the course of business, you must make a decision. Though it is evolving, it is still *your* moral principles that should guide the business decision.

The best approach to your moral principles is to see them as the fruit of all your experience and thought. As such, they should be trusted to push you in directions consistent with the "examined moral self." In addition, reflecting about the insights derived from new experiences and new suggestions gives you the opportunity to improve on your moral principles.

To drive home this point about reexamining our moral principles, think about the moral principles James Rouse, the subject of the Values in Action Box, would have probably had when he was 14. Had he stubbornly held onto these principles on some mistaken understanding that they were who "he really is," we all would have lost his many contributions. Fortunately, Rouse did allow his character, his moral principles, to mature along with other aspects (such as physical and mental facets) of his life.

---

### VALUES IN ACTION
#### James Rouse

When James Rouse retired in 1979, his company, the Rouse Company, was by most standards an impressive success story. Forty years after its beginning as a small real estate firm in Baltimore, the company owned over 60 regional malls, had developed several nationally acclaimed downtown shopping areas, and had successfully planned and built an entire city, Columbia, Maryland. Yet, James Rouse, the leader whose ideas had shaped this company's direction and who was responsible for the company's success, told interviewers that he was most proud of the benefit that he had brought to lives of the people who shop, work, and live in his buildings.

When Rouse would publicly explain his business decisions, his sentences were robust with references to "community," "beauty," and "service to mankind." Yet, we often wonder, "Do people like Rouse fulfill what their words promise, or are all these nice sentiments just a clever front for public relations?" Let's look at particular decisions Rouse made as founder and president of a large real estate development company. By examining his actions, we can attempt to see whether Rouse's actual decisions seem to substantiate their public justification.

Rouse's concern for the larger community was evident early in his career. After a stint in the Navy during World War II, he returned to the real estate firm he had started with a partner in 1939. By the end of that decade, he was well known in Baltimore for his participation in multiple efforts to revitalize and rebuild the downtown and slum areas of that city. In 1953, President Eisenhower appointed him chairman of the task force on federal housing.

In the 1950s, Rouse turned his firm's attention to shopping areas in suburbia. Rouse saw a need for a marketplace that would give a sense of community to people in increasingly fragmented suburban areas. Although the retailers Rouse approached were initially skeptical about his ideas, Rouse opened the first enclosed regional shopping mall in the country in 1958 at Harundale, New Jersey.

We tend to identify modern malls with crass consumerism; Rouse himself made critical comments about the many malls built all over America in the following decades. But we should also recognize the consideration for human

*(continues on the next page)*

(continued)

needs that sparked Rouse's idea concerning an enclosed shopping center. This consideration led Rouse to include community meeting spaces inside each mall he designed: spaces for concerts, counseling centers, even churches.

Rouse's concern for suburban humanity continued into further projects. He protested the "frantic, fractured living, the loneliness amid the flurry of modern activity, the rising delinquency among middle-class children, increasing neurosis, alcoholism, divorce, the destruction of nature." Rouse acted on this criticism of suburbia in a highly visible fashion: in 1963, he announced the building of a new city in Howard County, Maryland, between Baltimore and Washington, D. C. Columbia, Maryland, was designed after hundreds of hours in consultation with fourteen consultants in sociology, education, health care, and other disciplines. The purpose of the town's design was to encourage a healthy sense of community.

Rouse also took on the task of rehabilitating dilapidated public squares in several large cities. He successfully transformed these areas into "festival marketplaces" where small vendors could sell their wares in an attractive environment. Not only did these marketplaces, which include Faneuil Hall in Boston and Harborplace in Baltimore, draw crowds of people, but the success of Rouse's developments sparked economic growth in the surrounding cities, bringing a new sense of civic pride to the urbanites.

Of course, it is possible to point out the other motives behind the Rouse Company's activities and claim these as "the top" priority. The same business talents that made Rouse's projects successful made these projects highly profitable. It is impossible for us to guarantee that all of Rouse's inspiring explanations of ethical motivation were not smoke screens for a thirst for status and financial success.

But we should recognize the consistency in Rouse's words and actions regarding his concern for the community. Even after Rouse retired, he did not simply congratulate himself for his service to mankind and retreat to enjoy the profits he had accrued in that role. Instead, he founded the Enterprise Foundation, a foundation that supports the efforts of nonprofit organizations to provide housing for low-income families. In 1990, Rouse became the advisor for another project: the redevelopment of Sandtown-Winchester, an entire inner-city neighborhood in Baltimore. Although Rouse died in 1996, Enterprise Foundation continues the ongoing work of rebuilding and assisting neighborhoods according to Rouse's "vision for the transformation of a neighborhood."

*References:*

David Bollier, *Aiming Higher: 25 Stories of How Companies Prosper by Combining Sound Management and Social Vision* (Amacon, New York: 1996), 314–27.

http://www.therousecompany.com /whoweare/history/index.html

http://www.enterprisefoundation.org/about/whoweare/founders/ind

## PRINCIPLES WRAP-UP

A central theme of this book is the need to have a system of ethical decision making that permits businesspeople to be thoughtful, quick, *and* ethical. To this end, chapter 1 introduced you to FILOP, and chapters 6 through 9 have taken you through the first four steps of this process. This chapter finished the last step: principles. The basis for moral principles is your personal vision about the world you would like to assist in creating. Although there are many visions of a better world that other people wish you to adopt, you are ultimately in charge. YOU should decide what kind of world you wish to help build. As you consider your ideal world, think about both the interests of those affected by the production and consumption of the good or service (such as the employees, investors, and customers) and the interests of the environment.

As we have continually emphasized, you do not have a lot of time to make an ethical business decision. The unusual speed required of businesspeople when they try to do good work is advanced not only by an immediate application of FILOP but also by a previously developed appreciation of the last step of the process: moral principles. The moral principles that define your character are something that you should determine a long time before an actual business dilemma arises. These moral principles are the habits of mind that you have selected as the foundation for your ethical identity.

## CRITICAL THINKING QUESTIONS

1. This chapter places a lot of ethical responsibility on the individual businessperson. To what extent are we being honest with ourselves when we say that we are sometimes "forced" to engage in unethical conduct at work? Is the ambiguity of "forced" important here?

2. What elements of FILOP might cause a business manager to make a decision that would be inconsistent with his or her moral principles?

## ENDNOTE

[1] See Kenneth Labich, "No More Crude at Texaco," *Fortune* 205 (September 6, 1999), available at 1999 WL 7940749; see also "A Better Chance Presents Recognition Award to Texaco Chairman Peter I. Bijur," *Business Wire* (June 18, 1999). For updated information about Texaco's diversity efforts, go to Texaco's Web site, texaco.com.

# CHAPTER 11

# Using FILOP to Consider the H. B. Fuller Dilemma

**THE FOCUS:**
How does FILOP direct us toward good work?

## FILOP (PRONOUNCED FI-LOP)

Business ethics can be improved with the assistance of these practical, logical steps.

| | |
|---|---|
| **F**ACTS | What are the facts shaping this particular dilemma? |
| **I**SSUE | What are the ways in which you can frame the ethical dilemma? |
| **L**AW | What laws are relevant to this ethical dilemma? |
| **O**PTIONS | How do I identify the options for action in response to an ethical dilemma? |
| **P**RINCIPLES | How does my sense of who I want to become shape my behavior as a businessperson? |

This chapter is part review and part demonstration. We promised you a practical, nontechnical approach to business ethics that you could apply in actual business settings. Now, it's time to deliver. You may be wondering how you will know whether our suggested guidelines are successful. In other words, what is the goal for an ethical system? Our objectives for this book are that you will become more ethical than you otherwise would be, that the world will become a better place as a result of your decision, and that, at the same time, you will feel proud of your own role in the community.

Contemporary newspapers are full of accounts of business behavior that damages the image of businesspeople in general. Yet, regardless of our vision of the good and the right, that vision requires the good work of businesspeople. Business activity is an inevitable component of our aspirations. Of course, you want to make a good living, but you also have a role to play in demonstrating to the rest of the community that buying and selling activity can take place in an atmosphere of trust.

We have already noted that a major problem with most approaches to ethics is that they are bulky; they do not fit the needs of the people and setting to which they are to be applied. Instead, they are more appropriate for an academic seminar room. A distinct advantage of the seminar room is the availability of long periods of thinking time between the introduction of the ethical dilemma and the necessary point of decision.

But business decisions must be made daily, and each has ethical components. What should we sell? How should we raise capital? Who should we fire and hire? How should compensation packages be structured? How much responsibility should we accept for the apparent effects of our operations? What picture of our financial condition should we share with the public? How honest should I be in my interactions with other employees and customers? Unlike students in a seminar, businesspeople do not have the luxury of large amounts of time for contemplation; they need to act.

To help you conserve time, our approach suggests that you prepare for good work far in advance of the need to figure out the ethical position with respect to a particular ethical dilemma. Although we are urging you to apply FILOP as your guide to practical business ethics, much of the usefulness of FILOP starts long before you face a particular business dilemma. For example, once you grow comfortable with the classical ethical guidelines through contemplation and practice, they become a reliable guide to consideration of the Options (step four of FILOP) you face at work.

## A RECAP OF KEY LESSONS FROM THE FOUNDATIONS CHAPTERS

If you wait until a moral dilemma arises to begin thinking about how to make an ethical decision, you have probably waited too long. The business world is fast paced; rarely do you have the luxury to sit and ponder the situation. Consequently, you must lay the foundation for future decisions before you are confronted with difficult choices in the workplace.

Our book begins by calling your attention to the importance of considering "the other" when making any ethical decisions; indeed, such a consideration is the foundation for ethical thought. As a result of this other-centered philosophy, ethical decisions must reflect a fair weighing and sorting among the numerous effects of a decision on various stakeholders.

We also discussed that this weighing and sorting takes place within an American business context. To aid the decision-making process, you should be aware of the special characteristics of this business culture in which you hope to flourish.

A better understanding of the specific business context, as discussed in chapter 2, serves as significant background information for our ethical considerations. H. B. Fuller, a large, multinational firm based in Minnesota, is one example of a company that functions in the American business culture. As a result, the nature of their ethical dilemma and the desirability of alternative decisions are shaped by that context. However, when you are considering the specific business context, you should also be aware of the prevailing culture within the corporation with which you are interacting. Individual firms *within* the prevailing national business culture, such as H. B. Fuller, may provide varying degrees of expressive freedom in which a businessperson is able to influence the very firm that is shaping the ethical dilemma itself. For example, a bureaucratic ethic in your firm both prevents certain options while permitting others.

Navigating inside these cultural boundaries at work can be tricky; you need practical strategies. Before anything else, you need to establish an anchor for an ethical guideline. That is, you should develop an awareness of and commitment to your own personal ethics. Without an understanding of your own ethical perspective, it is too easy to simply obey whatever orders your boss hands you. In chapter 3, you learned that one of the best ways to understand your ethical perspective is through the language of values. Which values do you prefer and how much weight do you give them? In other words, what are your value priorities? Finding your value priorities in advance of confronting ethical situations allows you to more quickly arrive at an answer that reflects who you want to be. Preparation will help you stay focused amidst the rush to make business decisions. Instead of simply obeying orders, your thoughtful, focused decisions will reflect your ability to accept responsibility for the ethical implications of an action.

In addition to preparation, a second strategy to make better ethical decisions is to apply the classical ethical guidelines outlined in chapter 4. Whether you choose the "Golden Rule," the "Public Disclosure Test," or the "Universalization Test," you are considering other members of the community in your decision. Although these guidelines are not foolproof, they offer a quick indication of the possibilities for good work. Combining these first two strategies is most effective. Thus, by practicing the application of these classical ethical guidelines *before* you are called on to make important decisions, you can enhance your ability to speedily arrive at more ethical business decisions.

Yet another way to prepare yourself for an ethical dilemma is to find a moral mentor model within your organization. A moral mentor can be a source of inspiration for you and others in the workplace. With the realization that ideal moral mentors are rare, you should not hesitate to discover "pretty good" moral mentors as models of good work. Such a model can be of great help when you are faced with a difficult decision because of the strength of their personal example.

The use of these three strategies allows you to prepare ahead of time for ethical decisions, and they are essential in creating a foundation for the more focused strategies tailored to each individual dilemma (FILOP). This preparation gives you a much greater chance of resisting the numerous pressures pushing you to take the ethical low road. Those pressures will always be around, and the people behind the pressure know how tempting financial and status gains can be. We can resist those pressures only when we have prepared in advance to repel them. Specifically, once we have taken the preparatory steps toward good work, FILOP can then direct us to the specific business option that will be most consistent with the partnership between the examined self and the external business environment. Let us demonstrate by reviewing the Fuller case.

---

## Key Lessons from the Foundations Chapters

*Remember these lessons from chapters 1 through 5 as you apply the FILOP process!*

- Business ethics requires a partnership between your sense of the good and the business culture.
- American culture's emphasis on individualism yields both positive and negative consequences for business decision making.
- Managers who work in organizations in which a bureaucratic ethic thrives are in danger of climbing the corporate ladder at the expense of their sense of morality.
- Corporate ethics codes serve a variety of purposes. Managers must have realistic expectations about these codes and avoid cynicism if they discover the code is little more than a company defense mechanism.
- Ethics disasters are complicated and usually involve problems with both people and organizations. They also involve problems that are larger than people and organizations.
- Doing good work requires preparation in terms of thinking about who you are and wish to become. It is important for you to think about your value priorities.
- When you are faced with an ethical dilemma, you can call on classical ethical guidelines to help you make a decision.
- Moral mentors in business serve as essential models, revealing to us that businesspeople can and do behave consistently with the highest ethical traditions.
- Although almost any business decision can be seen as self-serving in terms of financial well-being, businesspeople do not leave their sense of the good at home when they go to work in the morning either.

## USING FILOP: APPLYING IT TO THE H. B. FULLER CASE

### Here Again is the H. B. Fuller Case from Chapter 1.

Forty million children live in the streets of Central America. These children, orphans and runaways, survive by finding small jobs, begging, stealing, and prostituting their bodies for food. In an economy with rampant unemployment and with few government or charity programs to help them, their lives are constantly threatened with cold, hunger, and fear. Vulnerable to attacks from both nature and other human beings, these children must sleep in doorways, abandoned buildings, and sewer pipes and are often physically and sexually abused, even by the police.

Around 70 percent of these Central American street children have found escape from the pain of these conditions by addiction to glue. The children buy solvent-based contact cement intended for shoe making and repairs, which is packaged by retailers in small plastic bags and baby food jars. When the children inhale the fumes of this glue, they experience relief from incessant hunger and are consoled in their loneliness.

However, this euphoria comes at a high cost. The fumes also destroy their lungs, livers, and brains. The chemicals in the glue, especially toluene, one of the solvent bases used in manufacturing the glue, are highly toxic. Not only does their use as narcotic agents burn the skin, nose, throat, and eyes, but also, once inhaled, the fumes go quickly through the bloodstream to the brain. Side effects include memory loss, hearing loss, brain damage, and, sometimes, sudden death. Addicts frequently lose physical coordination and suffer muscle weakness and permanent nerve damage. The chemicals also interfere with blood cell production, inducing a life-threatening form of anemia. Death can result because inhaling the glue sometimes leads to sudden liver failure or cardiac arrest.

The physical harm of these chemicals is not even necessarily the most serious hazard to those who sniff the glue. Children intoxicated by these narcotics are also much more vulnerable to death from sources other than just the toxic fumes. For example, children high on glue are more likely to drown in drainage ditches and sewers or be killed in traffic or by violence.

In the early 1980s, newspapers in Honduras began to run stories about child addicts. These newspapers referred to the children as "los resistoleros"—after Resistol, a line of glues manufactured by H. B. Fuller S. A., a subsidiary of Kativo Chemical Industries, S. A. Kativo is one of Central America's 500 largest corporations and is wholly owned by H. B. Fuller Company of St. Paul, Minnesota.

Although Resistol glues may be a popular choice of addicts, they are by no means the only product so abused—addicts in Honduras and other Central American countries also abuse glues, paint thinners, and other chemical products made by other companies.

However, despite Kativo's protest of the label, the name Resistoleros stuck. The strong marketing position of H. B. Fuller's products turned into a marketing nightmare as child addiction became synonymous with the Resistol glue products. Child advocacy groups, most noticeably Covenant

House (or Casa Alienza in Spanish-speaking countries), began to organize protests against H. B. Fuller and other companies who were marketing the solvent-based glues destroying the street children of Central America.

Despite H. B. Fuller's reputation in the United States as a corporation devoted to ethical integrity and the concern for the wider community, the company's response to the public outcry in Latin America was less than satisfactory. Although the company did stop using toluene, the highly toxic solvent, in some of the adhesives, the substitute for toluene, cyclohexane, is only slightly less poisonous when inhaled, causing many of the same irreversible damages to the health of the street children.

H. B. Fuller looked even worse when its chief competitor, another multinational corporation, stopped selling solvent-based glues in Central America, offering instead a water-based adhesive. Henkel Corporation is based in Dusseldorf, Germany. When its company image came under increasing fire from both the Central American and German press, Henkel decided to switch to non-solvent-based products, first in Central America, then globally.

In 1992, H. B. Fuller's board of directors announced that the glue would be discontinued "wherever these products are known to be abused as inhalants." This statement was initially welcomed by the press, but ended up hurting H. B. Fuller's case further, as availability of the Resistol glues in Central America continued almost unhindered. H. B. Fuller stopped retail sales only in Honduras and Guatemala—the two countries in which Casa Alienza is active. Production and marketing continued in four other Central American countries, and in Honduras and Guatemala, street children could buy the glue from retailers who purchased the glue in large drums and repackaged it.

Efforts were also made to have H. B. Fuller add an irritant to the toxic glues that would make them too obnoxious to inhale. Airplane glue manufacturers in the 1960s added oil of mustard to their glue to avoid abuse of the glue as a narcotic. H. B. Fuller refused to reformulate its glues with this oil. In March 1989, the Honduran Congress even passed a law requiring oil of mustard to be included in all solvent-based glues made or imported for sale in the country. However, H. B. Fuller protested changing its formula, and the law was not enforced.

H. B. Fuller's mission statement declares, "The H. B. Fuller Company is committed to its responsibilities, in order of priority, to its customers, employees, and shareholders. H. B. Fuller will conduct business legally and ethically, support the activities of its employees in their communities, and be a responsible corporate citizen." It is possible that this statement is no more than corporate wallpaper covering crass profit seeking, but the company's history in other areas seems to indicate otherwise. H. B. Fuller's consistent policies as an employer and community benefactor have earned it 13th place in *Business Ethics* magazine's "100 Best Corporate Citizens" for 2002. This knowledge raises an important ethical question: How closely linked are H. B. Fuller's decisions about glue in Central America to this corporate responsibility? To better answer this question, we must first examine several reasons for H. B. Fuller's continued sale of a solvent-based glue.

One of H. B. Fuller's protests is that the legitimate users of Resistol in Central America will be harmed if the product is discontinued. Solvent-based contact cements provide rapid set, strong adhesion, and water resistance—characteristics H. B. Fuller has tried without success to match with a water-based glue. If the glue is not available for legitimate public and industrial use, economic growth in Central America might be hindered.

At the same time that solvent-based adhesives are vital to some Central American businesses, drug addiction is so prevalent among street children that they will turn to any available narcotic substance. If shoe glue were not available, H. B. Fuller argues, street children would get high on the paint thinners and other solvents used even now as alternative narcotic substances.

Furthermore, in 1994, when Fuller substituted cyclohexane for toluene in its glues, the price of the glue also increased by 30 percent. In addition to the increase in price, cyclohexane also lacks the sweet smell of toluene. Although Casa Alienza is right to point out that cyclohexane is still highly toxic, H. B. Fuller argues that this change in formula has made the glue less attractive to children than other manufacturers' glues available on the streets.

In the 1980s, when the effort was made to persuade Fuller to add allyl isothiocyanate (oil of mustard) to its glues, Fuller presented evidence that the additive was significantly hazardous to the health of employees and consumers. Oil of mustard was found to be carcinogenic in studies run with rats. Furthermore, a toxicology report offered evidence that the chemical was extremely destructive to the tissue of the upper mucous membranes and the upper respiratory tract, eyes and skin; caused burns, nausea, dizziness, and headache; and could be fatal if swallowed or inhaled. Finally, adding allyl isothiocyanate would shorten the shelf life of the glues to a maximum of six months.

In further attempts to demonstrate their concern for the problem of glue addiction, H. B Fuller executives have met with both government leaders and antidrug advocates in Central America. In 1987, the company started community affairs committees with Kativo employees in Central America, stating, "We want to be a company with recognized values, demonstrating involvement, and commitment to the betterment of the communities we are a part of." As part of their involvement, the company has made public statements and helped draft legislation in favor of increased education for street children about drug abuse. H. B. Fuller also makes regular contributions to homeless shelters for street children in Central America.

A thorough examination of this dilemma will show that drug addiction of Central American children is part of a larger problem of poverty, neglect, and abuse found in these countries. But how do H. B. Fuller's decisions either relieve or exacerbate the problem? Is the supposed concern for "community" shown by Fuller and its subsidiaries genuine? Or is the company taking advantage of current conditions in Central America to further its own profits?

When we first introduced this case in chapter 1, we included a set of questions for you to consider. All of them can be addressed indirectly by considering the larger question: What strategy should H. B. Fuller use in response to the extensive use of Resistol among children in Central America? In order to answer this all-encompassing question, we will use the FILOP guideline.

1. Awareness of the **F**acts of the ethical dilemma
2. Appreciation for the scope of the **I**ssue
3. Understanding of the relevant **L**aw governing the issue
4. Consideration of the **O**ptions available
5. Selection of applicable ethical **P**rinciples

## FACTS

When you face a decision as a businessperson, that decision is made in a context. Misreading the context is like running with a broken leg or, perhaps more accurately, running a marathon using the wrong map. The facts, as you identify them, are the context on which the rest of the process relies. If the facts are all wrong, your understanding of the issue and the options from which you can choose will be severely compromised.

So the first step in FILOP is to gather as many relevant facts as you can in the time you have available. Ordinarily, you will never have more than a few of the facts that pertain to your decision, but you owe it to everyone involved to discover as many relevant facts as is practical.

With regard to the Fuller case, though, we have given you many relevant facts. Think for a moment about the facts that seem especially relevant to the question: *What strategy should H. B. Fuller use in responding to the extensive use of Resistol among children in Central America?* One example of a set of facts that seems relevant to this question is the set that tells us what H. B. Fuller has already done to respond to

---

### Facts Review

- A fact is a building block or piece of information. It is a statement about the way the world is.
- Many facts shape an issue, but only certain facts are pertinent in evaluating a dilemma.
- Ignore irrelevant facts. If possible, try to add to your list of available facts.
- Caution: You will not be able to find every potentially relevant fact.
- Generally, ask yourself the "W" questions—Who is involved in the dilemma? What has happened? Where? When? Why?

the problem. For example, we know the company has already met with government and antidrug officials. We also know that the company has changed the formulation of the glue to make it less attractive to abusers and to raise the price. These two examples show what you should be doing in the first step of FILOP—find the most relevant facts. From here, you should generate a comprehensive list of relevant facts that are available to you.

In addition to clarifying and summarizing the most important facts you have on hand, you may need to add to your list of facts. Think of questions you may have after reading the case as we have presented it. For example, you may wonder whether any additional countries have passed legislation similar to the 1989 Honduran statute that prohibits importing of any glue that contains the substance Toluene or does not have mustard oil included in its formula. This question is significant because Fuller management will have a difficult time holding itself out as a servant to the people in locations where the distribution of Resistol is illegal.

You may also want additional information about drug use among youth in Central America. Suppose you find a recent survey of drug usage among street children.[1] The survey reported that of the 520 street children surveyed, 504 said they used glue, 201 took Crack, 151 drank alcohol, 65 used marijuana, 32 took cocaine, another 32 said they used hallucinogenic drugs, and 10 used propane gas. Clearly, most children are abusing more than one type of drug. How might this set of facts affect Fuller's course of action? One the one hand, Fuller may fairly decide that these youth are going to attempt to find some sort of drug to use. Hence, Resistol is not to a certitude causing any drug problem. Yet, as a seller that wants to choose a path rooted in ethical traditions, Fuller cannot ignore the number of children using its product. It appears that the availability of the glue is enhancing the ease of drug use.

Now, think of additional questions. We'll get you started.

1. What social conditions make it difficult for children in Central America to "say no to drugs"?
2. How will a decision to pull out of the Central American market affect employees and legitimate customers?
3. What will small shoe manufacturers do if Fuller pulls the product? Does the company have alternatives?
4. What are the environmental effects of the glue?

Business decision makers never have all the relevant facts. But the point of this initial step in FILOP is that facts provide the basic structure of an ethical dilemma. Gather as many as are practical in the available time, then move on to the next step.

## ISSUE

Reading the Fuller case would convince anyone that Fuller has an ethical problem. But the specific way in which we word that problem will determine the decisions we will need to make.

The more authority you have in an organization, the more you can approach the ethical dilemma as a broader, more societal, ethical problem. Authority permits you to see the issue in its broader scope, to consider various consequences to multiple stakeholders. Such authority provides you with the responsibilities and opportunities necessary when tackling the broad issues. Consequently, the top management at Fuller can frame the issue in such relatively abstract forms as the following.

- Should a firm continue to provide a product to its consumer base, even when that product is a public relations nightmare?
- Is a responsible firm obligated to consider the unplanned consequences of the use of its products when those consequences can be seen as the result of the poor choices of unintended consumers?
- Should a multinational corporation primarily obey the laws and social norms of the country in which its headquarters are located or the countries in which its products are consumed?
- Should a firm admit the problems associated with its products or expend its primary energies debunking the alleged harm caused by the product?

These issues are relevant primarily to the people at the top of an organizational hierarchy because only they can take actions to address these issues. Other customers, suppliers, and employees of the firm may have

---

**Discovering Issues Review**

- When discovering issues, you are arranging the facts, transforming them into the statement of your problem/ethical dilemma.
- An issue is a statement of your dilemma in question form. Try to start with the word *should*.
- Make sure that the way you present the question allows you to search for alternative answers.
- Find other ways to frame the ethical dilemma. Practice going from abstract to specific.
- Realize that your own value priorities affect the way you phrase an issue.
- Your ultimate goal is to frame the issue in a way that highlights the ethical questions at issue and that directs your attention to the actions you can take in response.

strong opinions about these issues, but they lack the power on an individual level to redirect the firm's policies.

Many people involved in the dilemma need to frame the issue in a more personal, concrete fashion. They are not in a policy-making position at the top levels of a business organization. Hence, for them, the issue must be framed in terms of their stock holdings, their jobs, and their consumption patterns. The issues that they would face in a scenario like the Fuller case would resemble the following.

- Should I allocate discretionary expenditures primarily toward finding some more benign form of the questionable product we are selling, or should I leave product line responsibilities to others?
- Should I work for a firm that knowingly markets a product that damages the health of tens of thousands of young people?
- Should I own stock in a firm that needs to improve its product line? By owning their stock, am I putting myself in a position to move the firm toward good work, or am I a willing participant in the demise of Central American urban youth?
- Do I have a responsibility to make Fuller management aware that my consumption dollars will be spent on the products of only those firms that place health or environmental concerns uppermost?

The issue that you decide to address focuses your attention on one question while diverting your gaze away from other potential issues. Whatever thinking goes into doing good work, the outcome will do so only within the boundaries provided by the framing of the issue. Once you are satisfied that you have determined the issue most relevant to you and the world you want to help create, it is time to find the relevant law that governs alternative responses to that issue.

## LAW

Law and ethical decision making are not identical. The evolution of laws suggests that the law is always moving in response to emerging understandings of good work. Law provides, however, a current reading of the minimal ethical standards required of business. When we say that particular business behavior is "against the law," we are announcing the community's minimal standards. Although ethical business behavior may extend beyond these legal minimums, businesspeople have, at the very least, a responsibility to respect the limits spelled out by the law. Hence, doing good work depends on discovering the relevant law.

Let's go back to the general question we raised when we first presented the case: *What strategy should H. B. Fuller use in responding to the extensive use of Resistol among children in Central America?* Before answering this question, you may want to know the answers to these legal questions.

---

### Review of How to Find Relevant Law

---

- Remember, the law generally sets a baseline for your behavior (e.g., unless you/the company wants to be punished and experience the resulting negative bad publicity, you need to behave in accordance with the law).
- The most efficient ways to find the law are to
  - Ask an attorney.
  - Educate yourself using a legal environment of business textbook.
  - Engage in a careful search for law on the Internet using a search engine such as Findlaw.com or yahoo.com.
  - Study, then use a more sophisticated approach like a lawyer or law a student would use.
- Remember—the law is merely a starting point. You might want to do *more* than the law allows.

---

1. What does the Honduran law that governs the sale of adhesive products prohibit?
2. Does any federal law in the United States address the use of oil of mustard? If so, would this law apply to company operations outside the United States?
3. Do any countries in Central America have labeling requirements for adhesive products?
4. Can Guatemalan plaintiffs sue H. B. Fuller in the United States because it is the parent company of Kativo Chemical Industries?

To review the possible ways to find relevant law, let's consider the last question: Can Guatemalan plaintiffs sue H. B. Fuller in the United States because it is the parent company of Kativo Chemical Industries? As a first step, either ask an attorney or read a legal environment of business textbook to find out what key terms a lawyer might use when thinking about this question.

Either of these two approaches should yield these as key terms: jurisdiction, multinational, and "product liability." The legal term *jurisdiction* refers to a particular court's power to hear a case. Rules with regard to jurisdiction will explain whether it is fair to make H. B. Fuller answer for Kativo in a U.S. court. The term *multinational* is important because we want to know legal rules for companies that operate outside the United States. The phrase *product liability* is important because, at its core, any lawsuit about the glue is likely to allege that H. B. Fuller should compensate users for harm they suffered as a consequence of using a defective, harmful product.

Using yahoo.com, we searched for: jurisdiction multinational, and "product liability." This search yielded several articles that allowed us to refine our search.[2] From skimming these articles, we discovered that we needed to do a new search, this time using the search terms "forum non conveniens" and "United States." The legal phrase "forum non conveniens" answers questions about whether a lawsuit should be dismissed because it is inconvenient for a company to answer in a particular jurisdiction (e.g., Minnesota, the location of H. B. Fuller's primary place of business) when most of the investigation of the relevant facts will take place far away from the jurisdiction in which the lawsuit will take place (e.g., the investigation here will take place mostly in Guatemala).

Searching for "forum non conveniens" and "United States" led us to a key document,[3] which tells us about a 1996 Minnesota case, *Polanco* v. *H. B. Fuller Co.*, challenging Fuller's behavior in Central America. A court dismissed this case because of lack of jurisdiction over H. B. Fuller's actions in another country. In particular, the court pointed out that the investigation of key facts would take place in Guatemala. Additionally, the court expressed its view that the citizens of Guatemala, not the United States, should decide the appropriate standards for products manufactured in that country.

Thus, we now know that the answer to our fourth legal question is "no." Guatemalan plaintiffs cannot sue H. B. Fuller in the United States. Now, see whether you can answer the other legal questions we listed.

The law does not tell a firm which work is good, but it does alert managers, owners, customers, employees, environmentalists, and other affected parties to previous determinations of the minimal requirements for business ethics.

## OPTIONS

Those at H. B. Fuller who have the decision-making authority to determine product lines, component composition, and marketing strategy have major ethical responsibilities consistent with the authority they

---

### Options Review

- Ethical dilemmas have a large array of possible solutions. Refrain from thinking there are just two—yes and no, do it or don't do it
- Strategies for coming up with alternative paths may include
  - Finding allies
  - Reviewing the company mission statement and/or code of ethics
  - Reminding yourself of the various interests that might be affected by certain options (e.g., shareholders, current company employees)
  - Finding paths to profit that are less ethically troubling
  - Trying to build on arguments you have heard people higher up in the hierarchy make
  - Considering whether you could secretly set the stage for some public pressure
  - Focusing on the firm's long-run profitability

possess. Like all of us contemplating an ethical dilemma, the extreme options are especially vivid. Fuller does not depend on Resistol for its existence. Thus, one available option is for Fuller to abandon that particular market to its competitors. At the other extreme, Fuller could "stay the course," hoping that laws against its behavior in Latin America will be poorly enforced and that it can persuade its critics of the overall social benefit of its line of adhesive products.

However, as chapter 9 suggested, a large array of possible options between the two extremes provide greater decision-making flexibility. By looking at multiple options, those with authority inside a firm can be more creative in constructing good work. For example, they could direct their research team to work toward the discovery of a nontoxic, effective adhesive, make large investments in information campaigns that warn potential users of Resistol of the dangers of brain damage, or work publicly to fight against the population pressures, unemployment, and distributional problems in Latin America. That latter option is ultimately more beneficial because it tackles the root problems that make the abuse of Resistol so popular in the first place. But then again, like most fundamental solutions, it is also much more expensive than more superficial forms of good work.

Individual employees, workers, owners, and consumers, who play a role in Fuller's business activities, have different options to consider. The ethical dilemmas they face require them to wonder to themselves whether they wish to continue to associate with a firm that produces Resistol, even though Fuller has known for a long time about the extent to which its product is destructive to Latin American youth. Furthermore, if these individuals decide to continue their associations with H. B. Fuller, they must decide whether and how they will work to transform Fuller's policy toward Resistol. Should they seek the advice of a moral mentor, suggest at every occasion how much more profitable alternative product lines are, or become a whistle-blower in an attempt to rescue the firm from its current course of action? Such options are but a few of the potential actions that a responsible person should consider.

## PRINCIPLES

Each person who has a role to play in H. B. Fuller's future has some degree of responsibility for the future of Resistol and those whom it both benefits and harms. How individuals decide to fulfill this responsibility will be shaped by their personal moral principles, the subject matter of chapter 10.

In our review of the idea of principles, we have presented what we call a "principles toolbox," which includes three sets of tools—(1) thinking about principles in terms of values as we explained in chapter 3, (2) relying on the classical ethical guidelines we presented in chapter 4,

## Principles Toolbox

*Values*

- Values are positive abstractions that capture our sense of what is good or desirable.
- Examples of values that often shape business decision making: honesty, freedom, security, justice, efficiency.
- You will need to provide alternative definitions for the values you present.

*Classical Ethical Guidelines*

- The Golden Rule—treat others the way you would want them to treat you. What's important here is an awareness that others matter.
- The Public Disclosure Test—we should care what thoughtful, virtuous people think of us. Suppose your decision were to be printed in the newspaper. How would the public react? How would you feel if you knew the public would know what you intend to do?
- The Universalization Test—consider those other people whom our actions affect. What would the world be like if everyone copied our decision? Were others to follow my example, would the world be a better place?

*Ethics Theories*

- Utilitarianism—Do that which leads to the best consequences for everyone involved.
- Deontology—Do that which you are motivated to do for the sake of duty.
- Virtue ethics—Do that which is consistent with the type of person you wish to become.

and (3) relying on the ethics theories we explained in the appendix to chapter 4. Which set of tools you choose to use when thinking about the "P" in FILOP may depend on the circumstances of the ethical dilemma you face and your comfort level in using one set of tools over another. At times, thinking about values, value conflicts, and value priorities may seem like a natural fit for you and your situation. At other times, the facts might call for you to consider the Public Disclosure Test, one of the classical ethical guidelines. These guidelines might make a lot of sense to you. Finally, there might be times when thinking about virtue ethics, one of the primary ethics theories, will help you make a morally sound decision. Relying on the deeper philosophical theories might be especially satisfying to you. All three sets of tools play a role in helping you develop a sense of self by doing good work.

With regard to the Fuller case, you should think about values. For example, those whose vision of a better world focuses on material success may not be bothered by the questionable honesty associated with distributing a product that harms vulnerable populations who are unaware of the neurological damage. A more passionate commitment to honesty when it conflicts with material success might push a Fuller employee or stock owner to either refuse to associate with Fuller or work to make certain that Resistol is used with awareness of its full range of effects.

You may also want to apply the classical ethical guidelines to the facts and issues, as you have articulated them. For example, you might want to apply The Golden Rule and consider the strategy H. B. Fuller should pursue if the company believes children in Guatemala matter as much as children in the United States.

Finally, you may want to think about ethics theories. What course of action would yield the best consequences for everyone involved? If H. B. Fuller's decision making were guided by a sense of moral duty, what would the company do? What steps would managers at H. B. Fuller need to take to become the kind of managers who demonstrate virtue, acting on the habits of courage, discipline, wisdom, and fairness?

Moral principles, made useful through the tool sets of values, classical ethical guidelines, and ethics theories, represent the personal core or ethical foundation that the human agent brings to business decisions. You select moral principles only after reflecting long and hard about the kind of world that would be encouraged were those value preferences, classical ethical guidelines, or ethics theories to be the basis for our collective future. For example, a dedication to individual responsibility as a core value would emphasize that H. B. Fuller coerces no one to use its products. That point would stimulate those who value individual responsibility over social responsibility to support the choice by Fuller to produce and distribute Resistol. On the other hand, those who habitually value social responsibility over individual responsibility would support social sanctions against H. B. Fuller on the grounds that the vulnerability of Latin American youth places responsibility on the community to protect the health of children because they are poorly equipped to protect themselves.

This final step of FILOP highlights the important role that is played by your sense of self in doing good work. Even though you are part of a business culture that you did not create and to which you must adjust, you are a very important determining factor in shaping the quality of business decisions. Your moral mentors and your moral principles propel you toward particular forms of good work. The perception of the business community as an essential member of the larger community depends on your being ever watchful that businesses aim toward good work.

## REVIEWING THE PRIMARY THEMES OF THE BOOK

- Business ethics requires a partnership between your sense of the good and business culture.
- Doing good work requires preparation in terms of thinking about who you are and who you wish to become.

- Moral mentors in business serve as essential models, revealing to us that businesspeople can and do behave in ways consistent with the highest ethical traditions.
- Although almost any business decision can be seen as self-serving in terms of financial well-being, there are other motivations. Businesspeople do not leave their sense of the good at home when they go to work in the morning.
- Business ethics can be improved with the assistance of practical, logical steps, like those provided by FILOP.

## ENDNOTES

[1] The information in this illustration is fictional.

[2] For example, International product liability litigation: Jurisdiction and forum nonconveniens in England, www.c.r.ntu.ac.uk/journal/pdf/nlj7_1/018.pdf; Surfing the Net in Shallow Water: Product Liability Concerns and Advertising on the Internet, www.fdli.org/pubs/Journal%20Online/53_2/art2.pdf; Product Safety Regulation: Casting the Net Wider, Deeper, www.ashursts.com/pubs/pdf/2028.pdf

[3] We first found a site, www.gigalaw.com/archives/0210/gigalaw.discuss.0210.00070.html, which led us to www.dgslaw.com/articles/339255.html, which told us about a case, *Polanco v. H. B. Fuller*. With the name of a case as a search term, we found an article that told us what the case said. See www.faegre.com/articles/article_92.asp.

# Index